PRACTICING PUBLIC MANAGEMENT

A CASEBOOK

PRACTICING PUBLIC MANAGEMENT

A CASEBOOK

Second Edition

C. Kenneth Meyer
University of Oklahoma

Charles H. Brown
Pennsylvania State University

Mitchell Beville, Randall Preheim, and Walter Scheffer contributed to the first edition of this book.

St. Martin's Press • New York

Editor: Larry Swanson
Project Editor: Beverly Hinton
Production Supervisor: Stacey Donohue
Cover Design: Darby Downey
Cover Art: Lorraine Williams

Library of Congress Catalog Card Number: 88-60537

Manufactured in the United States of America.
32109
fedcba

For information, write:
St. Martin's Press, Inc.
175 Fifth Avenue
New York, NY 10010

ISBN: 0-312-00329-3

PREFACE

The principal aim of the second edition of *Practicing Public Management: A Casebook* has not changed from that of the first edition: to present students with a variety of administrative situations and problems for analysis.

The second edition contains sixty-one cases that present a variety of problems ranging from minor difficulties encountered in day-to-day management situations to more difficult problems involving principle and policy. A number of cases from the first edition have been replaced by ones that consider more contemporary issues or that better involve the student in administrative decision-making. New to the second edition are fourteen minicases, situations presented in 150 to 300 words that do not require extensive background for analysis and that enable the text to cover a wider range of topics. The text's forty-seven major cases require students to engage in considerable preparation and intensive study in order to analyze the often complex problems of public management they present.

The casebook deals with management problems of a timeless quality—careless or indifferent employees and supervisors, policy determination, personality conflicts, boredom, and improving efficiency and productivity. It also addresses issues of contemporary origin—the increasing number of women in the work force and in management-level positions, equal opportunity, workfare, affirmative action, polygraph testing, alcohol and drug abuse, community economic development, employee rights, environmental problems, and others.

In an effort to illustrate a broader spectrum of new and old administrative problems and situations, the number of topics covered is increased from eighty-two in the first edition to more than one hundred in the second edition. As an aid to instructors in selecting cases according to topics an alphabetically arranged *Index of Topics* is provided. The topic listings are followed by the case numbers in which they are presented with an asterisk indicating those in which they receive major emphasis. An additional aid is an appendix, *Case Histories Keyed to Topics*, which lists the cases by number and title according to the table of contents; topics taken up in the cases are given, again with an asterisk identifying those receiving major emphasis.

Each case is accompanied by a set of questions and instructions intended to stimulate thinking about and discussion of the problems under consideration. In addition, each major case contains a carefully selected bibliography directing students to works that deal with the administrative theories, concepts, and practices presented. The bibliographies will help students to analyze the cases as well as become better acquainted with the literature of public management.

The casebook is adaptable to all levels of instruction from the two-year junior college to the university and graduate school. It may be used as a supplement to instruction by textbook and lectures or as the primary text for a course employing the case-study approach, as the focus of a graduate seminar or colloquium, or as an aid to an in-service government-training program. The cases included in the text have been created to reflect the real-life experiences of administrators of the kind students may face in the entry- and middle-level positions they will obtain upon graduation.

We are grateful to the following students and administrators who contributed ideas, information, and material used in the cases: Harry Allison, Gary Anderson, Stan Anker, Michael J. Baker, Vicki Brooks, Elaine T. Davis, Steven Feimer, Mary J. Frasier, Vern Guericke, William Hartman, Jim Julin, Deborah Louison, Kim Weber Mulinix, Jeffrey Pederson, Duane Petzoldt, Gail H. Poe, Regina Pryce, Daniel P. Richter, Cathie Rodman, Gregory Sogaard, S. R. H. Spicer, Mildred Juanita States, Kent W. Sudman, Marina Sukop, Carolyn Thompson, Marvin L. Wagner, and Mark Williams.

Thanks are also given to Larry Swanson, editor at St. Martin's Press, for his support and for recommending that the second edition be thoroughly revised and updated; and to Beverly Hinton, the project editor, for the careful attention which she gave this edition. The authors acknowledge the many useful comments and ideas which were contributed by the reviewers: Carolyn Ban, State University of New York at Albany; Dennis Dresang, Robert M. La Follette Institute of Public Affairs, University of Wisconsin-Madison; Daniel Guerrero, California State University at Dominguez Hills; Eugene B. McGregor, Jr., Indiana University at Bloomington; Linda Richter, Kansas State University; Ralph F. Shangraw, Jr., The Maxwell School, Syracuse University; C. Richard Swaim, University of Baltimore; Ronald Sylvia, University of Oklahoma at Norman. Of course, special thanks are due to those students and instructors who utilized the first edition of *Practicing Public Management: A Casebook* and for their positive suggestions which have been included in this book. We give special thanks and appreciation to Sheila L. Black for meticulously typing the new material.

C. Kenneth Meyer
Charles H. Brown

CONTENTS

MINICASES

INDEX OF TOPICS

The text gives major emphasis to topics in cases marked by asterisks.

PRACTICING PUBLIC MANAGEMENT

A CASEBOOK

PART I

THE CASE-STUDY APPROACH TO TRAINING FOR PUBLIC MANAGEMENT

The Role of Public Administrators

In the early years of the United States, jobs in the government depended on the principle of "to the victor belong the spoils." Appointments of middle- and lower-level administrators, to whom the case studies in this book are directed, were made by those who won elections. But as the population grew, as the country became industrialized, as services performed by the government expanded, and as public affairs became more complex with the adoption of controls and regulations considered desirable, the method of filling positions with party supporters was recognized as inadequate.

The continuity needed in public service could not be achieved when there were wholesale turnovers in employees after elections nor could competent ones always be found if job eligibility was based chiefly on allegiance to a political party. Incompetency, inefficiency, and even corruption became so prevalent by the middle of the last century that agitation developed to replace political patronage with a civil-service system. This was finally achieved in the federal government with passage of the Civil Service Act of 1883, but states and cities were slower to effect such reform and indeed the merit system has reached some of them only in the past few years. Public service as a recognized profession requiring academic training is a more recent development, and though university-level instruction in the field began as early as 1911, its greatest growth has occurred in the past fifteen or twenty years.

The need for specialized training to perform the complex role of public administrators is based on significant differences between management in government and management in business and industry. It is sometimes argued that management is the same everywhere because it basically deals with the operational relationships among people, but this notion is an oversimplification. The organizational structure in which government managers work is much more complicated than that of business or industrial managers, even those in the huge multinational corporations that have developed in recent years. Corporation executives are subject to a small board of directors and their competency is measured fairly easily by such items as sales records, production figures, and, finally, the profit or loss registered in the annual report. On the other hand, it is difficult to gauge managerial effectiveness in government because its performance cannot readily be measured by the rules of business and because the goals of public service largely consist of intangibles. The conditions that make the role of public-management administrators more difficult than that of private-sector administrators include the following:

Multiple Direction and Control. The supreme power in a business or industrial concern is vested usually in a small and closely knit board of directors, but in government it is divided broadly into three branches—the legislative, the executive, and the judicial—and it may be further diffused among a host of regulatory agencies, commissions, and authorities. Administrators in the public sector often find themselves subjected to pressures from conflicting centers of power and public opinion.

Impermanence and Change. Top officials in government are elected for specified terms. Policies and goals may shift suddenly with a change in the majority control of Congress, a state legislature, a county commission, or a municipal body or with the election or appointment of a new person to office in the executive branch. Often the work of the bureaucracy goes on only slightly affected by these turnovers, but occasionally aggressive and reforming officials may make demands that are difficult for middle- and lower-level managers to meet.

Legal and Procedural Constraints. The rules and regulations established by lawmaking bodies to ensure honesty, protect the rights of employees, and minimize error are numerous and involved and therefore are difficult to understand. Private-sector managers, even in the largest corporations, seldom find themselves so entangled in red tape as those in the public sector.

Measurement of Accomplishment. The most obvious and therefore most frequently mentioned distinction between public and private management is that one is a service enterprise and the other a profit enterprise, but this is an inadequate standard by which to judge their respective effectiveness. The government builds roads and dams, purchases and uses office machines and supplies, provides services for the public, and engages in many other activities that differ little from those of private organizations. Though ultimately there is no profit, such factors as costs, productivity, and efficiency can be determined and compared with those of private enterprise, as they should be. Nevertheless, when public interest is put in the balance it compensates for the occasions when work done by the government seems to be unduly expensive or inefficient. The reason is that private enterprise has left to the government the performance of services for which no profit could be made or that were so vital that the people did not wish to leave them to the vagaries of the marketplace of unaccountable private enterprise.

Expectations of the Public Regarding Government Employees. Higher ethical standards are demanded of government workers than of those in business or industry. Gifts, pay-offs, conflicts of interest, and nepotism commonplace in business are not only condemned as unbecoming to public officials but are also illegal under a number of laws regulating their conduct.

Surveillance of Operation. An important aspect of private enterprise is that it *is* private. It is subject to certain regulations in the public interest, but generally its records are not open to outsiders, its owners and managers ordinarily do not have to divulge their plans and prospects, and there are few restrictions upon who may be hired or fired. The operations of the government, on the contrary, are subject to constant scrutiny—by legislators and city council members, by the news media, by interest groups, and by the public.

The Training of Public Administrators

Although the foregoing discussion of the role of public administrators emphasizes only a few highlights, it is sufficient to indicate that the skills required are exceptional. As a consequence, in recent years there has been a rapidly developing trend of professional training for public-service jobs. This has accompanied the adoption of civil-service and merit systems in state and local governments similar to those established earlier in the federal government and also has paralleled the higher educational requirements demanded for other employment in our technological society. A high-school diploma once signified adequate education for most jobs, but after World War II a bachelor's degree became a more frequent requirement and today master's and doctor's degrees, formerly needed only in academic institutions, are common in business, industry, and government.

Public-administration and public-affairs programs, now firmly established in universities and colleges, are directed toward educating and training students in the professional skills they will need, but this curriculum provides only a part of their required preparation. They must learn also about the political, social, and economic milieus in which government functions; they must be trained in logic and in the statistical and other quantitative skills that individual performance requires; they must be able to communicate orally and in writing; and they must develop the psychological insights needed for understanding and influencing individual and group behavior. Over the years the instructional technique that most successfully combines proficiency and knowledge in these areas with administrative-management practice has been the case study.

The method has long been followed in law schools—indeed has dominated the instruction in them—according to the theory that by examining the precedents established in the settlement of legal suits and actions general principles will develop. With adaptations it was used in the first quarter of this century in business schools with the same idea—that the analysis of actual situations would result in generalizations that could be applied in similar situations. It has since been adopted in such fields as social work, educational administration, financial administration, and public administration.

In a survey of two hundred training directors on the effectiveness of nine different instructional methods for various training objectives, the case-study method had the best overall score. The other eight methods listed in the order of effectiveness were conference discussions, role playing, sensitivity training, business games, programmed instruction, films, television lectures, and lectures with questions. The training objectives rated were knowledge acquisition, changing attitudes, problem solving, interpersonal skills, participant acceptance, and knowledge retention. Case study ranked first in problem solving; second in knowledge acquisition, participant acceptance, and knowledge retention; and fourth in changing attitudes and interpersonal skills.*

In public-administration programs, unlike those of law and perhaps other fields, the case-study method has seldom been the core of the instructional system; more often it has been a supplement. Most collections of case studies are designed to supplement the standard textbooks, assigned outside readings, and lectures traditionally employed in classroom instruction. Its chief aim has not been to arrive at general principles but to enable students to share some of the real-life experiences of management.

In the study of law the cases considered are to be found among those actually introduced into and disposed of in the legal and judicial process, but in other fields they come from the experiences of actual participants who supply the information for accounts describing an illustrative situation or problem. The cases vary in length from a few hundred words to several thousand. Usually they are narratives about the people whose personalities and backgrounds are briefly given and whose thoughts and actions are related as the situation develops in a postulated office or agency of government. All the names used are, of course, fictitious.

Case studies, to be sure, are no substitute for experience, but their simulation of experience can be instructive. In one semester students are introduced to a variety of experiences that might otherwise take them years to encounter in a job. By identifying with the people in a case history students develop the ability to look at a situation or problem from different points of view, and their broadening empathy is further enhanced by hearing the

* Stephen J. Carroll, Jr., Frank T. Paine, and John M. Ivancevich, "The Relative Effectiveness of Training Methods—Expert Opinion and Research," in William F. Glueck, *Personnel: A Book of Readings,* Dallas, Tex.: Business Publications, 1979, pp. 236–247.

views of their classmates in the analytical discussions of the policies or perplexities that the cases present. They receive some practice in scientific or systematic thinking by learning to look at problems and situations objectively, by examining the facts available, and by considering a variety of solutions or proposed courses of action for a particular difficulty. They may thus become more flexible in putting abstract rules or administrative procedures and techniques to the test of practical application.

There are some deficiencies and dangers in the case method of which students should be aware. The situational narratives must always be simplifications. All the facts in a situation, conflicts among individuals, and emotional interplay among the participants cannot be set forth in a case history. It is not life but a clouded mirror of life. Solutions that seem so practicable in classroom discussion, courses of recommended conduct that seem so irreproachable, and conclusions that seem so cogent often will not work in everyday affairs. Sometimes they are defeated by the contrariness of organizational members or by the constraints of the system. Thus students who excel in classroom explication should not let themselves be deluded into thinking they have mastered the art or craft of management.

Using Case Histories

The case-study method was developed to approximate the way people derive their information and make decisions in life. Most school instruction by textbook and lecture is prescriptive; it is measured by what the student retains in memory and can transmit on examination. Case study is essentially self-learning through simulated experience. Its goal is not primarily the acquisition of a measurable body of knowledge or information but rather the development of attitudes and training in purposive thinking. Its success depends largely upon the lively interchange of information, ideas, and opinions brought out in classroom discussion. But this discussion must not be just a free-for-all or brainstorming session. It demands preparation by the participants and direction by a leader, either the instructor or an elected or appointed member of the class. To obtain the most out of the examination of cases, therefore, students should observe the following rules:

> Come to the class meeting prepared. Read the case history carefully and determine what the main issues are, speculate as to the motivations of the people involved, and seek to define the reasons why the situation or problem arose. Find out what the literature of public management offers on the topics related to the case by reading the works listed in the selected bibliographies appended to each case in this volume.
>
> Be a vocal participant in the class discussion. Since this is a self-learning exercise, letting other class members do the analysis and suggest the various approaches

to handling a situation or solving a problem will hinder your development in trying new concepts, expressing new ideas, or looking at new administrative or organizational practices. You should contribute as much as possible and be ready to learn new things not only about administration but also about yourself.

Interact with classmates by criticizing their ideas. Courtesy and civility are important in interactions among people but so is assertiveness. Cross-examine class members on their ideas, ask probing questions about the implications of their proposals, and measure these by the hallmarks of practicality, necessity, ethicality, and legality. Other students and teachers may be so obsessed with attempting to find answers that they fail to ask "What is the question?" By playing the role of Doubting Thomas you can help your class associates clarify the issues.

Consider the discussion an opportunity to achieve self-understanding. Feel free to get thoroughly involved and be open in expressing your own beliefs and feelings. Case analysis, however, is more than the projection of a series of attitudes exemplified in statements beginning with such expressions as "I believe . . . ," "I feel . . . ," or "I am sure . . ." Try to understand the sources of your beliefs, feelings, and convictions and be receptive to those of others before adopting a final stand. Self-understanding may come from asking such questions as these: What does the problem or situation presented in the case mean to me? Is there anything in my own experience that would shed light on the problem or situation? Have I let my emotions or biases dominate my thinking about a problem or situation?

Keep a log or diary of your observations and experiences. If maintained chronologically, this journal on rereading will make possible a comparison of your first thoughts on a topic with those finally held and to trace the changes that occurred, if any. It will enable you to see in retrospect what influences prevailed: your reading in the field, the comments of your instructor, the opinion of fellow students, or whatever may have been a factor in forming your attitudes. Self-questioning will help you follow the honored injunction "Know thyself."*

The procedures that may be followed in studying case histories are numerous, and the instructor and class members will probably wish to use different ones to prevent analysis from becoming routine and to experiment

* Dr. Robert B. Denhardt of the University of Missouri-Columbia recommends the keeping of an administrative journal as a means of bridging the gap between theory and practice in public administration. "Through careful use of the Administrative Journal," he says, "you should be able to bring together theories of the individual and the organization on the one hand, and the way you think, feel, and act in administrative situations on the other." He suggests a journal consisting of four main sections and an appendix. The first (Outer Experience) is used to record occurrences relating to public organization; the second is used to record reflections and generalizations about these occurrences; the third (Inner Experience) is a first-person account of how the Outer Experience affected the writer emotionally, physically, and intellectually; the fourth is devoted to reflections and generalizations on the inner experience; and the appendix (Period of Growth) is devoted to a reconsideration of the four sections after an extended period of time to enable the writer to take a long view of his or her personal and professional development. See "The Administrative Journal: Theory and Method," in *Innovations in Teaching Public Affairs and Administration,* Richard Heimovics and Ann-Marie Rizzo, eds., Kansas City-Miami, 1981.

to discover more fruitful approaches. The same method will not do for all histories contained in the casebook. Whatever the approach, students should take extensive notes for their personal log or diary and for reconsideration when they are alone and not affected by the classroom environment. Very often one finds that ideas that seemed at the time to be irresistible will turn out to be irrelevant or trivial.

Sometimes there could be an unrehearsed consideration of a case, which could be announced at the start of a class or group session and followed by discussion after members have had a chance to read it. The spontaneous expression of points of view and suggestions for courses of action to be taken about a situation or problem will result in a lively discussion that will stimulate ideas.

But probably a more effective use of the case histories would be to assign them before classroom discussion so that students may have an opportunity to obtain information bearing on the particular problem or situation to be considered and to organize their thoughts about it. Sometimes they could be asked merely to be prepared to take part in a general discussion. Alternatively, one or more students or a team might be asked to give a presentation analyzing the topic and making recommendations followed by a general class critique. Or the instructor may wish to make a presentation in which a personal analysis and proposed course of action are given. Another method would be for the instructor or an appointed or elected student to lead a discussion in which the situation or problem is clarified and suggestions for handling it are elicited by conducting a Socratic dialogue.

To avoid making the classroom discussions too academic, the practical or applied point of view may be introduced by occasionally inviting practicing administrators to take part. The guests might participate as members of the class and tell how they would deal with the matter, or they might observe the discussions and conclude the class consideration of a history by evaluating the points brought out by the students and setting forth their own views as to the best course of action. Another way of bringing in a professional viewpoint would be for students to interview public officials—a valuable experience in itself—about a case history to obtain their views and comments for presentation to the class.

Not all the case histories would have to be taken up in class sessions because this is time-consuming. More ground can be covered, if the class and instructor think it desirable, by having members write reports on additional cases to be submitted to the instructor for evaluation and criticism or, if the paper load is too great for the instructor, to assign these cases individually to students for their written criticism.

In the foregoing suggestions on how the case histories might be used, considerable writing is urged. The reason is that it is easier to strip a situation, problem, or perplexity to its essentials; to order one's thoughts; to check on the validity of facts and observations; and to note omissions by using the opportunity for examination and reexamination that putting things on paper affords. The language and construction should conform to the practice of the average educated person in speech and writing. Especially to be avoided is the jargon employed in many official reports and memos known as "governmentese," "gobbledygook," or "bafflegab," which not only retards communication but also interferes with clear thinking.

Analyzing Case Histories

Each of the histories in the casebook presents a problem of difficulty or describes a situation about which action has been taken or is indicated. At the end several questions and instructions are presented as a guide to studying the particular case. These are not intended to be exhaustive, but rather are designed to start a fermentation process leading to other questions and ideas.

For a fuller consideration of a case, and especially for cases arising in actual administration, a systematic method of analysis should be followed that includes (1) assembling facts bearing on the problem, (2) clarifying it by defining the issues, (3) proposing and evaluating suggested solutions or courses of action, and finally (4) determining which one seems best in view of the circumstances. This method is known as problem solving, a classic statement of which was made by the pragmatic philosopher and educator John Dewey in 1910.* As mentioned before, training directors polled on the effectiveness of different instructional methods ranked case study first in developing problem-solving skills. These are important because so much administration consists of making decisions regarding problems, difficulties, and dilemmas large and small that constantly arise.

A great virtue of the problem-solving method is that students learn to view the perplexities arising in day-to-day administration as objectively as possible. Also, they learn to avoid prejudgment and bias and free themselves of emotionalism. A good administrator is not merely a thinking machine. The manager is concerned with human situations and deals with people who behave like people—that is, who sometimes do things that do not make sense, who cannot be persuaded by logic, and who cannot be manipulated like chess pieces on a board.

Mental activity goes on continuously during a person's waking and sleeping hours, but this stream of consciousness hardly constitutes thinking. Only when the images, notions, and impressions arising in the brain are subjected to order does one engage in purposive thought. The problem-solving technique is employed to obtain this consequential sequence.

* John Dewey, *How We Think,* Boston: D. C. Heath and Co., 1910. The book was extensively revised in a new edition published in 1933.

John Dewey in his description of the problem-solving method distinguished five steps or phases. These are: (1) the recognition of a problem, (2) the definition and clarification of the problem, (3) the rise of possible solutions, (4) the development by reasoning of the implications of the solutions, and (5) further observation and experiment leading to acceptance or rejection of the solutions. Dewey recognized that this process as outlined is an oversimplification. Thinking is too complex to be so well ordered. In what Dewey called "reflective thinking" about a problem or situation the phases do not follow one another in set order and indeed may be so interrelated that they cannot be separated. Nevertheless, the procedure can be helpful in coming to grips with perplexities encountered in the casebook histories and in management.

In developing the first phase of problem solving it is wise to classify at the start the area of management in which the case history belongs. A rough guide can be found in the topical listing in the appendix: accountability, communication, job satisfaction, recruitment, and so on. More than one of these areas may apply to individual cases and students may wish to add others not covered in the listing.

Once the basic dilemma or difficulty in a case is defined, it should be submitted to analysis for clarification. Various questions will come to mind in this task: What are the facts in the case? How did the difficulty arise? Who are the people involved? What are their motivations and interests? What are their needs? Was the problem brought about by personality conflicts? If blame can be placed, who is to blame? Are there rules and regulations governing the case? Should the matter be brought to the attention of higher authority? Will the situation finally resolve itself? Is any action called for at all?

If the administrator decides that something must be done, he or she next should consider what possible courses are available and submit them to careful analysis as to which would be best to follow in the circumstances. Again, asking questions will prove helpful in the diagnostic process: What are the likely consequences of the decision? Is the course of action a temporary expedient or a long-term solution? Is the solution feasible? What has to be done to put it into practice? Does it involve the expenditure of money or alteration of existing rules and regulations? Will it be acceptable to the people involved? Will permission to put it into effect have to be obtained from higher authority? Does the decision on what to do conform with regular practice? What group will be best served by the decision—the public, the department, or its employees? Is it in the interest of good government? Is it ethically right? Is it equitable for all those concerned?

In diagnosing a situation or problem and seeking a remedy, the administrator must examine personal motivations. Administrators will frequently be tempted to take the easy way out, to vacillate and delay rather than come to grips with the difficulty immediately. Perhaps administrators will attempt a cover-up or fail to present the matter to superiors for fear of exposing their own inability or weakness. They may resort to merely palliative measures when more fundamental ones are required. They may rule in favor of people they like and against those they dislike. They may put their own personal interests above those of the employees they supervise and the public and government they serve. Difficult though it may be, an attempt to resist these inclinations must be made. In an administrative career, a long-range reputation for probity, square-dealing, and decisiveness will do the manager more good than running for shelter when storms arise in the department.

PART II

CASE HISTORIES FOR ANALYSIS

1

It's Not Easy at the Top

Rose Marie Matlock majored in political science at the large urban university that she attended. Interested in politics from childhood, she had ambitions of becoming a political reporter, perhaps even a Washington correspondent. To this end, she took several courses in journalism, including news reporting and writing, editing, and feature writing.

Upon graduation, the only journalistic job she could get was on the women's section staff of a newspaper in a city of 50,000. It was not what she had hoped for but it would give her some experience in the field and, in time, perhaps she would be transferred to the city news staff. After several months of writing about engagements and weddings, doing occasional features on the domestic arts and fashions, and editing and headlining syndicated articles on homemaking, Matlock began to feel frustrated and took a civil-service examination for a position in Washington as a public information specialist. To her delight, she was offered a job in the Department of Agriculture. Perhaps more doors, she thought, would be open to her in the capital than in her home state.

Excited by living in a city like Washington at the center of world-shaking events, Matlock enjoyed her job. In preparing news and informational releases, writing articles for consumer publications, and, after several years, becoming assistant editor of an interdepartmental magazine, Matlock felt that she was doing important work and thought only with mild regret occasionally of the failure to achieve her ambition of becoming a political writer.

And yet she believed she had not reached her potential. Seeking greater opportunity and more challenging work, she applied for the position of director of publications in a division of the Department of Housing and Urban Development. Examining her own qualifications for the executive-level position, Matlock decided that she met its major requirements: she was thoroughly familiar with most phases of publication work, she was interested in other people, and she believed she could lead and guide them. Further, she believed in the social value of the department and was eager to meet the challenges of the position. She was highly gratified, therefore, when she was notified she had received the appointment.

On her first day on the job Matlock held a staff meeting and complimented members on the reputation that the division had won and explained that no immediate changes would be made—they should carry on as usual. She said that in a few weeks she hoped to talk to each of them individually to familiarize herself with their jobs, their goals, and their interests. Her office door, she added, would always be open for consultation.

After several months, the shine had begun to be rubbed off the new job, the day was not long enough to meet all of the demands of staff members. They consulted her on endless matters of major and minor importance: type size and style for article titles, bulletin formats, and sexist and racist phrasing. The number of questions presented to Matlock on a typical day was overwhelming and her ability to make decisions suffered. She found herself making such responses as "Let me think about it and I'll get back to you," "I'll go over it and let you know," and "That's all right; use your own judgments." Matlock also became a sounding board for staff members' complaints about coworkers: Betty Ray did not submit her copy in on time to meet the printer's deadline; Oscar Bellows had been asked to write an article of 1,500 words and had turned in one of 2,500 that had to be cut; Matthew King's work contained numerous spelling errors and something should be done about it.

Matlock had tried at first to take a friendly interest in all staff members in the belief that understanding their problems would assist her in making assignments and in evaluating and directing their work. Several, however, took advantage of this by relating woeful tales of family problems or the break-up of an affair with a live-in companion. Although Matlock felt she should give a sympathetic ear to these, she found it increasingly difficult to listen without feeling impatient.

A perfectionist in her own work, Matlock felt that she should check carefully each publication for content, typography, format, and suitability before giving final approval. But her day was so taken up with conferences with staff members, office-matter rulings, and consultations with other department heads that she frequently worked late at the office and took material to look over at home.

Finally, a year and a half after she had assumed her executive position so optimistically and ambitiously, Matlock decided she could no longer go on. She had lost weight, and she was nervous and short-tempered. Each morning she felt unable to face another day at the office. Matlock decided that in becoming director of publications in the Department of Housing and Urban Development, she might have over-reached herself, and it was time to reassess her capabilities.

Questions and Instructions

1. What managerial faults was Matlock guilty of? What did she do right?
2. How could Matlock have better handled the difficult situations she faced as an executive?
3. What personality traits make a good executive?
4. Do you think Matlock possesses the qualities needed to make a good or satisfactory executive?
5. Before deciding to give up on her job, what should Matlock do? Do you think she gave up too easily?

Selected Bibliography

Beck, Arthur C., and Hillmar, Ellis D., *Positive Management Practices: Bringing Out the Best in Organizations and People,* San Francisco, Calif.: Jossey-Bass, Inc., 1986.

Bennis, Warren, "Leaders: The Strategies for Taking Charge," *Public Management* 69 (January 1987): 11–12.

Bennis, Warren, and Nanus, Burt, *Leaders: The Strategies for Taking Charge,* New York: Harper & Row, 1985.

Blades, Jon W., *Rules for Leadership,* Washington, D.C.: U.S. Government Printing Office, 1986.

Brown, David S., "The New Managers and Their Responsibilities," *The Bureaucrat* 16 (Spring 1987): 45–46.

Caudle, Sharon, "The Bedrock Capping 'Uppity Women,'" *The Bureaucrat* 14 (Summer 1985): 27–30.

Chusmir, Leonard H., and Durand, Douglas E., "Stress and the Working Woman," *Personnel* 64 (May 1987): 38–43.

Ciabattari, Jane, "When It's Your Turn to Be Boss," *Working Woman* 12 (March 1987): 109–14.

Cleveland, Harlan, *The Knowledge Executive: Leadership in an Information Society,* New York: E. P. Dutton, 1985.

Forrester, Randolph J., "Things They Never Covered in the MPA Program (and How to Cope)," *Public Management* 69 (April 1987): 20–21.

Iaconetti, Joan, "Seven Delegating Mistakes and How to Avoid Them," *Working Woman* 12 (July 1987): 24–27.

Lawler, Edward E., III, *High-Involvement Management: Participant Strategies for Improving Organizational Performance,* San Francisco, Calif.: Jossey-Bass, Inc., 1986.

McSpedon, Joseph H., "Standards to Avoid Employer Retaliation Charges," *Labor Law Journal* 33 (January 1982): 36–45.

Pastin, Mark, *The Hard Problems of Management,* San Francisco, Calif.: Jossey-Bass, Inc., 1986.

Peter, Laurence J., *The Peter Prescription: How to Make Things Go Right,* New York: William Morrow, 1972.

Ritti, R. Richard, and Funkhouse, G. Ray, *The Ropes to Skip and the Ropes to Know: The Inner Life of an Organization,* New York: John Wiley & Sons, Inc., 1987.

Townsend, Robert, *Further Up the Organization—How to Stop Management from Stifling People and Strangling Productivity,* New York: Alfred A. Knopf, 1984.

Weinberg, Barbara L., "Moving Up and Around in Local Government Management," *Public Management* 68 (October 1986): 11–13.

2

If It's Legal, It's O.K.

Rudolf Swartz, executive assistant to Governor Susan Forney, was directed by her to investigate a situation reported in a newspaper exposé that six Highway Department employees who were fired three years earlier for filing false travel claims had been reinstated to their jobs at higher salaries. Governor Forney's administration had been marked by several minor scandals, and she was worried that the fallout from this new one might harm her chances for re-election in the fall.

Checking the facts in the situation, Swartz found that the six employees had been charged in district court with filing false claims totaling $5,500. At their trial they pleaded guilty to all counts and received two-year deferred sentences on their promise to repay the state the money they had illegally received. Two of the employees were construction superintendents and the others were equipment operators. Swartz's investigation revealed that restitution had been made and that when the deferred sentences had run their course the guilty pleas were expunged from official records, the practice with such sentences under state law. The six employees returned to their former jobs one week after the legal process was completed.

During an interview with Wayland Johnson, director of the department, Swartz was told that Johnson rehired the six employees after being advised by his legal counsel that no laws had been violated. "The workers were highly competent and efficient," Johnson said. "I'm not proud of them, but their experience on the job made their re-employment practical. I don't hold any personal animosities. They paid their debt to society. Is there a law that says that if you violate a public trust, you can't go back to work?"

Johnson also told Swartz that he did not expect an incident of travel-claim fraud to reoccur. The earlier incident had resulted he explained, in tighter surveillance on travel claims in more frequent audits. Johnson noted that the six employees had applied for jobs and were rehired by the Central Division engineer, Angus McCormick, who had assured him that despite their previous dishonesty he considered them worthy citizens. "McCormick told me that he spoke to each of them about whether they realized what they had done was wrong," Johnson said. "He believed they had learned their lesson and, as they were experienced people, the state had an investment in them."

Swartz discovered that apparently no law had been broken when the former workers were re-employed. Attorney General Anthony Bellini told him: "Legally, I see no prohibition. A deferred sentence is not considered a conviction, and it is expunged from the record as if it was never there. Philosophically and morally, I don't have anything to say. Johnson's running his department. If he thinks he can get good work out of them and can check on them, that's his decision." From Frederick Larson, head of the Office of Personnel Management, Swartz learned that, under the State Merit System, rules prohibited the re-employment of a worker convicted of a crime involving moral turpitude. Even so, Larson saw no legal objection to the re-employment of the six workers because their convictions had been declared as if they did not exist.

Reporting to Governor Forney, Swartz said he believed the incident would not be damaging to her administration or re-election, because the offenses had been minor ones blown out of proportion by the press. "I hope," he added with a laugh, "the workers have been limited as to how much job-related traveling they're required to do."

Questions and Instructions

1. Are you convinced by the statement of the highway department director that the six employees had paid their debt to society and deserved to be returned to their jobs?
2. Just because there was no legal bar to the rehiring of the six employees, do you think doing so was morally acceptable?
3. What political reasons may have influenced the decisions of the highway director and the division engineer to rehire the employees?
4. Do you think that the loophole in the state law that made re-employment of the six employees legal should be closed?
5. If you were the governor's assistant, what would you advise her to do about the situation?

Selected Bibliography

Bailey, Stephen K., "Ethics and the Public Service," *Public Administration Review* 24 (December 1964): 235–43.

Banfield, Edward C., "Corruption As a Feature of Governmental Organization," *Journal of Law and Economics* 18 (December 1975): 587–605.

Blick, Larry N., "Ethical Complexities," *Public Management* 66 (February 1984): 7–9.

Boling, T. Edwin, and Dempsey, John, "Ethical Dilemmas in Government: Designing an Organizational Response," *Public Personnel Management* 10 (No. 1, 1981): 11–19.

Bowman, James S., "The Management of Ethics: Codes of Conduct in Organizations," *Public Personnel Management* 10 (No. 1, 1981): 59–66.

Cooper, Terry L., "Hierarchy, Virtue, and the Practice of Public Administration: A Perspective for Normative Ethics," *Public Administration Review* 47 (July/August, 1987): 320–28.

Gawthrop, Louis C., "Toward an Ethical Convergence of Democratic Theory and Administrative Politics," in Chandler, Ralph Clark, ed., *A Centennial History of the American Administrative State,* New York: The Free Press, 1987. pp. 189–216.

Lewis, Carol W., *Scruples and Scandals—A Handbook on Public Service Ethics for State and Local Government Officials and Employees in Connecticut,* Storrs, Conn.: The University of Connecticut, 1986.

McCown, Andrew J., "The Challenge of Meeting High Ethical Standards," *Public Management* 66 (February 1984): 2–4.

Peters, Charles, and Branch, Taylor, eds., *Blowing the Whistle: Dissent in the Public Interest,* New York: Praeger, 1972.

Rohr, John, *Ethics for Bureaucrats: An Essay on Law and Values,* New York: Marcel Dekker, 1978.

Toffler, Barbara Ley, *Tough Choices: Managers Talk Ethics,* New York: John Wiley & Sons, Inc., 1986.

Wakefield, Susan, "Ethics and the Public Service: A Case for Individual Responsibility," *Public Administration Review* 36 (November/December 1976): 661–66.

Waldo, Dwight, "Reflections on Public Morality," *Administration and Society* 6 (November 1974): 267–82.

Warwick, Donald D., "The Ethics of Administrative Discretion," in Fleischman, Joel L.; Leibman, Lance; and Moore, Mark H., eds., *Public Duties: The Moral Obligations of Government Officials,* Cambridge, Mass.: Harvard University Press, 1981. pp. 93–127.

3

Special Privileges for Officials?

Sarah Jefferies had worked in the rehabilitation agency of the State Welfare Department for almost twenty years and had become the administrative secretary to the agency manager, Edward Foster. Jefferies always received superior job-performance ratings from her supervisors and had several letters of commendation for assuming responsibilities beyond those given in her job description. Foster, who had managed the agency for five years, was considered a capable person in the job and respected for his ability "to get the job done right." The central office frequently depended on him for assistance.

During the past nine months Jefferies had noticed that Foster and other officials often reported to work late in the morning and left the office early in the afternoon. Every agency employee earned ten hours of annual leave a month and could receive payment for the unused portion of accumulated leave at the end of each year. In addition, employees received nine paid holidays a year. Overtime was compensated for by allowing employees to take the equivalent time off. Jefferies was responsible for recording employee hours and leave time and felt that the agency officials were taking more time off than allowed by the state. Her coworkers also noticed this and were becoming upset. At a water-fountain conference Jefferies was selected by the other employees to speak with Foster about the situation.

Jefferies told Foster that some of the employees were disturbed by the agency officials' disregard for the rules governing office hours, leave time, and compensation time. She also informed him that with his approval one official improperly received two weeks' compensation. Foster explained that administrators had more privileges than subordinate staff members. "They are not punching a time clock," he said, "and if they get their work done, that's all that counts."

After her discussion with Foster, Jefferies wondered what she should do.

Questions and Instructions

1. Suggest several courses of action that are open to Jefferies in resolving her dilemma.
2. What are the legal and moral implications of the perceived abuses? Are they too trivial to bother with?
3. Does Jefferies have an obligation to "blow the whistle" about the abuses? If she decides to do so, should she tell Foster of her intention?
4. Should Foster consider more carefully the impact of his behavior on the organization?
5. Would you suggest that the agency policy governing tardiness, absenteeism, and sick leave be applied equally to all employees or differentiated according to administrative rank?
6. Should a flexitime approach be recommended in resolving the issues raised in this situation?

Selected Bibliography

Barad, Cary B., "Flexitime Under Scrutiny," *Personnel Administrator* 25 (May 1980): 69–74.

Elbing, Alvar O.; Gadon, Herman; and Gordon, John R. M., "Flexible Working Hours: It's About Time," *Harvard Business Review* 52 (January/February 1974): 18–33.

Graham, George A., "Ethical Guidelines for Public Administrators: Observations on the Rules of the Game," *Public Administration Review* 34 (January/February 1974): 90–92.

Holley, William H., et al., "Employee Reactions to a Flexitime Program: A Longitudinal Study," *Human Resource Management* 15 (Winter 1976): 21–23.

Meier, Kenneth J., *Politics and the Bureaucracy: Policymaking in the Fourth Branch of Government,* North Scituate, Mass.: Duxbury Press, 1979. Ch. 7, "Controlling Bureaucracy: Ethics and Participation," pp. 162–85.

Mosher, Frederick C., *Democracy and the Public Service,* 2nd ed., New York: Oxford University Press, 1982. Ch. 7, "Merit, Morality, and Democracy," pp. 202–19.

Odiorne, George S., *Personnel Administration by Objectives,* Homewood, Ill.: Richard D. Irwin, 1971. See "Discipline by Objectives," pp. 415–31.

Presthus, Robert, *The Organizational Society,* rev. ed., New York: St. Martin's Press, 1978. Chs. 6, 7, and 8, pp. 143–251.

Rainey, Glenn W., Jr., and Wolf, Lawrence, "Flex-Time: Short-Term Benefits, Long-Term . . . ?" *Public Administration Review* 41 (January/February 1981): 52–63.

Ronen, Simcha, and Primps, Sophia B., "The Impact of Flexitime on Performance and Attitudes in 25 Public Agencies," in Bozeman, Barry, and Straussman, Jeffrey, eds., *New Directions in Public Administration,* Monterey, Calif.: Brooks/Cole Publishing Co., 1984. pp. 269–80.

Wagel, William H., "Flexible Work Schedules That Work for Everyone," *Personnel* 64 (June 1987): 5–10.

4

An Illegal Order

Upon receiving his bachelor of public administration degree from Central State University, Jerry Grissom felt fortunate when he obtained a job with the State Department of Social Services in the county office near the university. He would be able to gain experience and to earn money while continuing work on his master's degree. Having married as an undergraduate and become a father shortly after entering into the graduate program, he needed the job to support himself and his family as well as to continue his education for a career in government service.

Bright, energetic, and ambitious, Grissom was a young man on the make: he knew where he wanted to go and how to get there. Employment in the county Social Services office was not one of his goals but a means to an end—a stepping stone to a higher administrative post in the state or preferably the federal government.

Although Grissom tended to choose his friends for their usefulness to him and not for the enjoyment of their company, he was well liked, for he almost always was cheerful and entertaining. Quick to grasp a situation and highly articulate and industrious, Grissom had impressed his university professors, who regarded him as a student with the highest potential.

His job with the Social Services Department was not demanding. His main responsibility was inspecting and checking complaints against licensed day-care centers and registered home-care centers in the district. Upon receiving a complaint against a center, he would interview the complainant and then make an inspection to see if any state regulations were being violated. If he found infractions, he would write a report and submit it to the head of the county unit, Adolf Schumann. If Schumann approved it, a notice was sent to the offender warning that if the infractions were not corrected within thirty days his or her license would be lost.

Grissom found Adolf Schumann somewhat forbidding and not so easily charmed by him as most other people he met. Consequently, Grissom was always especially careful in writing up his reports and painstaking in his other work. Although not an outgoing person, Schumann from time to time praised him for his work. Grissom felt sure he would get a good recommendation when he left the county office.

Grissom's rosy prospects were darkened when an unfavorable situation resulted from his following up on a routine complaint made against a registered home-care center operated by Susan Parmenter. His inspection turned up several minor violations—she occasionally accepted more children than she was licensed to care for, trash that might be a fire hazard had been permitted to accumulate, and there was no sink with running water in the area where babies were changed. None of these were serious, but Grissom informed Parmenter that they would have to be corrected. He explained that regulations required that a written notice of the violations be sent to her and she would have thirty days to correct them or run the risk of losing her license.

The report on Parmenter's center was among several similar ones and Grissom had almost forgotten about it when he was called into Schumann's office and found the department head sitting at his desk with the report in his hand.

"This report is utterly uncalled for," Schumann told Grissom. "I can't see anything here that calls for a warning of suspension of the operator's license."

"Well, it's just routine," Grissom replied. "The violations do exist and I was merely following regulations in reporting them."

"I don't want to discuss the matter," Schumann said. 'Your petty fault finding amounts to harassment. Mrs. Parmenter is only trying to make a few dollars by taking care of children in her home. She's not operating a professional day-care center. Just tear up the report and let her alone."

Grissom left the office in a mild state of shock. His reports had been questioned on occasion, but this was the first time he had been ordered to withdraw one. The violations he had found at the Parmenter home were so easily corrected that he did not see why Schumann had made a big issue of them. He did learn why a few days later. He had made a few inquiries and discovered that Mrs. Parmenter's brother was Homer Schmidt, a county commissioner and a close friend of Schumann's.

Questions and Instructions

1. If you were involved in a situation similar to Grissom's, would you quietly tear up the report?
2. Is there any substance to Schumann's view that the violations were so minor that sending out a notice to Parmenter hardly seemed worthwhile?

3. What course of action is open to an employee when ordered by a superior to disobey regulations even if over a minor matter?

Selected Bibliography

American Society for Public Administration, *Professional Standards and Ethics,* Washington, D.C.: American Society for Public Administration, 1979.

Appleby, Paul H., *Morality and Administration in Democratic Government,* Baton Rouge, La.: Louisiana State University, 1952.

Barnard, Chester, *The Functions of the Executive,* Cambridge, Mass.: Harvard University Press, 1938.

Berg, Larry L.; Hahn, Harlan; and Schmidhauser, John R., *Corruption in the American Political System,* Morristown, N.J.: General Learning Press, 1976. Ch. 2, "Corruption and the Responsible Citizen," pp. 31–58.

Boyarsky, Bill, and Boyarsky, Nancy, *Backroom Politics,* Los Angeles, Calif.: J. P. Tarcher, 1974. Ch. 1, "Introduction—The People Who Can Make Life Miserable for Us All," pp. 1–17, and Ch. 4, "Corporations above the Law," pp. 71–96.

Caiden, Gerald E., and Caiden, Naomi J., "Administrative Corruption," *Public Administration Review* 37 (May/June 1977): 301–9.

Cobb, Anthony T., "Informal Influence in the Formal Organization: Perceived Sources of Power Among Work Unit Peers," *Academy of Management Journal* 23 (March 1980): 155–61.

Mertins, Herman, Jr., and Hennigan, Patrick J., *Applying Professional Standards and Ethics in the '80s,* Washington, D.C.: American Society for Public Administration, 1982. See "Conflicts of Interest," pp. 17–18, and "Public Disclosure and Confidentiality," pp. 20–21.

White, Bernard J., and Montgomery, B. Ruth, "Corporate Codes of Conduct," *California Management Review* 23 (Spring 1981): 92–96.

Young, Stanley, "Politicking: The Unsung Managerial Skill," *Personnel* 64 (June 1987): 62–68.

5

Managerial Conflicts

The Graphics and Photography Division of Midstate University provided services for the academic, business, and maintenance divisions of the institution. It was divided into five units: Graphics Production, Printing and Duplicating Services, Photographic Services, Equipment Maintenance and Distribution, and Educational Films Library. The division employed twenty-five staff people full time and from fifteen to twenty students part time.

The division was not happy. The unit supervisors were empire builders of the first order who jealously contended for more funds and more employees. Meetings of unit heads with the division director were marked by bickering and there was little cooperation among the units. Because there was little esprit de corps among the division administrators, there was likewise little among the employees.

The director of the division was Dr. Olaf Johanssen, a likable man who in the fifteen years he had held his position had been generally viewed as a weak administrator. Now sixty-three years old and planning to retire at sixty-five, Johanssen had increasingly relaxed his control over the division, leaving administrative and personnel matters chiefly to Lester Best, the assistant director.

Best, who was thirty years old, had held his position for five years and was extremely eager to get ahead. To his superiors, he had always shown a respect that bordered on servility, but with his coworkers he was thoughtless, tactless, inconsiderate, and arrogant.

Difficult personnel problems had arisen particularly in the Photographic Services unit, supervised by Jerome Christianson, and in the Equipment and Maintenance unit, supervised by Donald Waterman. The smallest unit of the division, Photographic Services employed three adults and usually one or two students. Christianson, age thirty-one, was highly qualified in education and professional experience for his job. He had begun work for the unit six years before as a Photographer I and within a few months had been made supervisor. Because of cuts in appropriations throughout the entire university, a promotion for Christianson was not immediately foreseeable and his pay increases had not kept pace with the cost of living.

Because Christianson's unit was small, he had closer contact with his staff than most supervisors and was sympathetic to their personal problems. A current problem concerned Andrew Polk, age twenty-six, the newest employee in the unit. Christianson and Polk had been good friends for several years. A former newspaper photographer, Polk took a job as a photo lab technician to earn money while doing graduate work in journalism at the university. Polk's work was decidedly superior and he was well liked throughout the division. Early in his employment Polk was called upon by the assistant director, Best—who was acquainted with his work as a newspaper photographer—to take pictures, assignments that were not included in his job description. He received overtime pay for these special assignments.

Toward the end of Polk's six-month probationary period he discussed the possibility with Christianson of being raised to the Photographer I level. Often called upon to perform Photographer I duties, he felt he should receive overtime pay commensurate with that rank when taking pictures. Christianson agreed and told him: "Best is using your talents as photographer but he isn't paying you the Photographer I scale. I think he should. Why don't you ask him about raising your salary?"

The next day Polk was in the main office picking up his mail when Best approached him about another assignment. Polk replied, "I'd be glad to help you out, Lester, but I feel it's only fair that I get paid overtime on the Photographer I scale rather than the lab-technician scale."

Best, surprised that a person still on probation would make pay demands, protested: "But you forget that during your interview we stated that from time to time you would be asked to perform overtime duties."

"Well, I remember that Johanssen did say I would be asked to on occasion," Polk said, "and I'm willing to do so. However, he made a point that he didn't want me doing the work of a photographer because others might complain I wasn't hired for that type of work. I'm willing to do the work. I'd just like to get paid for it."

"Well, we will just have to see about that," Best said and walked away in a huff.

Next morning Christianson was called to Johanssen's office, where he found the director and Best awaiting him. Johanssen said that Best reported that Polk had been insubordinate and that he should be reprimanded by Christianson.

Christianson returned to his own office and explained to Polk that he was to do whatever was asked of him. "I know it isn't fair," he said, "but that's the way this place works. Maybe after a few months I can get you raised to Photographer I."

During the next four months, Polk performed all tasks requested by Best and Johanssen without complaint. Both he and Christianson kept a record of extra duties performed to use as "ammunition for a promotion" when additional funds became available for another Photographer I position.

Meanwhile, Donald Waterman in the Equipment and Maintenance unit had been having problems. Now sixty years old, Waterman had worked in the division for eighteen years. He planned to take an early retirement "because this damn place will never shape up."

Three weeks before, one of Waterman's technicians resigned because he was "tired of waiting for two years for a promotion from Johanssen." Five days before the effective date of resignation, the division director raised the position from Electronics Technician I to a II. The office rumor was that the promotion was pushed through to make the position more attractive and easier to fill, since the university's salary scale made it difficult to hire technicians.

Hired for the job was Roscoe Flinch, age forty-two, a TV repairperson who in accepting had negotiated a deal by which he would receive a raise after his first month of employment. This speedy raise would give him a salary $1500 higher than that received by Waterman after eighteen years of service. Waterman was furious and exclaimed on first learning about it: "How can I supervise him when he makes more than I do?" He was so nettled that he determined to take it easy during the two years before he retired.

A few weeks later employees were surprised to observe Flinch taking pictures of various activities of the division. Andrew Polk was curious and asked him, "What are you doing? I didn't know you were a photographer."

Flinch grinned and said, "Best wants some pictures for a slide show illustrating the services the division provides and asked me to prepare them."

Polk went to Christianson's office and told him of the project. Angrily Christianson rushed to Johanssen's office and confronted him. "What the hell is Flinch doing with a camera?" he asked. "He's not working in the photography unit."

"Well, he is working on a slide show for us," Johanssen said.

"That's what I hear. Why wasn't I told about the project and why wasn't the photography unit given the job?"

Passing by the open door of the office, Best heard Christianson's protest and quipped: "Maybe he is interested in photography, Jerome."

Christianson realized he was a victim of another of the division's unaccountable administrative procedures and, too overwhelmed to say more, returned to his own office. He had lost another skirmish in the civil war being waged in the Graphics and Photography Division.

Questions and Instructions

1. In general, what are some of the administrative problems of the division?
2. Evaluate the leadership styles of Olaf Johanssen and Lester Best and the administrative abilities of Jerome Christianson and Donald Waterman.
3. In view of the attitudes of the director and assistant director, what courses of action might the supervisors have taken to prevent the situation in the division from arising and developing as it did?
4. What does the situation in the division reveal about the overall administration of the university?
5. If you were vice-president of administration at the university and became aware of the discord in the division, how would you deal with it?
6. Most grievance procedures established by institutions apply only to nonadministrative employees. Should there also be a grievance procedure for administrators?

Selected Bibliography

Blau, Peter M., "Strategic Leniency and Authority," in Golembiewski, Robert T.; Gibson, Frank; and Miller, Gerald, eds., *Managerial Behavior and Organization Demands,* Itasca, Ill.: F. E. Peacock Publishers, 1978. pp. 158–61.

Bozeman, Barry, "Strategic Public Management and Productivity: A Firehouse Theory," *State Government* 56 (No. 1, 1983): 2–7.

Brinks, James T., "The Comparable Worth Issue: A Salary Administration Bombshell," *Personnel Administrator* 26 (November 1981): 37–40.

Filipowicz, Christine A., "The Troubled Employee: Whose Responsibility?" *Personnel Administrator* 24 (June 1979): 17–22.

Freedman, Sara M., and Montanari, John R., "An Integrative Model of Managerial Reward Allocation," *Academy of Management Review* 5 (July 1980): 381–90.

Kramer, Fred A., *Dynamics of Public Bureaucracy—An Introduction to Public Management,* 2nd ed., Cambridge, Mass.: Winthrop Publishers, 1981. Chs. 10, 11, and 12 provide a useful overview of various types of executive, legislative, and judicial controls.

Lau, Alan W.; Newman, Arthur R.; and Broedling, Laurie A., "The Nature of Managerial Work in the Public Sector," *Public Administration Review* 40 (September/October 1980): 513–20.

Lutz, Carl F., "Efficient Maintenance of the Classification Plan," *Public Personnel Management* 2 (July/August 1973): 232–41.

March, James G., and Feldman, Martha S., "Information in Organization as Signal and Symbol," *Administrative Science Quarterly* 26 (June 1981): 171–86.

Porter, Lyman W.; Lawler, Edward E., III; and Hackman, J. Richard, *Behavior in Organizations,* New York: McGraw-Hill, 1975. See "Conflict Resolution," pp. 463–66.

Remick, Helen, "The Comparable Worth Controversy," *Public Personnel Management* 10 (No. 4, 1981): 371–83.

Schulkind, Gilbert, "Monitoring Position Classification—Practical Problems and Possible Solutions," *Public Personnel Management* 4 (January/February 1975): 32–38.

Watts, Patti, "Preretirement Planning: Making the Golden Years Rosy," *Personnel* 64 (March 1987): 32–39.

6

Going Bare

For two consecutive years, Jefferson County commissioners were faced with budget-busting insurance costs. Their insurance company notified them that this year's renewal cost of a $1 million general liability coverage would rise from $37,303 to $127,843; the year before the cost had been only $8,001. Anticipating another increase for the coming year, the commissioners had budgeted $50,000 for insurance but were appalled to find the sum was $77,843 under what was needed.

While seeking ways of meeting the problem of greatly increased insurance costs, they decided, as many counties and municipalities were doing, on "going bare," a term in the risk business meaning "uncovered." To reduce hazards in the meantime, they directed Daniel Hayashi, damage control officer, to institute a safety program to prevent accidents and eliminate dangers that could result in injuries.

Hayashi's duties had largely consisted of checking for damage to bridges and roads and deciding priorities on maintenance and repair work, and he was ignorant of what his new job involved. He soon learned there was a term to describe it—*risk management*. It was, he read in a magazine article, a program to minimize the exposure of local government units to risk because of increased liability litigation and the practice of insurance companies setting exorbitant rates beyond their means or refusing to provide coverage at all.

Hayashi saw as his first problem finding out what his responsibilities were and how he could meet them. He discovered that until recently counties were not required to follow federal safety regulations set by the Occupational Safety and Health Administration. Now that they were, Hayashi, in written directives and talks, attempted to keep county employees informed about these regulations. He did the same with respect to a new law requiring employees to be informed of hazardous materials with which they worked.

Hayashi started his educational program with the county road crews whose work, he felt, was where risk was highest. He was gratified by the workers' responses. "I think they're pleased that we're concerned," he reported to the commissioners. "They seem to be thinking of themselves more as professionals and there is higher morale. That has its own benefits because good morale creates greater efficiency."

At the same time, Hayashi kept a watchful eye for safety violations and inspected county buildings for hazards. This aspect of safety had been largely neglected before because public buildings were exempt from fire codes. He found elected officials cooperative in his efforts, especially after they were told that since the county had no insurance they might be sued personally. "It's a bad situation to be in," the district attorney had told him. "You run for office and after you begin serving the people, you find everything you own is on the line." In one county, Hayashi learned that the three commissioners prepared letters of resignation effective the day the county's policy expired because they were so afraid of being liable should someone decide to sue.

Prominent in the state and national news at the time were the multimillion dollar damages juries seemed willing to award and the multiplication of suits. Physicians were major targets, and some retired from practice because they could not afford the high cost of coverage. But the excessive costs were brought home to everyone because automobile rates rose sharply, policies were canceled for no apparent reason, and many persons were unable to find a firm willing to sell them coverage. As a result, most states were considering tort reform legislation to set limits on liability awards, and state legislatures and the U.S. Congress were being urged to pass laws regulating the insurance business.

Jefferson County, so far as Hayashi knew, had never been sued for damages in the hundreds of thousands or millions of dollars that now seemed rampant. But even on a lesser scale jury awards and settlements could be injurious. In a neighboring county, a suit asking $100,000 for an alleged false arrest was filed; in another, some twenty suits ranging from $50,000 to $100,000 were brought because a planning commission inadvertently omitted details in a legal notice concerning the location of a natural gas processing plant; and, in a third, the driver of an automobile won a jury award of $5,800 though he had bypassed a barricade and signs warning that a bridge was washed out and had ended up in a ditch. Risk-management programs, no matter how good, could not entirely prevent such legal actions, but nevertheless Hayashi considered them worthwhile.

As a neophyte in risk management, Hayashi did not think himself qualified to decide on what should be done about the insurance situation. Going bare, of course, was not a solution. He found in some counties that selective coverage was obtained—the counties were going only partially unclad. For example, one county dropped all policies except for the sheriff's department, which was insured at an annual cost of $11,000 for defense and settlement of claims against its deputies and jail employees. He also discovered that insurance pools for municipalities and counties were being established about the country, but there were enough gaps in coverage that joining a pool, even if one were established in the state by the county commissioners' association, would probably not be the complete answer. Another possibility was to self-insure, which some cities and counties were doing by selling tax-exempt bonds to fund primary insurance reserves from which claims could be paid. Was a final solution contained in proposed regulatory legislation, state or federal, or in the cap on liability awards being urged by insurors and fought by trial lawyers? The dilemma, Hayashi thought, might be around for a good while.

Questions and Instructions

1. Even though Jefferson County did not have the $77,843 needed above the budgeted amount of $50,000 for renewing its insurance, were the commissioners acting responsibly in letting the policy lapse?
2. How do you account for the fact that counties surveyed by Daniel Hayashi seemed to find it so difficult to raise the extra funds, often under $100,000, required to continue their insurance?
3. What other areas in county government, besides those receiving Hayashi's attention, could be included in a risk-management program?
4. Draft a risk-management program for a city.
5. Why might it be harder for a small city to self-insure through the issuance of bonds than a large city?
6. What are the weak points of each method mentioned for obtaining more reasonable insurance costs—self-insurance, pools, legislation, and so forth?

Selected Bibliography

Bieber, Robert, "Are Risk Managers Needed in Cities?" *Public Management* 67 (February 1985): 7–10.

Cornia, Gary C.; Timmins, William M.; and Varley, David A., "Cooperation between Personnel and Budget Offices During Position Requests and Reclassifications," *State and Local Government Review* 17 (Winter 1985): 180–87.

Danziger, James N., and Ring, Peter Smith, "Fiscal Limitations: A Selective Review of Recent Research," *Public Administration Review* 42 (January/February 1982): 47–55.

Geller, Kenneth S., "Municipal Liability under Section 1983: A Thumbnail Sketch," *Public Management* 68 (November 1986): 9–12.

James, Frank E., "Insurance Pooling," *Public Management* 67 (February 1985): 6.

Le Croy, Charles E., "Excess Insurance Alternatives Provide Risk Management," *American City & County* 101 (January 1987): 16–18.

Muzychenko, Jay, "Where Did All the Insurance Go?" *Public Management* 68 (November 1986): 3–5.

Pupkin, Barry A., "Local Government and Antitrust: A Strategy for Reducing Liability," *Public Management* 67 (April 1985): 13–14.

Rosenbloom, David H., "Public Administrators' Liability: Bench v. Bureau in the Contemporary Administrative State," *Public Administration Quarterly* 10 (Winter 1987): 373–86.

Stipak, Brian; McGowan, Robert P.; and Stevens, John M., "Effect of Fiscal Stress on Attitudes of Local Executives," *State and Local Government Review* 17 (Winter 1985): 188–92.

Wiesenthal, Eric, "Public Liability Crisis Sparks Tort Reform," *Public Administration Times* 9 (March 1, 1986): 1, 3.

7

An Equitable Sick-Leave Plan

Slashes in federal aid programs to cities, a decline in revenue from a two-percent sales tax, and higher costs in everything from cleaning supplies to wages had brought hard times to the elected officials of Spring Valley. The combination of these factors made it seem impossible for Robert Donizetti—the city manager—and the budget committee of the City Council to provide a balanced budget for the city.

Situated in a northeastern state, Spring Valley had a population of twelve thousand, a declining one that matched its declining revenue. In casting about for means to finance the small city's operations, Donizetti saw few opportunities for increasing the revenue. In the past year one of its chief employers, the Acme Manufacturing Company, had been forced to close its local factory, and all parts of the local economy had been affected by a state wide business recession. Hence, Donizetti went carefully over departmental budgets seeking ways to cut costs and eliminate waste.

One area in which Donizetti decided savings could be effected was through changes in policy concerning sick leave. The city's work force consisted of only about 150 full-time employees, and figures in Donizetti's office showed that sick leave in the past six years averaged 7.34 days per year per employee. This was not only costly in dollars in terms of Spring Valley's budget but meant a loss of labor efficiency and productivity. His statistics showed that female and older employees used more sick leave than males and younger workers. Donizetti prepared tables of sick-leave averages by age and sex for the budget committee (see Tables 1 and 2).

Spring Valley had not had many labor conflicts. Employee relations were handled through the personnel director, William Danforth, and the City Employees' Association, whose president was Joshua Blum. In respect to sick leave, the city had in recent years agreed to include in it family care, doctor appointments, and emergency time off for such events as funerals.

After study of the problem, Donizetti recommended that the City Employees' Association and the personnel department together devise a sick-leave incentive program. It would serve as a means of reducing sick leave,

Table 1. Sick Leave in Spring Valley by Sex, 1983–88

Year	*Male*	*Female*
1983	6.1	7.9
1984	5.9	7.7
1985	6.4	8.4
1986	6.3	8.7
1987	6.5	8.5
1988	6.8	8.9

as a deterrent to sick-leave abuse, and as an equitable plan for the several uses of sick leave.

On June 6 the personnel department presented its proposal. Under its plan, employees would be reimbursed on February 1 of each year for 20 percent of the sick-leave credits accumulated during the past year. An employee would have to have built up forty-five sick-leave days in order to draw cash payments, a move intended to reduce turnover in employment in the city.

The City Employees' Association made a counterproposal that included a choice by the employee to consider sick leave as vacation time or else to triple it and add it to retirement service. Unused credits diverted to retirement were to be made at a rate of 100 percent.

The main point of contention at this stage concerned the percentage of sick-leave credit for which an employee might be reimbursed. The city offered no alternative to minimum yearly reimbursement while the employees demanded that some sort of retirement-related incentive be adopted. After several fruitless negotiations, the two parties agreed to present the problem to a fact finder. His or her findings and suggestions for resolution of the issues would be used as a basis for further negotiations. The fact finder chosen, Alfred Cartaret, conducted private hearings with both parties and submitted his report on July 15.

Table 2. Sick Leave in Spring Valley by Age, 1983–88

Year	*Under 30*	*Over 30*
1983	5.1	6.8
1984	5.3	8.4
1985	5.7	8.1
1986	5.5	7.7
1987	5.8	8.3
1988	5.6	8.6

Questions and Instructions

1. Assume that you are the fact finder in the case. Analyze the sick-leave problem in Spring Valley and propose a plan equitable to both parties.
2. If you were the city manager, entrusted with pursuing the best interests of the city, which provisions in the proposal would you accept and which would you attempt to change?
3. Assume that you are the union negotiator. Which provisions would you accept and which would you attempt to change?

Selected Bibliography

Advisory Commission on Intergovernmental Relations, *Recent Trends in Federal and State Aid to Local Governments,* Washington, D.C.: U.S. Government Printing Office, 1980. pp. 3–25.

———, *1980 Changing Public Attitudes on Governments and Taxes,* Washington, D.C.: U.S. Government Printing Office, 1980. pp. 1–7.

Cascio, Wayne F., and Awad, Elias M., *Human Resources Management: An Information Systems Approach,* Reston, Va.: Reston Publishing Company, 1981. pp. 486–528.

Donaldson, William V., "Managing Shrinking Cities: Cincinnati," *Bureaucrat* 10 (Fall 1981): 56–58.

Hunt, J. G., and Hill, J. W., "The New Look in Motivation Theory for Organizational Research," in Golembiewski, Robert T.; Gibson, Frank; and Miller, Gerald, eds., *Managerial Behavior and Organization Demands: Management as a Linking of Levels of Interaction,* 2nd ed., Itasca, Ill.: F. E. Peacock Publishers, 1978. pp. 81–97.

Lawler, Edward E., III, "New Approaches to Pay: Innovations That Work," in Glueck, William F., ed., *Personnel: A Book of Readings,* Dallas: Business Publications, 1979. pp. 279–87.

Lewis, Carol W., and Logalbo, Anthony T., "Cutback Principles and Practices: A Checklist for Managers," *Public Administration Review* 40 (March/April 1980): 184–88.

Nesbitt, Murray B., *Labor Relations in the Federal Government Service,* Washington, D.C.: The Bureau of National Affairs, Inc., 1976. See "Administrative and Sick Leave," pp. 194–96.

Perry, James L., and Hunt, Carder W., "Evaluating the Union-Management Relationship in Government," *Public Administration Review* 38 (September/October 1978): 431–36.

Song, Youngdahl, and Yarbrough, Tinsley E., "Tax Ethics and Taxpayer Attitudes: A Survey," *Public Administration Review* 38 (September/October 1978): 442–52.

"Why Not a Rational Sick Pay Leave Policy?" *American City and County* 95 (April 1980): 51–53.

8

The Far Side of Fifty

At the age of fifty-six Hazel Ridgeway became unhappy with her job as a cartographic drafter in the Engineering Division of the State Department of Transportation. She had joined the staff twenty-one years ago and now held what some of her friends considered a good job—a decent salary, excellent fringe benefits, and interesting work. But somehow they did not seem enough.

Ridgeway expressed her dissatisfaction in a letter to a friend: "For the next ten or fifteen years of my work life I want something more—I'm not sure what. Maybe something different—a change of scene perhaps or even entering some other type of work. I don't think I can do as a woman in another department told me she had done—accept the situation and not think about it any more. That doesn't seem to satisfy me or some other women of my age I know."

Engaging in a new hobby, becoming an activist in some movement, perhaps women's rights, involving herself in politics, enrolling as a part-time student in the local university to work toward a master's degree—none of these possible activities that occurred to Ridgeway to add interest to her life seemed attractive. Nor could she devote herself to family affairs. Except for a few years when her two children were young, Ridgeway had always worked in her field. Now her children had their own successful careers and her husband enjoyed his work as an accountant.

In the past, Ridgeway had not been much interested in a management-level job, believing the chance of getting one remote. Now, however, she thought there might be an opportunity for advancement because of the resignation of Donald Porter as chief of the cartographic section. On numerous occasions Ridgeway had served as back-up supervisor for Porter, and had always received good performance ratings and salary advances. She felt that her chances of promotion had improved because many ambitious if perhaps younger women were climbing up the professional ladder. If she did succeed in getting the job it would offer challenges that would improve her outlook on her profession. So she decided to submit an application.

It was not long before Ridgeway discovered that the selection procedure for a new chief of cartographics was not being routinely followed. The Department of Transportation had an internal promotion policy, but in this case Jerome Makins, head of the Engineering Division, was going outside to fill the classified-exempt position and had appointed a search committee to seek applicants. Ridgeway was pleased to be one of three finalists but disappointed when a 35-year-old man, Leonard Black, was chosen for the position.

With no previous management experience and fewer than ten years of employment background, Black did not seem to Ridgeway to have credentials equal to her own. She protested to the deputy director of the Department of Transportation, asserting that she had been discriminated against because of her age—she did not want to raise the issue of sexual discrimination—but was told he would not intervene in the selection. For one thing, he told her, Black might sue if his appointment was rescinded. She replied tartly that she felt she also had a cause for a suit.

The vague dissatisfaction that Ridgeway had felt about her job now turned to anger, and her spirits were raised by the prospects of a fight. She engaged a lawyer to file a complaint with the Equal Employment Opportunity Commission (EEOC), asking that she be given the job of section chief or an equivalent one. Shortly thereafter Ridgeway suffered what she considered retaliation for making her EEOC complaint. For the first time in her years with the section, she received a poor job evaluation and only a token raise when there was an across-the-board salary increase.

Failing to settle the case through negotiation with Transportation Department officials, the EEOC brought suit in the United States District Court. Testimony at the trial showed that engineering division chief Makins had pressured the selection committee to hire Leonard Black, and that he had told Porter, the retiring head of the cartographic section, he was sorry there was no way "to keep old Hazel Ridgeway from applying for the job because of equal opportunity laws." Evidence revealed that, though Ridgeway had never held a management position herself, she had frequently served as back-up supervisor to Porter and had successfully maintained production standards. Witnesses also testified that Black at the job interview had acknowledged he had very little supervisory experience. After joining the cartographic section he had enrolled in courses in public management at the local university to make up for this lack.

The jury took about two hours to reach a verdict that the Transportation Department had engaged in willful age discrimination and retaliation. In subsequent negotiations the Department of Transportation agreed to a settlement by which Ridgeway would receive $92,500 in salary adjustment, expenses, and legal fees in addition to a promotion to a supervisory position. It had taken Ridgeway three years to win her fight but, even though there had been times of discouragement, she had been rescued from the doldrums that preceded it and had the satisfaction in the end of being a victor.

Questions and Instructions

1. Do you believe that the frustrations and disappointments felt by Hazel Ridgeway are common among working women today?
2. In the present conditions prevailing as to the employment of women, what can a woman of Ridgeway's age expect to attain?
3. Is it harder for a man than for a woman, after passing the middle years, to accept the truth of having failed to be as successful as he had hoped to be?
4. Is early retirement an acceptable solution to the problem of the older employee who has feelings of frustration or failure about his or her career?
5. What options are available to older employees who feel that they have been by-passed for promotions and are seldom consulted in policy-making decisions, or who see younger workers getting ahead at a quicker rate than they did in their early careers?
6. What counts most in successful management, experience and knowledge of an older person or the ambition and enthusiasm of a younger person?
7. What courses of action are open to an executive who doubts that an older employee is physically or mentally fit for promotion or is not competent to handle a better job?

Selected Bibliography

Avolio, Bruce J.; Barrett, Gerald V.; and Sterns, Harvey L., "Alternative to Age in Assessing Occupational Performance," *Experimental Aging Research* 10 (No. 2, 1984): 101–5.

Baroni, Barry J., "Age Discrimination in Employment: Some Guidelines for Employers," *Personnel Administrator* 26 (May 1981): 97–101.

Brandon, Billie, and Snyder, Robert A., "ADEA Update: Case Law and 'Cost' As a Defense," *Personnel Administrator* 30 (February, 1985): 116–19.

Faley, Robert H.; Kleiman, Lawrence S.; and Longnick-Hall, Mark L., "Age Discrimination and Personnel Psychology: A Review and Synthesis of the Legal Literature with Implications for Future Research," *Personnel Psychology* 37 (Summer 1984): 327–50.

Goetschin, Pierre, "Re-shaping Work for an Older Population," *Personnel Management* (June 1987): 39–41.

Gryski, Gerard S., and DeCotiis, Allen R., "The Relationship of Demographic Factors to Job Satisfaction," *State and Local Government Review* 15 (Winter 1983): 38–43.

Hanlon, Martin D., "Age and Commitment to Work," *Research on Aging* 8 (June 1986): 289–316.

Hayward, Mark D., and Grady, William R., "The Occupational Retention and Recruitment of Older Men: The Influence of Structural Characteristics of Work," *Social Forces* 64 (March 1986): 644–66.

Kieffer, Jarold A., "Mini-Symposium on New Roles for Older Workers: The Neglected Option," *Public Administration Review* 44 (September/October 1984): 433–52.

Lewis, Gregory B., "Changing Patterns of Sexual Discrimination in Federal Employment," *Review of Public Personnel Administration* 7 (Spring 1987): 1–13.

Lynch, Terri, "The National Association of Older Worker Employment Services: Activities and Policies," *Public Administration Review* 44 (September/October 1984): 444–47.

Mathys, Nicholas J.; LeVan, Helen; and Schwerdtner, Frederick, "Learning the Lessons of Age Discrimination Cases," *Personnel Journal* 63 (June 1984): 30–31.

Morrison, Malcolm H., "Work and Retirement in an Aging Society," *Daedalus* 115 (Winter 1986): 269–93.

O'Brien, Fabius P.; Robinson, Jerald F.; and Taylor, G. Stephen, "The Effects of Supervisor Sex and Work Environment on Attitudes Toward Older Employees," *Public Personnel Management* 15 (Summer 1986): 119–30.

Rhodes, Susan R., "Age-Related Differences in Work Attitudes and Behavior: A Review and Conceptual Analysis," *Psychological Bulletin* 93 (No. 2, 1983): 328–67.

Waldman, David A., and Azvolio, Bruce J., "A Meta-Analysis of Age Differences in Job Performance," *Journal of Applied Psychology* 71 (No. 1, 1986): 33–38.

Wolf, James F.; Neves, Carole M.; Greenaugh, Richard T.; and Benton, Bill B., "Greying at the Temples: Demographics of a Public Service Occupation," *Public Administration Review* 47 (March/April 1987): 190–98.

Zanar, Louis P., "Recent Amendments to the Age Discrimination in Employment Act," *George Washington Journal of International Law and Economics* 19 (No. 17, 1985): 165–97.

9

A Campaigner for Equal Rights

Dawson Bryan had worked ten years in the building-construction trade in Parkhurst when he joined the Code Enforcement Department of the city as a code-compliance inspector. In a few years he had worked up through the two grades of compliance inspector and the positions of safety officer and assistant director of the department and last year he was named director.

By city ordinance, the duties of the department were to inspect construction, alteration, or remodeling of any buildings and the installation of electric wiring, gas and water lines, plumbing, and air conditioning; to act as designee of the county Health Department for the enforcement of health provisions in the city code; and to enforce housing regulations, safety regulations, and sign regulations.

A big, burly man, Bryan took a no-nonsense attitude toward his job and the fifteen employees in the department. Tact was not a word in his vocabulary. When he gave instructions, he was inclined to shout as he had done when working outdoors in the building trade. The employees in the department were used to his high-decibel communication and paid no attention to it. On the whole, the department was well managed, was strict in enforcing the codes despite being understaffed, and worked very well as a team. It was an all-male enclave in a city government that since the adoption of an equal-opportunity and affirmative-action ordinance had been increasingly infiltrated in recent years by women employees in departments, like street cleaning and maintenance, that had never seen them before.

The male stronghold in code enforcement was breached when the Department of Personnel sent Bryan a new Compliance Inspector Grade 1 named Kate Grunwald. Bryan immediately got on the telephone to protest to Martin Everest, director of personnel, that the work of inspection was so specialized no woman could handle it. Everest replied that Grunwald was fully qualified, in fact better qualified than some of the male inspectors because she had studied electrical engineering in a university for two years and only three or four of his present staff had any college work. "Anyway," Everest said, "read Articles III and IV of our union contract dealing with nondiscrimination and affirmative action. You'll see why we were glad to hire Grunwald." (See Exhibit 1 at the end of this case.) Bryan replied he did not need to read a book to learn that a woman in his department meant trouble.

Kate Grunwald was not the type to ask any special favors on the job. She had quit the university after two years when she married and her husband, a petroleum-engineering senior, upon graduation had taken a job in Kuwait. Five years later their marriage ended in divorce, and Grunwald, who gained custody of their son, was irregularly employed for a time in construction work, where she encountered difficulty because of being a woman. She had noted the subordinate position of women in the Kuwaiti society and had suffered from sex bias on the job in the United States. She therefore became an ardent activist in the women's movement and took part in the political and feminist activities of the National Organization for Women (NOW). She had adopted a belligerent attitude toward what she perceived as sex bias.

On the job, Grunwald was first assigned to checking on complaints, most of them reports of health nuisances, and not on routine inspection of the electrical wiring, gas and water lines, and plumbing in new construction that she considered herself best qualified to do. She was reliable and competent, and Bryan could not find any reasonable fault with her work. Nevertheless, the relationship between the two might be accurately described as restrained hostility.

After Grunwald had been six months on the job, a vacancy occurred for a Grade 2 compliance inspector. She mentioned to Bryan that she intended to apply for the job, but he tried to discourage her by saying she ought to have more experience before seeking a promotion. Nevertheless, Grunwald submitted an application to the Personnel Department. When asked for a report on her work, Bryan told Everest, the personnel director, that she was doing all right as far as he could see, but disrupted the peace of the department by expressing her views on women's rights and had taken time off during a busy spring-inspection season to attend a regional convention of NOW. "All the more reason for promoting her," Everest said. "We don't want a bunch of women libbers picketing City Hall on her behalf."

A few months after receiving her promotion, Grunwald decided to apply for another vacancy in the department, that of safety officer, a supervisory position with a higher salary. She was dissuaded from doing so by Bryan on the ground that two other compliance inspectors with more seniority were already applicants. A year later the safety-officer position became vacant again and Grunwald, against the advice of Bryan, applied for it.

A week later she obtained sick leave, but it was revealed afterward that she had spent part of the time attending, as an observer for the county chapter of NOW, a conference at the state capital of the American Federation of State, County, and Municipal Employees planning a campaign to support comparable worth legislation. Although comparable worth—the concept of equal pay for work of comparable value—was not applicable to her own job, Grunwald was interested in its benefits to the thousands of women victims of discriminatory pay scales.

When Grunwald returned to her job, Bryan angrily told her she had no business taking sick leave to engage in political activity, which was forbidden in the city charter. Equally angry, Grunwald told Bryan that he was a sexist and that most city departments were in violation of the equal-rights and affirmative-action provisions of the charter in respect to the employment of women. The only political activity forbidden in the city charter, she said, was a prohibition against employees taking part in city elections.

A few days after this confrontation, the most heated that had taken place between Grunwald and Bryan, she learned that she had not received the promotion to safety officer.

Shortly afterward, Grunwald filed a complaint with the Equal Employment Opportunity Commission alleging that she had been passed over for promotion on grounds of sex discrimination. She charged that she had been discouraged from seeking promotions by the head of her department and that she was a victim of discrimination when she failed to get promoted when she had applied for a higher position. She also questioned the qualifications of a male who, she alleged, was given the job of safety director without applying for it. She cited her department head's criticism of her support for women's rights as prima facie evidence of discrimination. She asked for advancement in position equal in pay and authority to past positions she had sought and for assurances there would be no retaliation resulting from her complaint.

Questioned by a newspaper reporter about her complaint, Grunwald said, "Women are not hired by the city for managerial positions on an equal basis with men. I'm interested in seeing more women selected as department heads. I'm going all the way with this complaint for the good of all women."

Questions and Instructions

1. Was the personnel director remiss in failing to do more than tell Bryan to read the union contract clauses on affirmative action to help prepare for the acceptance of a woman in the Code Enforcement Department?
2. What decision do you think the Human Rights Commission will reach on Grunwald's complaint under the Civil Rights Act of 1964? (See Exhibit 1 in Case No. 13, "Pressing a Harassment Suit.")
3. Is the fact that Grunwald took sick leave to attend a meeting on com-

parable worth legislation sufficient grounds for a reprimand or denial of a promotion?

4. Do you think Grunwald was right in going directly to the EEOC with her complaint instead of seeking redress through grievance procedures outlined in the city's contract with the American Federation of State, County, and Municipal Employees Union? Explain.
5. Do you think Grunwald would make a good department head or supervisor?

Selected Bibliography

Brown, Marsha, "Getting and Keeping Women in Non-Traditional Jobs," *Public Personnel Management* 10 (No. 4, 1981): 408–11.

Burns, Ruth Ann, "Women in Municipal Management: Opportunities and Barriers," in *The Municipal Year Book 1981,* Washington, D.C.: International City Management Association, 1981. pp. 167–74.

Cruz, Nestor, "'Realpolitik' and Affirmative Action," *Public Personnel Management* 9 (No. 3, 1980): 192–95.

Gettings, Robert, "Litigation as a Tool for Social Change," *Journal of Health and Human Resources Administration* 2 (February 1980): 313–19.

Hackman, J. Richard, and Lawler, Edward E., III, "Employee Reactions to Job Characteristics," *Journal of Applied Psychology* 55 (June 1971): 259–86.

Holley, William H., and Feild, Hubert S., "Equal Employment Opportunity and Its Implications for Personnel Practices," in Glueck, William F., ed., *Personnel: A Book of Readings,* Dallas: Business Publications, 1979. pp. 349–58.

Kovach, Kenneth A., "Women in the Labor Force: A Socio-Economic Analysis," *Public Personnel Management* 9 (No. 4, 1980): 318–26.

Menges, Edward H., Jr., "The Lakewood, Colorado, Personnel System: Creating an Environment for Productivity," *Public Personnel Management* 9 (No. 4, 1980): 257–67.

Preffer, Jeffrey, and Davis-Blake, Alison, "The Effect of the Proportion of Women on Salaries: The Case of the College Administrators," *Administrative Science Quarterly* 32 (March 1987): 1–24.

Rosen, Benson, and Jerdee, Thomas H., "On-the-Job Sex Bias: Increasing Managerial Awareness," *Personnel Administrator* 22 (January 1977): 15–18.

Ruzicho, Andrew J., "The Weber Case—Its Impact on Affirmative Action," *Personnel Administrator* 25 (June 1980): 69–72.

Schleh, Edward C., "Using Central Staff to Boost Line Initiative," *Management Review* 65 (May 1976): 17–23.

Slack, James D., "Affirmative Action and City Managers: Attitudes Toward Recruitment of Women," *Public Administration Review* 47 (March/April 1987): 199–206.

Smith, Russel A.; Edwards, Harry T.; and Clark, Theodore R., *Labor Relations in the Public Sector: Cases and Materials,* 2nd ed., Indianapolis, Ind.: Bobbs-Merrill, 1979.

Sutton, Robert I., and Rafaeli, Anat, "Characteristics of Work Stations As Potential Occupational Stressors," *Academy of Management Journal* 30 (June 1987): 260–76.

Taub, Nadine, "Dealing with Employment Discrimination and Damaging Stereotypes: A Legal Perspective," *Journal of Social Sciences* 41 (No. 4, 1985): 99–110.

Tomkins, Adrienne, "Sex Discrimination: Adrienne Tomkins, Stenographer," *Civil Liberties Review* 5 (September/October 1978): 19–24.

Exhibit 1. Union Contract Articles on Civil Rights

Article III

Non-Discrimination

Section 1. No employee or an individual being considered for employment shall be favored or subjected to discrimination by management or by the Union because of race, creed, color, sex, or national origin, relationship to any person or persons, or political or union activities, other than those prohibited by this Agreement.

Section 2. Management and the Union agree not to interfere with the right of employees to become or not to become members of the Union and further, will urge the employees that there will be no discrimination or coercion against any employee because of Union membership or non-membership.

Article IV

Affirmative Action

Section 1. The City and the Union are committed to the concept and practice of equal employment opportunity as a necessary component of merit principles, which is a phase of affirmative action.

Section 2. The Affirmative Action commitment will be supported by positive and aggressive practices and procedures, which will insure non-discrimination and equal-employment opportunity for racial and ethnic minorities, the disadvantaged, and women in securing admission in the City employment force and promotional opportunities at all job levels.

Section 3. The general objectives of the City and the Union in affirmative-action practice will be:

a. to engage in continuous planning and monitoring of the effects of practices in order to eliminate and prevent the occurrence of arbitrary, discriminatory practices and policies related to employment, membership, and promotion; and

b. to take positive steps to solicit applicants for employment and membership from minority groups and women's organizations.

10

Parking Meters—A Perennial Problem

Once again the town of San Juan looked forward to the annual show put on by the City Council. The *Evening Gazette* printed the agenda for the next meeting, which included the item "Replacement of Parking Meters," and the bulletin board of San Juan Cable Television announced that it would cover the meeting. The show, which occurred as regularly as the Pioneer Days festival and was almost as much fun, always packed the council chamber.

The issue over the parking meters was whether to keep the seven hundred old and obsolete meters, which frequently were inoperable and which accepted only pennies, nickels, and dimes, or to replace them with new meters that would accept nickels, dimes, and quarters. The question of whether to install new meters taking coins of larger denomination that would produce more revenue was almost as controversial as that raised twenty-five years before when the installation of the meters was first considered. The council had brought up the matter of replacing the old meters on five previous occasions, and the debate had always resulted in a stalemate.

Mayor Arthur Enriquez wanted to avoid the circus atmosphere of previous discussions of the parking-meter problem. When he called the council to order with a rap of the gavel, he was a little dismayed by the television cameras and lights and the standing-room-only crowd in the chamber. After approval of the minutes, the mayor introduced the second item on the agenda, "Replacement of Parking Meters."

"The discussion of the advantages and disadvantages surrounding the parking meters has been going on for five years," Enriquez said. "The debate is not on whether San Juan will have meters, for that has been established. The debate centers on whether we will replace the old meters with new ones—meters that will accept larger coin denominations. This is no time to become angry over the meters. Let us reason together and resolve our differences in a manner that will benefit the citizens of San Juan."

Enriquez then introduced the new city manager, Joseph Stevenson, who would make a preliminary report on the question of replacing the meters.

Stevenson was aware that his predecessor had been fired by a vote of three to two because of his support of replacement. He did not intend to get into similar trouble by submitting a proposal either for or against the meters.

He began by saying that to an outsider the controversy over the parking meters might appear inflated and unnecessary, but to the citizens of San Juan it was a matter of principle. He related that more than twenty-five years before, when the city first considered installing meters, citizens were outraged. They felt that the streets belonged to the public and they should not be charged for using them. But after the installation of the meters, drivers got accustomed to putting their coins in the slot and thought nothing of it. But about fifteen years ago parking in the downtown district became a serious problem because the population had grown from 10,500 to more than 25,000 people. Today, Stevenson continued, the small cost for parking was no deterrent to misuse of parking space. Spaces that should be open to customers and clients of downtown stores and firms were taken up by the cars of business professionals and their employees. The downtown parking problem went beyond the question of replacement of meters. "In the early days," he said, "meters were used to regulate parking and were not an instrument of city-revenue enhancement." There might be other solutions to the problem, such as municipal or privately operated parking lots or garages. He did not believe the meter question could be answered this evening. The air had to be cleared and he would have to develop a plan for the council to consider. To this end, he had developed an "Administrative Plan of Action." He then distributed to the council-members and the audience a list of objectives and studies that should be made. (See Exhibit 1 on p. 55.)

Stevenson's temporizing proposal was effective, and those who had come to the council meeting expecting fireworks were disappointed. Several of the councilmembers briefly stated their points of view and only a few of the people in the audience were sufficiently aroused to take the floor.

Adam McKnight, a business leader and councilmember from a ward that included the downtown area, said, "Parking meters are merely devices that regulate the use of limited parking space in high-use parts of the town. We're a friendly town. We want farmers and people from neighboring towns and small communities to come to San Juan and shop. We're not money-hungry people. We don't need new and more expensive gadgets complicating our way of life. Leave the more expensive meters to those who live in big cities."

Elizabeth Howard, a councilmember from a well-to-do residential district, disagreed with McKnight. She saw "no reason why San Juan should remain stagnant or not keep up with the demands of the time." Revenue was generated from parking meters, she said, and this revenue would purchase the new meters and increase the city's coffers as well. "Who among us can't afford to spend fifteen- or twenty-cents for parking these days?" she asked rhetorically.

Philip Hemphill, a councilmember and an implement dealer, reported the complaint of a rancher who had recently priced a John Deere tractor. "He would like to purchase the tractor from my dealership," Hemphill said, "but he was angry over receiving a parking ticket last Saturday. It seemed like every time he came to town he got a parking ticket."

After forty-five minutes of comment from the councilmembers and members of the public, Mayor Enriquez entertained a motion to table the parking-meter issue until the next monthly meeting. It carried unanimously. City Manager Stevenson breathed a sigh of relief. He had a little time left to survey the situation, find out the facts and figures, and come up with proposals to solve the problem.

Questions and Instructions

1. If you were Stevenson, what would you do first? Why? Is the administrative plan of action an adequate one? Have any factors been overlooked? If so, what are they?
2. What would you do to keep a good relationship with the council?
3. The day after the council meeting, you go into the Rainbow Cafe next to City Hall. Councilmembers Howard and Hemphill are sitting in a booth and they invite you to join them for a cup of coffee. In the course of the conversation Hemphill turns to you and asks, "How do you personally stand on the meter question?" What will be your response? What are the implications associated with your response? Discuss.
4. What methods will you use to obtain public opinion about the parking meters? Telephone survey, mailed questionnaires, newspaper poll, or some other form of survey method? What are the advantages and limitations associated with random versus nonrandom sampling techniques?
5. Evaluate the outcome possibilities presented in objective four of Exhibit 1 at the end of this chapter. What assumptions are reflected in the entries? Do you agree or disagree with their stated impact? What other impacts might be added to the outcome table? Elaborate.
6. Develop a model by which parking-meter policies may be evaluated in the future. What are the assumptions upon which the model is based and what are their implications? Explain.

Selected Bibliography

Abney, Glenn, and Lauth, Thomas P., *The Politics of State and City Administration,* Albany, N.Y.: State University of New York Press, 1986. Ch. 9, "Council Intervention in Municipal Administration," pp. 176–94.

Davidson, Dan H., and Bennett, Solon A., "Municipal Purchasing Practices," *The Municipal Year Book 1980,* Washington, D.C.: International City Management Association, 1980.

Denhardt, Robert B., "Strategic Planning in State and Local Government," *State and Local Government Review* 17 (Winter 1985): 174–79.

Etzioni, Amitai, "Mixed Scanning: A Third Approach to Decision-Making," *Public Administration Review* 27 (December 1967): 387–88.

Fitz-Gibbon, Carol Taylor, and Morris, Lynn Lyons, *How to Design a Program Evaluation,* Beverly Hills, Calif.: Sage Publications, 1978.

Hatry, Harry P.; Winnie, Richard E.; and Fisk, Donald M., *Practical Program Evaluation for State and Local Governments,* 2nd ed., Washington, D.C.: The Urban Institute Press, 1981. Ch. 2, "What's the Program All About? Identifying Program Objectives, Evaluation Criteria, and Clientele Groups," pp. 13–24, and Ch. 4, "The Dirty Job—Data Collection," pp. 57–71.

Lathan, Gary P., and Yukl, Gary A., "A Review of Research on the Application of Goal Setting in Organizations," *Academy of Management Journal* 18 (December 1975): 824–45.

Meltsner, Arnold J., *Policy Analysts in the Bureaucracy,* Berkeley, Calif.: University of California Press, 1976. Ch. 7, "Communication," pp. 229–64, and Ch. 8, "Predicaments," pp. 265–94.

Merget, Astrid E., "The Era of Fiscal Restraint," in *The Municipal Year Book 1980,* Washington, D.C.: International City Management Association, 1980. pp. 178–91.

Morgan, David R., *Managing Urban America: The Politics and Administration of America's Cities,* 2nd ed., Monterey, Calif.: Brooks/Cole Publishing Co., 1984. Ch. 1, "The External World of the Urban Manager," pp. 13–41, and Ch. 3, "Urban Policy Making," pp. 64–89.

Murphy, Jerome T., *Getting the Facts, A Fieldwork Guide for Evaluators and Policy Analysts,* Santa Monica, Calif.: Goodyear Publishing Co., 1980. Ch. 7, "Summing Up and Applying Standards," pp. 161–80.

Newell, Charldean, and Ammons, David N., "Role Emphases of City Managers and Other Municipal Executives," *Public Administration Review* 47 (May/June 1987): 246–253.

Odiorne, George S., "How to Succeed in MBO Goal Setting," *Personnel Journal* 57 (August 1978): 427–29.

Quade, E. S., *Analysis for Public Decisions,* New York: Elsevier North Holland, 1975. Ch. 1, "Analysis and Public Decisions," pp. 1–12; Ch. 2, "What Sort of Problem? What Sort of Analysis?" pp. 13–31; and Ch. 7, "Effectiveness and Benefits," pp. 103–15.

Rice, Mitchell F., and Jones, Woodrow, Jr., "Municipal Service Suits, Local Public Services and Service Equality," *Midwest Review of Public Administration* 14 (March 1980): 29–39.

Steiner, Richard, "Communication between Government and Citizen: Open or Closed Book?" *Southern Review of Public Administration* 1 (March 1978): 542–61.

Svara, James H., "Dichotomy and Duality: Reconceptualizing the Relationship between Policy and Administration in Council-Manager Cities," *Public Administration Review* 45 (January/February 1985): 221–32.

Weiss, Carol H., *Evaluation Research,* Englewood Cliffs, N.J.: Prentice-Hall, 1972. pp. 1–59.

Wesemann, H. Edward, "Innovative Revenue Sources: The Entrepreneurial Municipality," *Public Management* 63 (January/February 1981): pp. 21–23.

Wikstrom, Nelson, "The Mayor as a Policy Leader in the Council-Manager Form of Government: A View From the Field," *Public Administration Review* 39 (May/June 1979): 270–76.

Exhibit 1. Administrative Plan of Action on Parking Meters

Objectives:

1. To assess the need for new parking meters as indicated by the cost of scheduled and unscheduled maintenance over a five-year period.
2. To analyze the economic advantages associated with the purchase and installation costs projected to the end of the next fiscal year.
3. To determine public attitudes on parking meters by conducting a poll or by using some other means of measuring public opinion.
4. To prepare a table of possible outcomes based on usage levels.

NEW METERS

Low Usage	*High Usage*
Medium revenue receipts Satisfied auto owners Low maintenance costs	High revenue receipts Dissatisfied auto owners Average maintenance costs

OLD METERS

Low Usage	*High Usage*
Low revenue receipts Satisfied auto owners High maintenance costs	Average revenue receipts Satisfied auto owners High maintenance costs

5. To prepare a proposal for the disbursement of meter revenue obtained from the present system and from a new metered system.
6. To examine the possibility of municipal parking lots or privately operated lots.
7. To prepare a final report and to make recommendations to the City Council.

11

A $5,000 Anonymous Phone Call?

Jim Johnson began work with the Health Facilities Program in December and after an orientation period became one of five environmental health sanitarians whose responsibility was to survey licensed medical facilities within the state to determine their compliance with licensure, Medicare, and other regulations. He was also responsible for providing part-time consultation to hospitals and nursing homes. Each survey team consisted of a registered nurse and an environmental sanitarian. The nurses were mostly mature, gray-haired women, while the sanitarians, although relatively young, tended to appear straitlaced and serious. Johnson, on the other hand, had curly brown hair that almost touched his shoulders and he wore faded blue jeans and sandals.

Johnson's supervisor was Tom Blake. "I'm a little concerned about Jim's effectiveness as a surveyor-consultant," he said to Frances Maner, his administrative assistant. "I'm afraid many of the people he will be working with will classify him as a worthless bum because of his casual way of dressing."

"But, Tom," countered Maner, "you know he was the most-qualified applicant we interviewed. We both agreed he was intelligent and that there was a great deal of promise hidden under his unorthodox appearance."

"I know," Blake said, "but he doesn't dress professionally!"

Johnson learned quickly and soon showed ample confidence and poise. He was fully capable of performing surveys after he had been on the job three months and showed potential for being a good consultant. Six months after being hired he attended a university for an intense, one-month specialized training course required of all health-facilities personnel conducting surveys under the Medicare and Medicaid programs. When Johnson returned, Blake noticed a marked improvement in his written reports and felt certain his survey activities would also show an improvement. After accompanying Johnson on two surveys, Blake decided he was doing as well as, or better than, any other sanitarian under his supervision.

One morning, while Blake was expressing his satisfaction in Johnson's work to Maner, she reminded him of his earlier reservations. "I know," he confessed, "but Jim has really proven himself, and now he has my full confidence."

"I think Jim will be the best sanitarian on our staff in a few years," Maner agreed. "Just wait and see."

A year after Johnson had been in the hospital and nursing-home program, Blake was called into the program director's office. Larry Dandurand, the program director, and Ralph Andrews, the chief inspector, were there, both looking upset.

"I received an interesting, although anonymous, phone call yesterday that I think deserves our attention," Andrews said. "It concerns one of the staff members, Jim Johnson."

Johnson was stationed in a district office in the eastern part of the state, sharing it with two other Health Department staff members, neither of whom was in the same program. Andrews said that the caller complained of all three persons engaging in horseplay while in the office, although this was not often since they were seldom there between 8 A.M. and 5 P.M. Andrews said that the caller phoned because he thought the central office should know about it.

"I tried to explain that because our staff was involved in survey activities they had to spend quite a bit of time away from the office," Andrews said. "The caller was quite persistent, insisting there was 'more productive work done by the inhabitants of a cemetery than done by the Health Department employees.'" Andrews said the caller ended the conversation with an accusation that Johnson was the worst offender and that he also was associating with undesirable persons, including drug users.

Blake proposed that the episode be ignored since the caller had refused to identify himself, but Dandurand made it clear that he had no intention of letting the matter drop and, since Blake was Johnson's supervisor, it was his responsibility to gather the relevant facts. Andrews suggested that Blake make discreet inquiries to substantiate the information given in the phone call. The idea of going behind Johnson's back to determine the accuracy of the phone call was repugnant to Blake. "Suppose I talk to Jim and ask him pointblank if what the caller said is true?" Blake asked.

"Fine," said Dandurand, "but let's get this thing cleared up right away."

After returning to his office, Blake tried to clarify the whole situation in his mind. He knew that Johnson did not spend any more time in his office than necessary. In fact, he recalled many unsuccessful attempts to reach him during scheduled office hours. When he had talked to Johnson about his absence from the office, Johnson admitted that he had some "problems" in "disciplining" himself to observe normal office hours. Realizing that he was very young to be placed in a field office without any direct supervision, Blake chalked up the irregular office hours as the price the program had to pay for running a decentralized operation. Besides, Johnson was getting the job done and that was the important thing. But Blake was upset that one of his sanitarians had been criticized by an anonymous phone caller.

The following week Blake visited Johnson at his office and related the whole story to him. "As far as I'm concerned your work is excellent and that anonymous phone call is of no consequence as far as your performance is concerned," Blake explained. He made it clear, however, that the program director was upset over the whole matter and that, as a state employee, Johnson would be closely scrutinized by the public.

Then Johnson admitted that earlier he had had problems keeping office hours but that in the past two months he had really tried to be in the office when not doing surveys. Blake knew this was true, since he telephoned all of the sanitarians at least once a week and during this period Johnson had always been there. Johnson said also that he did have two cousins who had been convicted of using drugs and that he saw both of them frequently. Johnson declared, "If the state is going to dictate who my friends have to be or the way I have to look, they can take this job and shove it."

"Jim, I assure you nobody in our office is trying to choose your friends," Blake said. "Whom you associate with is none of the state's business. What I really want to do is forget that phone call completely, but I did want you to know about the director's reaction, since it may have a bearing on your advancement potential in the Health Facilities Program." Blake looked Johnson straight in the eye and said, "As far as your personal appearance is concerned, it's a fact of life that external appearance affects the public's opinion about the quality of the work we do. Success is not always measured in terms of hard work and productivity."

At the end of the conference, Blake felt that Johnson had accepted the discussion constructively. But two months later Johnson resigned. Blake telephoned him to find out the specific reasons for this resignation. He learned that Johnson was not leaving state government for a larger salary and, in fact, had no other job lined up.

Johnson explained, "I just wanted to try doing something other than working for the state, and I guess I should make the change now, while I'm still young."

Blake asked him if the anonymous call had anything to do with his resignation, and Johnson said that it had helped him make the decision but was not a primary reason. Blake urged Johnson to change his mind and stay with the program, but after a long discussion he felt that Johnson's mind was made up and the resignation was irrevocable.

After working with Johnson for a year and a half, Blake was certain that the telephone call had far more to do with his resignation than he had admitted. If the phone call could be considered the primary reason Jim resigned, Blake told himself, then it cost the state at least $5,000 in money lost training Jim for the job.

Questions and Instructions

1. Since the phone call was anonymous, should it have been given any consideration at all?
2. How could the substance of the phone call be verified or disqualified by a discreet investigation? If the caller's information could not be substantiated, would it have been necessary to tell Johnson anything at all?
3. Would it have been wise for Blake to transfer Johnson to the central office where he would have had the benefit of direct supervision?
4. Should more emphasis have been placed on the observance of normal working hours when Blake became aware of Johnson's work schedule?
5. If you were Blake and had time to reflect on this incident, what policy recommendation would you suggest to prevent this type of problem from occurring in the future? Should the central office consider having a definite number of hours or specific times during the day when field personnel should be in the office? What are the implications of this type of policy?
6. Is it possible that Johnson's appearance was beneficial in his employee-client relationship? What should be said or done about an employee's personal dress or appearance?
7. Is a supervisor responsible not only for informing an employee of undesirable attitudes or behavior but also for designing a plan to correct or improve them?

Selected Bibliography

Argyris, Chris, "The Individual and Organization: Some Problems of Mutual Adjustment," *Administrative Science Quarterly* 2 (June 1957): 1–24.

Atherton, Roger M., "Centralization Works Best When Managers' Jobs Are Improved," *Human Resource Management* 16 (Summer 1977): 17–20.

Dawis, Rene V., "Personnel Assessment from the Perspective of the Theory of Work Adjustment," *Public Personnel Management* 9 (No. 4, 1980): 268–73.

Duckworth, Donald R., "Participation and Communication: The Key to Effective Customer Relations in Visalia," *Public Management* 69 (April 1987): 5–8.

Feldman, Daniel C., "A Socialization Process That Helps New Recruits Succeed," *Personnel* 57 (March/April 1980): 11–23.

Flynn, W. Randolph, and Stratton, William E., "Managing Problem Employees," *Human Resource Management* 20 (Summer 1981): 28–32.

Gould, Sam, "Career Planning in the Organization," *Human Resource Management* 15 (Fall 1976): 11–18.

Hall, Richard H., *Organizations: Structure and Process,* 2nd ed., Englewood Cliffs, N.J.: Prentice-Hall, 1977. Ch. 7, "Centralization," pp. 67–100.

House, Robert J., and Mitchell, Terence R., "Path-Goal Theory of Leadership," *Journal of Contemporary Business* 3 (Autumn 1974): 81–97.

Luthans, Fred, and Martinko, Mark, "An Organizational Behavior Modification Analysis of Absenteeism," *Human Resource Management* 15 (Fall 1976): 11–18.

Meier, Kenneth J., *Politics and the Bureaucracy: Policymaking in the Fourth Branch of Government,* North Scituate, Mass.: Duxbury Press, 1979. Ch. 5, "Bureaucracy and the Public's Expectations," pp. 108–29.

Ralph, Pierson M., "Performance Evaluation: One More Try," *Public Personnel Management* 9 (No. 3, 1980): 145–53.

Schleh, Edward C., "Using Central Staff to Boost Line Initiative," *Management Review* 65 (May 1976): 17–23.

Smith, Bruce L. R., and Hague, D. C., eds., *The Dilemma of Accountability in Modern Government: Independence Versus Control,* New York: St. Martin's Press, 1971.

Wright, Moorhead, "Individual Growth: The Basic Principles," *Personnel* 37 (September/October 1960): 8–17.

12

To Quit or Not to Quit

Case A. An Intolerable Situation

Ever since Jason Hendrix became director of the State Bureau of Investigation, Alonzo Mercedes, deputy director for five years, had found himself at odds with his superior. Mercedes had been a candidate for the position of director on the retirement of an old friend and associate, but he had not really expected to be appointed. He realized that a new governor, elected on the promise of making a clean sweep, would search outside the state to find a director without established political friendships and loyalties. The governor's choice was Jason Hendrix, a retired army colonel whose latest assignment had been in military intelligence.

Introducing a bit of military spit and polish into the bureau was in Mercedes's view not a bad thing, but he thought Colonel Hendrix overdid it at times. As experienced peace officers, most staff members understood the need for concise and explicit orders and did not mind commands rather than requests. They regarded the colonel, however, as a martinet rather than a leader. Hendrix's chief fault as an administrator, Mercedes thought, was that he would not listen to people. His usual response to difficult situations was: "I want action, not explanations." Thus, as chief intermediary between the director and the staff, Mercedes developed a smoldering resentment of Hendrix.

This resentment grew when employees formed a chapter of the Fraternal Order of Police (FOP). Colonel Hendrix, believing the FOP a threat to his authority and to the orderly performance of investigations, told Mercedes that he would "bust" Henry Dryfus, supervisor of the intelligence section, who was serving as interim president of the FOP chapter. Hendrix threatened to disband the chapter because two other agents were also officers. Later he issued a memorandum to staff members warning them against joining the organization.

In the past Mercedes had not regarded unionization favorably but, in view of the low morale brought on by Hendrix's fulminations, he decided to defend the FOP. He felt that his continuance as deputy director, after the director's typical display of unreason, would be intolerable. He therefore delivered a letter of resignation to Hendrix, and made it available to reporters who had heard of the dispute. The letter stated:

> I think employees should not be treated as you have done this past week. Bureau employees have the same guaranteed constitutional rights as everyone else. They should not be continually subject to your whimsical and irrational fits of anger nor should that be a repeated excuse for disregarding employees' rights.

Mercedes explained to reporters that he had decided to resign because he wanted to stop talk he was criticizing Hendrix because he wanted his job.

In response to reporters' requests for an interview, Hendrix prepared a statement read by a bureau spokesman. In it he said that he regretted Mercedes's resignation because he had been an asset to the agency, adding that he did not care to comment on the dispute over the FOP. "The bureau is bigger than any one person or any small group of people and is certainly as professional as any law enforcement agency in the nation," the statement said. "When this resignation is no longer newsworthy, the bureau will continue to work to the best of its ability with the resources available."

Case B. The Frustrated Assistant Director

After the Department of Human Welfare was faced with the need for reducing its expenditures six percent on orders of the governor because of declining tax collections, Herbert Ali, assistant director of Health Services, found himself constantly on the losing side in proposals to effect savings.

The tendency was, Ali believed, to cause the state's needy to suffer through decisions to reduce services rather than to eliminate waste in operations. For example, state welfare officers were ordered closed for one day a week for which employees were not paid, two emergency relief services were eliminated, and a home-heating program was suspended. It would be better, Ali felt, to reduce a top-heavy administrative force, delay a job reclassification program that would create promotions with pay increases, cut travel allowances, and in general save on operations costs rather than to "rob the poor and the needy."

Frustrated by the curt rejection of his recommendations, Ali felt that he could no longer find satisfaction in his job. His letter of resignation to the Welfare Commission said:

> Throughout my fifteen-year career with the department, I have believed that informed decisions can be made only when all of the facts, honest opinions, and best advice are gathered for evaluation. The decision-making process places an

absolute duty on employees, particularly those in management positions, to express their opinions to superiors in the performance of their job responsibilities. It is also the employee's responsibility, once having offered his or her advice, to carry out with professional dedication and best effort the ultimate decisions of the commission and the director.

Under the present circumstances, I find it increasingly difficult to fulfill these essential responsibilities. Unfortunately, the employee's opinion is often regarded by superiors as criticism or negativism. Given this situation, I have decided that I must resign.

Questions and Instructions

1. How do the motives of Alonzo Mercedes and Herbert Ali differ in their decisions to resign?
2. To what extent were their resignations a result of personality conflicts?
3. Was resignation with a critical blast against superiors an effective way to correct a situation that each felt was wrong?
4. What other courses of action were open to Mercedes and Ali to improve the situations they found unbearable?
5. Discuss the pros and cons of bringing before the public an internal conflict over policy within an agency or department of government.

Selected Bibliography

Balutis, Alan P., "Death by Reorganization," in Bozeman, Barry, and Straussman, Jeffrey, eds., *New Directions in Public Administration,* Monterey, Calif.: Brooks/Cole Publishing Co., 1984. pp. 329–36.

Barbour, George P., Jr.; Fletcher, Thomas W.; and Sipel, George A., *Excellence in Local Government Handbook,* Washington, D.C.: International City Management Association, 1984.

Baum, Howell, *The Invisible Bureaucracy: Problem-Solving in Bureaucratic Organizations,* Oxford, England: Oxford University Press, 1986.

Cayer, N. Joseph, "Managing Human Resources," in Chandler, Ralph Clark, ed., *A Centennial History of the American Administrative State,* New York: The Free Press, 1987. pp. 321–43.

Conant, James K., "Can Government Organizations Be Excellent Too?" *State and Local Government Review* 19 (Spring 1987): 47–52.

Frost, Taggard F., "The Sick Organization. Part I: Neurotic, Psychotic, Sociopathic," *Personnel* 62 (May 1985): 40–44.

Golembiewski, Robert T., *Humanizing Public Organizations,* Mt. Airy, Md.: Lomond Publications, 1985.

Johnson, Jerry W., "Interpersonal Relationships in the Office," *Public Management* 66 (July 1984): 4–6.

Nalbandian, John, "Performance Appraisal: If Only People Were Not Involved," *Public Administration Review* 41 (May/June 1981): 392–96.

———, "The Evolution of Local Governance: A New Democracy," *Public Management* 69 (June 1987): 2–5.

Nigro, Felix A., and Nigro, Lloyd G., eds., *Readings in Public Administration,* New York: Harper and Row, 1983. See "Techniques for Removal through Organizational or Management Procedures," pp. 151–55.

Pederson, Roy R., "Solving the Management Equation," *Public Management* 68 (August 1986): 8–9.

Roberts, Robert, "Last Hired, First Fired and Public Employees," *Review of Public Personnel Administration* 2 (Fall 1981): 29–48.

Rosenbloom, David H., *Public Administration and Law,* New York: Marcel-Dekker, 1983. See pp. 99–139 for a discussion of public employees expressing themselves on matters of public concern, and pp. 207–24 for a discussion of public employees' political and legal freedoms.

Sherman, V. Clayton, "Eight Steps to Preventing Problem Employees," *Personnel* 64 (June 1987): 38–48.

Truelson, Judith A., "Protest Is Not a Four Letter Word," *The Bureaucrat* 14 (Summer 1985): 22–26.

Vaughn, Robert G., "Public Employees and the Right to Disobey," *Hastings Law Journal* 29 (November 1977): 261–95.

13

Pressing a Harassment Suit

After several jobs with various small and unprofitable business firms, Mae Fiedler was pleased to be employed as a records clerk in the Union City Police Department. Here she had regular working hours, sick-leave pay, vacations, and health insurance, security she had not before enjoyed.

A disadvantage, however, was that she was frequently embarrassed by the indecent language used by her predominantly male coworkers and by their talk laced with sexual references. Noting this, the police officers often teased her by commenting on her appearance and by making suggestive remarks about wanting to be alone with her. A confrontation occurred one day: While walking along a hallway, Fiedler was stopped by three officers—Ernest Foster, Robert Aquinaldo, and Leslie Madison—who not only spoke indecently to her but touched the upper part of her body. Fiedler broke away from them and entered the records room. Looking back to see if they were following her, she saw Foster unzip his trousers and wave what she thought was his penis.

Fiedler reported the incident to Chief of Police Oscar Flanagan, as well as the indecent talk that went on in her presence. Although Flanagan promised to look into the matter, he told Fiedler that the officers were only having fun and meant no harm. But when the officers discovered that Fiedler had complained to the chief, they chided her for being a prude and posted on a bulletin board pornographic pictures of naked women bearing her name.

Seeking a way of stopping the harassment, Fiedler went to the city's Women's Resource Center for advice. Although the counselor assigned to Fiedler's case was sympathetic, she was not optimistic in regard to a favorable outcome. She explained that it was difficult to substantiate charges of sexual harassment and that most such court cases failed. Unfortunately, she continued, the cases were unsuccessful because administrators were averse to taking action, coworkers were reluctant to cooperate for fear of losing their jobs or chances of promotion, evidence satisfying legal requirements was difficult to obtain, and the complainant was sometimes treated as the one on trial. "It takes time, money, and energy to follow this type of case through to the end," the counselor said. "Are you willing to initiate action you may lose? If so, we can give you moral support and recommend an attorney to represent you. But the decision is up to you."

Fiedler told the counselor that she would think the matter over. Two days later, however, when the department refused to view the incident as one of sexual harassment, she made up her mind to pursue the case. As a result of an investigation by Chief Flanagan, Officer Foster was suspended for three days without pay for "excessive horseplay," and Officers Aquinaldo and Madison received only written reprimands. The opinion of the department was that there had been no indecent exposure. The object displayed before Fiedler was a fake rubber penis that Foster had been displaying to other officers as a joke.

On the advice of the Women's Resource Center counselor, Fiedler went to the district attorney to file a criminal complaint. He questioned her in such detail that she felt, as she had been warned, like an accused person undergoing cross-examination. The district attorney refused to take action against the officers, saying that Fiedler was making too much of what was nothing more than a harmless prank. He told her that the officers' actions were not punishable crimes, and that she did not have adequate proof for conviction.

Angered by the district attorney's view, Fiedler consulted a lawyer recommended by the Resource Center, Amanda Arnold. Subsequently, she filed a claim for damages against the city under a state tort claims act. Arnold's petition requested $100,000 in damages for violation of Fiedler's right of privacy. It declared that Foster "intentionally exposed himself, knowing that Fiedler was looking at him" and that Fiedler had the right to be free of "such oppressive, insulting, and degrading behavior."

Shortly after filing the claim, Fiedler received written notification of her transfer from the Police Department to the city's Garbage Department to fill a new position at the sewage treatment plant where collection trucks were unloaded. Believing that this action was taken in retaliation for her suit, Arnold filed a complaint with the Equal Employment Opportunity Commission (EEOC). It alleged sexual harassment and requested that the city rescind the transfer. Fiedler's fight became even more difficult when the EEOC denied the request for investigation because of lack of time. It said, however, she had the right to sue city officials in federal court.

After more than three months of frustration, Fiedler brought suit in the United States District Court, asking $500,000 in actual damages and $2 million in punitive damages. The petition cited the failure of the city to respond properly to Fiedler's initial complaint to Chief Flanagan and to her $100,000 claim for damages, and the failure of the district attorney to take proper action. The petition also asked the court to direct the city to reinstate Fiedler in her position as a records clerk in the Police Department, to order an end to the harassment, and to require the city to issue a statement against sexual harassment of women.

Questions and Instructions

1. In an age of sexual freedom, pornographic publications, plays, motion pictures, video casettes, and male and female nude dancers entertaining in nightspots, did Mae Fiedler take too seriously the actions of the police officers?
2. Could Fiedler have handled the situation at work differently to improve her relationship with the officers, or was her choice of action the most effective one?
3. Do the Civil Rights Act of 1964 and the Directive on Sexual Harassment issued by the Equal Employment Opportunity Commission even if followed provide enough protection for employees who find themselves in a situation like that of Fiedler's? (See Exhibits 1 and 2 on pages 69–71.)
4. Are the options available to employees who believe themselves victims of sexual harassment too complex and legally restricted to make it worthwhile to seek remedial action?
5. What punitive action should law codes provide against supervisors who take no action to stop harassment of employees by coworkers?
6. Which type of harassment is more difficult to deal with, the one which the victim suffers in the workplace or that which occurs in the effort to obtain redress?

Selected Bibliography

Biles, George E., "A Program Guide for Preventing Sexual Harassment in the Workplace," *Personnel Administrator* 26 (June 1981): 49–56.

Discoll, Jeanne Bosson, "Sexual Attraction and Harassment: Management's New Problems," *Personnel Journal* 60 (January 1981): 33–36.

Farley, Lin, *Sexual Shakedown: Sexual Harassment of Women at Work,* New York: McGraw-Hill, 1979.

Gordon, Francine E., and Stroker, Myra H., eds., *Bringing Women into Management,* New York: McGraw-Hill, 1975. Chs. 1, 2, and 3, pp. 7–58.

Hoyman, Michelle, and Robinson, Ronda, "Interpreting the New Sexual Harassment Guidelines," *Personnel Journal* 59 (December 1980): 996–1000.

James, Jennifer, "Sexual Harassment," *Public Personnel Management* 10 (No. 4, 1981): 402–7.

Kronenberger, George K., and Rourke, David L., "Effective Training and the Elimination of Sexual Harassment," *Personnel Journal* 60 (November 1981): 879–83.

MacKinnon, Catharine A., *Sexual Harassment of Working Women,* New Haven, Conn.: Yale University Press, 1979.

McIntyre, Douglas I., and Renick, James C., "Sexual Harassment and the States As Policy-Makers and Employers," *State Government* 56 (No. 4, 1983): 128–33.

Neugarten, Dail Ann, and Miller-Spellman, Monica, "Sexual Harassment in Public Employment," in Steven W. Hays and Richard C. Kearney, eds., *Public Personnel Administration: Problems and Prospects,* Englewood Cliffs, N.J.: Prentice-Hall, Inc., 1983. pp. 274–88.

Neugarten, Dail Ann, and Schfritz, Jay M., *Sexuality in Organizations: Romantic and Coercive Behaviors at Work,* Oak Park, Ill.: Moore Publishing Co., 1980. See Section II, "Sexual Harassment: The Problem," pp. 57–77, and Section IV, "The Legal Status: Sexual Harassment Under Title VII," pp. 109–57.

Quinn, Robert E., "Coping with Cupid: The Formation, Impact, and Management of Romantic Relationships in Organizations," *Administrative Science Quarterly* 22 (March 1977): 30–45.

Renick, James C., "Sexual Harassment at Work: Why It Happens, What to Do About It," *Personnel Journal* 59 (August 1980): 658–62.

Rosenbloom, David H., "Public Administrative Professionalism and Public Service Law," *State and Local Government Review* 16 (Spring 1984): 52–57.

Somers, Patricia A., and Clementson-Mohr, Judith, "Sexual Extortion in the Workplace," *Personnel Administrator* 24 (April 1979): 23–28.

Thurston, Kathryn A., "Sexual Harassment: An Organizational Perspective," *Personnel Administrator* 25 (December 1980): 59–64.

Warfield, Andrea.; Swartz, Rose Ann; and Wood, Duane, "Co-Worker Romances: Impact on the Work Group and on Career-Oriented Women," *Personnel* 64 (May 1987): 22–35.

Exhibit 1. Excerpt from Civil Rights Act of 1964

TITLE VII—EQUAL EMPLOYMENT OPPORTUNITY
DISCRIMINATION BECAUSE OF RACE, COLOR,
RELIGION, SEX, OR NATIONAL ORIGIN

Section 703.

a. It shall be an unlawful employment practice for an employer—

1. to fail or refuse to hire or to discharge any individual, or otherwise to discriminate against any individual with respect to his compensation, terms, conditions, or privileges of employment, because of such individual's race, color, religion, sex, or national origin; or

2. to limit, segregate, or classify his employees in any way which would deprive or tend to deprive any individual of employment opportunities or otherwise adversely affect his status as an employee, because of such individual's race, color, religion, sex, or national origin.

b. It shall be an unlawful employment practice for an employment agency to fail or refuse to refer for employment, or otherwise to discriminate against, any individual because of his race, color, religion, sex, or national origin, or to classify or refer for employment any individual on the basis of his race, color, religion, sex, or national origin.

c. It shall be an unlawful employment practice for a labor organization—

1. to exclude or to expel from its membership, or otherwise to discriminate against, any individual because of his race, color, religion, sex, or national origin;

2. to limit, segregate, or classify its membership, or to classify or fail or refuse to refer for employment any individual, in any way which would deprive or tend to deprive any individual of employment opportunities, or would limit such employment opportunities or otherwise adversely affect his status as an employee or as an applicant for employment, because of such individual's race, color, religion, sex, or national origin; or

3. to cause or attempt to cause an employer to discriminate against an individual in violation of this section.

d. It shall be an unlawful employment practice for any employer, labor organization, or joint labor-management committee controlling apprenticeship or other training or retraining, including on-the-job training programs, to discriminate against any individual because of his race, color, religion, sex, or national origin in admission to, or employment in, any program established to provide apprenticeship or other training.

e. Notwithstanding any other provision of this title, (1) it shall not be an unlawful employment practice for an employer to hire and employ employees, for an employment agency to classify, or refer for employment any individual, for a labor organization to classify its membership or to classify or refer for employment any individual, or for an employer, labor organization, or joint labor-management committee controlling apprenticeship or other training or retraining programs to admit or employ any individual in any such program, on the basis of his religion, sex, or national origin in those certain instances where religion, sex or national origin is a bona fide occupational qualification reasonably necessary to the normal operation of that particular business or enterprise, and (2) it shall not be an unlawful employment practice for a school, college, university, or other educational institution or institution of learning to hire and employ employees of a particular religion if such school, college, university, or other educational institution or institution of learning is, in whole or in substantial part, owned, supported, controlled, or managed by a particular religion or by a particular religious corporation, association, or society, or if the curriculum of such school, college, university, or other educational institution or institution of learning is directed toward the propagation of a particular religion.

f. As used in this title, the phrase "unlawful employment practice" shall not be deemed to include any action or measure taken by an employer, labor organization, joint labor-management committee, or employment agency with respect to an individual who is a member of the Communist Party of the United States or of any other organization required to register as a Communist-action or Communist-front organization by final order of the Subversive Activities Control Board pursuant to the Subversive Activities Control Act of 1950.

g. Notwithstanding any other provision of this title, it shall not be an unlawful employment practice for an employer to fail or refuse to hire and employ any individual for any position, for an employer to discharge any individual from any position, or for an employment agency to fail or refuse to refer any individual for employment in any position, or for a labor organization to fail or refuse to refer any individual for employment in any position, if—

1. the occupancy of such position, or access to the premises in or upon which any part of the duties of such position is performed, or is to be performed, is subject to any requirement imposed in the interest of the national security of the United States under any security program in effect pursuant to or administered under any statute of the United States or any Executive order of the President; and
2. such individual has not fulfilled or has ceased to fulfill that requirement.

h. Notwithstanding any other provision of this title, it shall not be an unlawful employment practice for an employer to apply different standards of compensation, or different terms, conditions, or privileges of employment pursuant to a bona fide seniority or merit system, or a system which measures earnings by quantity or quality of production or to employees who work in different locations, provided that such differences are not the result of an intention to discriminate because of race, color, religion, sex, or national origin, nor shall it be an unlawful employment practice for an employer to give and to act upon the results of any professionally developed ability test provided that such test, its administration or action upon the results is not designed, intended, or used to discriminate because of race, color, religion, sex, or national origin. It shall not be an unlawful employment practice under this title for any employer to differentiate upon the basis of sex in determining the amount of the wages or compensation paid or to be paid to employees of such employer if such differentiation is authorized by the provisions of section 6(d) of the Fair Labor Standards Act of 1938, as amended (29) U.S.C. 206(d).

Exhibit 2. Directive on Sexual Harassment Issued by the Equal Employment Opportunity Commission

Section 1604.11 Sexual harassment.

a. Harassment on the basis of sex is a violation of Sec. 703 of Title VII. Unwelcome sexual advances, requests for sexual favors, and other verbal or physical conduct of a sexual nature constitute sexual harassment when (1) submission to such conduct is made either explicitly or implicitly a term or condition of an individual's employment, (2) submission to or rejection of such conduct by an individual is used as the basis for employment decisions affecting such individual, or (3) such conduct has the purpose or effect of unreasonably interfering with an individual's work performance or creating an intimidating, hostile, or offensive working environment.

b. In determining whether alleged conduct constitutes sexual harassment, the Commission will look at the record as a whole and at the totality of the circumstances, such as the nature of the sexual advances and the context in which the alleged incidents occurred. The determination of the legality of a particular action will be made from the facts, on a case by case basis.

c. Applying general Title VII principles, an employer, employment agency, joint apprenticeship committee or labor organization (hereinafter collectively referred to as "employer") is responsible for its acts and those of its agents and supervisory employees with respect to sexual harassment regardless of whether the specific acts complained of were authorized or even forbidden by the employer and regardless of whether the employer knew or should have known of their occurrence. The commission will examine the circumstances of the particular employment relationship and the job functions performed by the individual in determining whether an individual acts in either a supervisory or agency capacity.

d. With respect to conduct between fellow employees, an employer is responsible for acts of sexual harassment in the workplace where the employer (or its agents or supervisory employees) knows or should have known of the conduct, unless it can show that it took immediate and appropriate corrective action.

e. An employer may also be responsible for the acts of non-employees, with respect to sexual harassment of employees in the workplace, where the employer (or its agents or supervisory employees) knows or should have known of the conduct and fails to take immediate and appropriate corrective action. In reviewing these cases the Commission will consider the extent of the employer's control and any other legal responsibility which the employer may have with respect to the conduct of such non-employees.

f. Prevention is the best tool for the elimination of sexual harassment. An employer should take all steps necessary to prevent sexual harassment from occurring, such as affirmatively raising the subject, expressing strong disapproval, developing appropriate sanctions, informing employees of their right to raise and how to raise the issue of harassment under Title VII, and developing methods to sensitize all concerned.

g. Other related practices: Where employment opportunities or benefits are granted because of an individual's submission to the employer's sexual advances or requests for sexual favors, the employer may be held liable for unlawful sex discrimination against other persons who were qualified for but denied that employment opportunity or benefit.

14

A Leave of Absence

John Harris, head of the Second Regional Office of the State Service Bureau, had decided to take a leave of absence to assume a temporary position on the governor's task force on reorganization. He estimated that he would be gone for nine months. He had been in charge of the regional office since it was created ten years before.

In the past, Harris had received excellent performance evaluations from his supervisors and was respected for his administrative ability. He felt that recently he had not been getting the support from the central office he had once received. He attributed this to his office's high turnover and decreased productivity for the past two years and feared that his superiors believed he had lost his administrative talent. He was beginning to think he had been selected for the task force so that he could be replaced in an indirect manner. Since he had worked with the bureau for seventeen of its twenty years, he could not believe he would be asked to transfer or resign.

Two weeks before he was to report to the task force, he asked Richard Rhodes, chief administrator of the central office, how his replacement would be selected. Rhodes told Harris that he could select his own replacement from a list of candidates submitted by the bureau and from Harris's qualified subordinates.

Harris decided to examine the qualifications of each candidate and select the one with the weakest background. This, he thought, would enable him to return to his old job when his assignment on the task force was completed. After reviewing the list of candidates, Harris narrowed his choice to three people: Linda Smith, administrative assistant from Region One; Maxwell Jones, administrative assistant from Region Seven; and William Marx, from Harris's office.

In reviewing Linda Smith's and Maxwell Jones's files, Harris decided that they were very ambitious young people who might become a threat to his position. Both Smith and Jones had a master's degree and Harris feared that they might be thought more competent than he. Therefore, he decided to appoint Marx, who, he felt, had an adequate background and qualifications that would satisfy his superiors but who would not pose a serious threat. Marx had been loyal to him for years and always seemed to display great respect. Thus Harris believed Marx would hesitate before attempting to undermine him. Harris left for his new assignment confident that he had made the right decision.

When Marx assumed Harris's position, he directed his efforts toward achieving efficiency. He reorganized the structure of the office and specified distinct work assignments for each employee. He appointed a personnel assistant and an administrative assistant.

Marx thus assumed a rigid and highly structured approach in his new managerial capacity and achieved excellent results after only two months. These were noted by his superiors, who expressed their appreciation for this attention to increased efficiency. However, after five months, problems began to develop that were unnoticed by Marx. Many of his subordinates began to feel they were being worked too hard. They believed that Marx was overly rigid and that a break was developing in their communications with one another.

Before two more months had passed, Richard Rhodes, chief administrator at the central office, received a message informing him that Harris would complete his assignment in two weeks and was preparing to resume his position at the Second Regional Office. Rhodes was faced with the problem of deciding whether to replace Harris with Marx. He had never had a problem with Harris in the past and still thought Harris was capable of resuming his old post. But, unaware of the staff criticism of Marx, he believed Marx had been doing a better job.

Rhodes realized he would never have thought of replacing Harris had the task-force assignment not come up, putting Marx in Harris's place. Rhodes was also aware of the problems confronting Harris's office at the time Harris was there but had passed them off believing they were caused by some external or coincidental factors—nothing Harris could not handle. However, when Marx's reorganization and strict managerial approach were implemented and highly positive results appeared, he began to question Harris's ability. He thought that perhaps Marx's approach was necessary at this time to correct the office's problems.

Questions and Instructions

1. Compare and contrast Harris's and Marx's management styles. For whom would you rather work?
2. Discuss several choices available to Rhodes in resolving the problem. What are some of the things Rhodes should consider before making a final decision?

3. How could Rhodes have prevented this problem from occurring?
4. Discuss the ethical implications of Harris's decision to choose the least-qualified person as his temporary successor?

Selected Bibliography

Balk, Walter L., "Toward a Government Productivity Ethic," *Public Administration Review* 38 (January/February 1978): 15–18.

Bavelos, Alex, and Barrett, Dermot, "An Experimental Approach to Organizational Communication," in Mankin, Don; Ames, Russell E., Jr.; and Gordsky, Milton A., eds., *Classics of Industrial and Organizational Psychology,* Oak Park, Ill.; Moore Publishing Co., 1980. pp. 476–94.

Bok, Sissela, *Lying: Moral Choice in Public and Private Life,* New York: Pantheon Books, 1978.

Boling, T. Edwin, and Dempsey, John, "Ethical Dilemmas in Government: Designing an Organizational Response," *Public Personnel Management* 10 (1981): 11–19.

Bowman, James, "Managerial Ethics in Business and Government," *Business Horizons* 19 (October 1976): 48–54.

Churchman, C. West, "The Myth of Management," in Matteson, Michael T., and Ivancevich, John M., eds., *Management Classics,* Santa Monica, Calif.: Goodyear Publishing Co., 1977. pp. 406–14.

Hurka, Slavek J., "Managers of Professional Departments in Teaching Hospitals: A Study of Satisfaction," *Journal of Health and Human Resources Administration* 3 (November 1980): 192–200.

Mosher, Frederick C., "Some Notes on Reorganizations in Public Agencies," in Lane, Frederick S., ed., *Managing State and Local Government: Cases and Readings,* New York: St. Martin's Press, 1980. pp. 117–37.

Prudent, H. O., "The Upward Mobile, Indifferent and Ambivalent Typology of Managers," *Academy of Management Journal* 16 (September 1973): 454–64.

Van Maanen, John; Lotte, Bailyn; and Schein, Edgar H., "The Shape of Things to Come: A New Look at Organizational Careers," in Hackman, J. Richard; Lawler, Edward E., III; and Porter, Lyman W., eds., *Perspectives on Behavior in Organizations,* New York: McGraw-Hill, 1977.

15

The Good/Bad Administrator

Timothy Kingsbury, secretary of the State Department of Natural Resources, considered it a coup when he hired George Krittenbrink as director of the Land and Water Resources Survey. The survey had grown in importance as the environmental consequences of increasing population became more worrisome, yet staff positions had been difficult to fill because the work was highly technical. Krittenbrink was a nationally known figure in his field and Kingsbury thought he could turn the survey over to him and devote his attention to matters that he knew more about.

For his part, Krittenbrink was glad to take the position, for it gave him an opportunity to ride his hobby horse of long standing: high- and low-altitude photography and remote-sensing pictures obtained by satellites circling the earth. He was a pioneer in applying such information about the earth to better use of land and other natural resources and had contributed authoritative articles to technical journals.

Krittenbrink's interest in this field had begun with aerial photography studies while studying geography in college and he had been excited by the prospects for obtaining more information about the earth's surface from hand-held cameras in the early Gemini and Apollo space flights. Later he familiarized himself with the advances made in 1972 when the National Aeronautics and Space Administration launched the first land-resource survey satellites—Landsat-1, -2, and -3, which provided a wealth of information about the planet.

The Land and Water Resources Survey had done more than most comparable programs in other states in the practical application of electronically recorded and transmitted data via satellite. Krittenbrink determined to make it the foremost program in the nation. When visitors inspected the survey and inquired how its work would help the state, Krittenbrink had a speech prepared for them, as if a guide in a museum. "There are roughly 230 million Americans depending upon approximately 2.3 billion acres of land," he would say. "This means that the per capita land share now is about 10.8 acres compared to a per capita share of nearly 17 acres in 1940. By the year 2000 the per capita land share will be 6⅔ acres. We need to use our land resources more effectively as our population grows and the amount of land taken out of production each year by highways, airports, and urbanization increases."

Satellite data, Krittenbrink would continue, would enable planners to identify land-use patterns and changes over time. He envisioned additional applications: monitoring crops for pest infestation and disease, solving hydrological problems, forecasting snow runoff, measuring water characteristics, providing regional indices of water availability, evaluating wildlife habitats, assessing damage in burned-out areas, identifying climatological patterns and trends, mapping thermal pollution, identifying soil characteristics associated with mineral exploration, predicting flood damage, locating new sources of fresh water, forecasting crop yields, conducting soil-conservation studies, detecting archeological sites, and assessing timber-stand vigor.

The day Krittenbrink took over as survey director, he addressed a staff meeting to explain his management policies and goals. He stressed the importance of completing projects expeditiously, of teamwork, and of meticulous attention to detail. The staff quickly learned that he was a strong-willed, nose-to-the-grindstone type of manager who believed that efficiency and organization produced successful results.

The staff of eight scientists and engineers came from diverse regions of the country and represented varied educational backgrounds, including geology; geography; civil, hydrologic, and electrical engineering; computer programming; and planning. Much of their work consisted of preparing and analyzing maps produced from information transmitted from satellites to the Goddard Space Flight Center, where it was placed on computer compatible tapes and readied for use in research and experimentation.

Each time the survey received a request from a city, county, or state agency, Krittenbrink evaluated the work to be done and assigned the project to members of the staff. He expected all projects to be completed on schedule and to meet his stringent quality specifications. When they were not, he was sharply critical and sarcastic in reprimanding the offender.

The most frequent victim of Krittenbrink's criticism was James Cartmill, a young, wisecracking geological engineer who, the survey director thought, lacked the serious purpose and devotion to detail required in scientific pursuits. On one occasion Cartmill failed to meet a deadline. The work had been proceeding according to schedule until the main-frame computer broke down, making Cartmill two days late in completing the assignment. Dismissing Cartmill's explanation that the delay was not his fault because it was caused by a computer malfunction, Krittenbrink angrily replied that he wanted results, not excuses.

The next day Krittenbrink called Cartmill to his office and brought up the matter again. "Cartmill," he said, "you're capable of good work but you've got to change your attitude. Science demands a holy dedication to work. It has no place for fun and games. You waste not only your time but that of others when you chat and joke with them."

Cartmill attempted to explain that the delay in completing the project had nothing to do with his relations with other staff members. A vital computer had malfunctioned, parts had to be flown in from Boca Raton, and a specialist had been called from Atlanta to make repairs, he said. "Cartmill, a man must take responsibility for the circumstances of his life," Krittenbrink replied. "He cannot let outside forces rule him. A man must anticipate external problems and control the exogenous forces in order to succeed." Recognizing that Krittenbrink was not going to accept his side of the story, Cartmill apologized and promised that in the future he would try to be the master of his fate.

Cartmill thought the matter was closed and was shocked when at the next staff meeting Krittenbrink scolded him before his fellow workers for nearly fifteen minutes. That Cartmill had taken lightly the injunction to control outside forces, Krittenbrink said, was clear from a flippant comment on being master of his fate. "Deadlines are a necessity of life," Krittenbrink said. "Without them we would not know what to do or when to do it. This is one characteristic of modern organizations that distinguishes them from the older ones. The professional engineer and technician pays attention to schedule and engages in contingency planning." The staff members returned to their work areas in quiet disbelief.

In the next few weeks Krittenbrink frequently reminded Cartmill of the need for adhering to work programs and once blamed him for the breakdown of a photographic copying machine because he had not followed a careful schedule of preventive maintenance. After a few months on the job, Krittenbrink extended his fault-finding to Donald Fletcher, a young engineer and friend of Cartmill, and three other staff members who all had excellent work histories and records for reliability. Toward the end of Krittenbrink's first year as supervisor, two engineers requested and received transfers to other departments. Cartmill, however, remained in the division, saying that he liked the work and could put up with the fault-finding of his superior.

It was not easy, for Krittenbrink had informed Cartmill that he was recording all work-related problems and transgressions in his personnel file. Cartmill's treatment did not go unnoticed by other staff members, and one morning during a coffee break they decided that, for self-protection, they should keep careful notes on the work they performed, on all problems associated with receiving computer tapes and related data sets, on machinery malfunctions, and on all regulations and project specifications ordered by Krittenbrink.

Joyce Harman, a new employee who had worked three years in the interior department of another state, observed the low morale in the division and the tense atmosphere that made it difficult to meet the exacting standards that the tasks required. Priding herself on being a well-educated and independent woman—she was active in the women's rights movement—Harman was not one to submit to the petty tyrannies of a male supervisor. When Krittenbrink made general criticisms of her work, she demanded specific proof. Krittenbrink, accustomed to the submissiveness of the other employees of the division, usually had no concrete justification and retreated to commenting on the need for expediting projects and for scientific accuracy in the work of the division.

After holding the job for three months, Harman took the initiative in arousing the division staff to protest Krittenbrink's unreasonable demands, selective persecutions, and general denigrations of them as people and professionals. They compiled a list of grievances with documentation that they submitted to Kingsbury, the Natural Resources Department secretary, requesting that Krittenbrink's supervisory behavior be evaluated and a formal hearing be held so that their concerns could be discussed. Kingsbury was surprised to learn about the trouble in the division. He had felt lucky to have as the director so dedicated and knowledgeable a person as Krittenbrink, who was praised by state agencies using the services of the survey. It now appeared to Kingsbury that efficiency and productivity might not be the sum total of good administration.

Questions and Instructions

1. As Kingsbury, what would you do first in taking up the problem? Would you talk first to the staff or to Krittenbrink?
2. Do you think that the differences between Krittenbrink and the staff can be reconciled?
3. Should Kingsbury come to the support of Krittenbrink? Consider both Krittenbrink's ability to get along with his staff and the productivity and quality of the work done by the survey.
4. Is there any justification for transferring Krittenbrink? What implications are associated with transferring the problem employees of an agency?
5. How does one supervise a supervisor? Should problem supervisors be treated similarly to or differently from other problem employees?
6. Is there any way for Krittenbrink to become a more effective administrator? If you were Kingsbury, what suggestions would you offer him in the way of improving his interpersonal relations?
7. Should Krittenbrink be dismissed from all supervisory responsibility? What are the implications of this decision? Elaborate.

Selected Bibliography

Abrahamson, Mark, *The Professional in the Organization,* Chicago: Rand McNally and Co., 1967. Ch. 2, "The Socialization of Future Professionals," pp. 17–57, and Ch. 4, "Professional Norms and Organizational Control," pp. 90–125.

Benveniste, Guy, *The Politics of Expertise,* Berkeley, Calif.: The Glendessary Press, 1972. Ch. 7, "How Experts Acquire Power," pp. 119–35.

Champion, Dean J. *The Sociology of Organizations,* New York: McGraw-Hill, 1975. Ch. 11, "Technological Change in Organizations and Adaptation of Members," pp. 248–80. Also, see "On Informal Communication Patterns: Their Origin, Functions, and Dysfunctions," pp. 181–90.

Giglioni, Giovanni B.; Giglioni, Joyce B.; and Bryant, James A., "Performance Appraisal: Here Comes the Judge," *California Management Review* 24 (Winter 1981): 14–23.

Handy, Charles B., *Understanding Organizations,* New York: Penguin Books, 1976. Ch. 2, "On the Motivation to Work," pp. 23–52; Ch. 8, "On Politics and Management of Differences," pp. 212–44; and Ch. 12, "On Being a Manager," pp. 358–79.

Kaufman, Herbert, *Time, Chance, and Organizations: Natural Selection in a Perilous Environment,* Chatham, N.J.: Chatham House, 1985.

Landau, Martin, and Stout, Russell, Jr., "To Manage Is Not to Control: Or the Folly of Type II Errors," *Public Administration Review* 39 (March/April 1979): 148–56.

Leavitt, Harold J., *Managerial Psychology,* 4th ed., Chicago: University of Chicago Press, 1978. Ch. 22, "Developing Managers: Applied Ideas about Influence, Learning and Groups," pp. 244–57; also, Ch. 12, "Authority: One Model for Influence," pp. 136–47, and Ch. 26, "Structure, People, and Information Technology: Some Key Ideas and Where They Come From," pp. 291–304.

Luthans, Fred, *Organizational Behavior,* New York, McGraw-Hill, 1973. Ch. 13, "The Nature and Impact of Technology," pp. 280–305.

Maslow, Abraham H., *Motivation and Personality,* 2nd ed., New York: Harper and Row, 1954. Ch. 5, "A Theory of Human Motivation," pp. 80–106.

O'Reilly, Charles A., III, and Weitz, Barton A., "Managing Marginal Employees: The Use of Warnings and Dismissals," *Administrative Science Quarterly* 25 (September 1980): 467–84.

Perrucci, Robert, "In the Service of Man: Radical Movements in the Professions," in Gerstl, Joel, and Jacobs, Glenn, eds., *Professions for the People,* Cambridge, Mass.: Schenkman Publishing Co., 1976. pp. 215–30.

Pinder, Craig C., and Schroeder, Klaus G., "Time to Proficiency Following Job Transfers," *Academy of Management Journal* 30 (June 1987): 336–53.

Stogdill, Ralph M., *Handbook of Leadership: A Survey of Theory and Research,* New York: Free Press, 1974.

Sutton, Harold, and Porter, Lyman, "A Study of the Grapevine in a Governmental Organization," *Personnel Psychology* 21 (Summer 1968): 223–30.

16

An Indecisive Decision

Two months ago, Tom Gordon was promoted to manager of operations of the Kennedy Recreation Center in Unionville. Gordon and his staff had been working overtime in planning the summer program. After discussing staffing requirements with the city's director of the Parks and Recreation Department, Gordon was granted an additional position. According to department policy, Gordon would be responsible for interviewing applicants and selecting the person to fill the new position.

Gordon was somewhat insecure in his job. His promotion had involved a transfer from another recreation center and he was relatively unacquainted with staff members at the Kennedy Center. He had recently learned that several of his colleagues had sought the position he now held. Other than that, nothing had occurred that would indicate there was any opposition to his appointment. Thinking he had to develop more self-confidence to become an effective leader at Kennedy, Gordon felt he should make his decision without consulting anyone else.

There were five applicants on the eligibility list. Gordon recognized one familiar name, Sam Cook. Gordon and Cook had been close friends several years before but had not kept in contact for some time. Gordon was aware that Cook had had some trouble with the law in his youth. When he was sixteen he had stolen a car and while being pursued by the police had had an accident in which several people were seriously injured. The accident occurred in the same minority community that the Kennedy Center served. Cook's employment record in the intervening years had been exemplary, however, and his employers had praised his job performance. He was married and had begun a family since Gordon last saw him.

The other applicants did not appear so well qualified as Cook. One who worked as a student intern in the Parks and Recreation Department received an unfavorable report from the manager of another recreation center. Another with previous experience had been discharged several years earlier and was reputed to have strong racial biases. The remaining two were college graduates with no work experience. While this lack of experience did not eliminate them, Gordon preferred a person with some on-the-job training.

After interviewing all of the applicants and checking their references, Gordon was convinced that Cook was the most qualified candidate. He felt that he could work best with Cook but was concerned about community reaction because of the incident in Cook's youth. Even if he had not been Cook's friend, Gordon would be inclined to hire him because he believed people were capable of rehabilitation and should not be denied equal consideration.

Questions and Instructions

1. Is Gordon unfair to those without experience?
2. Is Gordon too concerned with doing a favor for an old friend? Would choosing an old friend be a good idea?
3. Should Cook's past prevent him from being considered for the position? Would the fact that he now has a good work record be a point in his favor in the community?
4. Would Cook be best advised to seek a job at another location where his past would not be known?
5. Since Gordon has so many doubts about hiring Cook, should he reconsider his decision not to consult the Parks and Recreation director about the appointment?

Selected Bibliography

Blake, Robert R., and Mouton, Jane S., "Grid Organizational Development," in Mankin, Don; Ames, Russell E., Jr.; and Grodsky, Milton A., eds., *Classics of Industrial and Organizational Psychology,* Oak Park, Ill.: Moore Publishing Co., 1980. pp. 540–55.

Cronback, Lee J., "Selection Theory for a Political World," *Public Personnel Management* 9 (January/February 1980): 37–50.

Crowder, Robert H., Jr., "What (Not) to Ask in an Interview," *Public Management* 66 (June 1984): 18–20.

"Ethics: Dictates and Dilemmas," *Public Management* (Special Issue on ICMA Code of Ethics), 63 (March 1981): 2–22.

Klinefelter, John, and Thompkins, James, "Adverse Impact in Employment Selection," *Public Personnel Management* 5 (May/June 1976): 199–204.

Korman, Abraham K., "Personnel Selection: The Traditional Models," in

Korman, Abraham K., ed., *Industrial and Organizational Psychology,* Englewood Cliffs, N.J.: Prentice-Hall, 1971. pp. 179–204.

Madden, Carl, "Forces Which Influence Ethical Behavior," in Walton, Clarence, ed., *The Ethics of Corporate Conduct,* Englewood Cliffs, N.J.: Prentice-Hall, 1977. pp. 31–78.

Shoop, Robert, "Public Personnel Selection: A Matter of Consistency," *Public Personnel Management* 3 (July/August 1974): 341–43.

17

No Clean Sweep in Winchester

Under attack from a newly formed Tax Reduction League, the city of Winchester reduced the ad valorem tax by a rate that amounted to a municipal budget cut of 5 percent. Winchester is a city of 150,000 population in the upper Midwest. It is the center of a rich agricultural district but also is highly industrialized with a serious air-pollution problem.

Faced with instructions from the City Council to effect savings in the Department of Public Works in order to reduce fuel consumption and keep within the smaller budget, Superintendent Fleming Hartman thought hard about what services could be eliminated and what maintenance costs could be cut. He decided that major savings could be made in the street-cleaning department. Clean streets were desirable, he thought, but they were not essential as were other maintenance services. With the approval of the mayor and City Council, he established the sweeping schedule on a regular basis to the downtown streets and main thoroughfares. Residential streets were cleaned only in response to complaints and then only if they were close to an arterial street. He was able to sell four sweepers and two flushers and cut the work force from twenty-four to twelve. Fuel consumption was substantial in street cleaning—each sweeper used 5,000 gallons of fuel a year—and the sale of the equipment saved about 20,000 gallons.

The new street-cleaning plan went into operation in February. The first adverse reaction came after the last snowfall in late March. The sweepers took several days to clean up the sand and other abrasives, curb-deep in some places, that had been spread to improve driving conditions. Complaints poured into the office of the Public Works Department, the two local television stations showed films of the accumulated grit, the *Daily Bulletin* editorialized against the inefficiency of the street department, and the mayor telephoned Superintendent Hartman demanding that something be done immediately to get the public off his back.

The complaints did not end after the clean-up of sand. As spring advanced, unsightly litter accumulated, paper was blown into yards and against buildings and fences, beer and soft-drink cans tinkled as they were propelled down the street by the wind, and dust and soot sometimes filled the air. Moreover, the lake in Winchester's large Greenbriar Park became increasingly polluted from the streams and storm drainage flowing into it.

In the previous year the Tax Reduction League had been the voice of the people. It was now replaced by environmental groups and neighborhood associations crying out against the dirt and litter. "Clean Up Winchester" was the slogan adopted by these various groups. As a result the City Council gave street sweeping a high priority in drawing up the new budget. But though many were concerned about municipal aesthetics, many also were concerned about high taxes. A state-mandated property-reassessment program that would raise ad valorem taxes, the loss of federal funds, and finally inflationary costs made it difficult for the City Council to provide a balanced budget without a tax increase, anathema to the people. To avoid or minimize a tax increase, the council ordered department heads to develop user fees in budget areas where rates could be established to pay for programs.

Public Works Superintendent Hartman received an extra instruction in formulating his proposal: he was to do everything possible about meeting the pressures to keep Winchester's streets clean.

Questions and Instructions

1. What fees could a municipal public-works department propose? Should there be a special fee for street cleaning or could the fee be collected from other services performed by the city?
2. What street-cleaning program, including number of sweepers, flushers, and other equipment, work and supervisory force, and frequency of cleaning, would you propose for Winchester?
3. Discuss the possibility of contracting with a private firm for performing the street-cleaning job.
4. In what other areas of municipal management might private contractors replace city employees in performing services and maintenance?

Selected Bibliography

Florestano, Patricia S., and Gordon, Stephen B., "Public vs. Private: Small Government Contracting with the Private Sector," *Public Administration Review* 40 (January/February 1980): 29–34.

———, "Private Provision of Public Services: Contracting by Large Local Governments," *International Journal of Public Administration* 1 (1979): 307–27.

———, "Contracting with the Private Sector," *National Civic Review* 71 (July-August 1982): 350–57.

Honadle, Beth Walter, "Interlocal Cooperation," *National Civic Review* 71 (July-August 1982): 362–64.

Mehavy, Stephen L., "Intergovernmental Contracting for Municipal Police Services: An Empirical Analysis," *Land Economics* 55 (February 1979): 59–72.

Morgan, David R.; Meyer, Michael E.; and England, Robert E., "Alternatives to Municipal Service Delivery: A Four-State Comparison," *Southern Review of Public Administration* 5 (Summer 1981): 184–98.

Pitt, Robert, "Why Street Cleaning Is Worth the Effort," *American City and County* 95 (April 1980): 41–43.

Ridings, Richard L., "'User Fee' Pays for Clean Streets," *American City and County* 97 (February 1981): 43–44.

Savas, E. S., "An Empirical Study of Competition in Municipal Service Delivery," *Public Administration Review,* 37 (November/December 1977): 717–24.

———, *Privatizing the Public Sector,* Chatham, N.J.: Chatham House Publishers, 1982.

Sonenblum, Sidney; Kirlin, John J.; and Ries, John C., *How Cities Provide Services: An Evaluation of Alternative Delivery Structures,* Cambridge, Mass.: Ballinger Publishing Co., 1977.

"Street Sweeping Blues? Try Contracting the Service Out," *American City and County* 96 (September 1981): 55–61.

White, Geoff, and Palmer, Stephen, "Contracting Out and the Cleaning-Up Question," *Personnel Management* (May 1987): 44–47.

18

A Vigilante Arrest

Although Police Chief Arthur Bond of Metcalf, a city of 15,000 population in a ranching and farming area of a Southwestern state, was aware of town talk about the failure of his department to make arrests in a series of recent burglaries, he was surprised one morning to learn that four citizens had brought to the police station about 1 A.M. a youth they had "arrested" for suspicious conduct.

The men revealed that they were in the habit of patrolling neighborhoods for suspicious activity. That evening they had stopped the youth after he let a man out of his car in the southern part of town. The youth, identified as Lemuel Arbor, said he was on his way home after he and a high-school friend had attended a movie and drove around town for a while before going to their respective homes. Arbor said that he had driven only a few blocks on East Tenth Street when a car came alongside his, with flashing lights and honking horn, and forced him to the curb. Arbor related that the passenger in the car held a pointed gun at him and demanded: "Get out of your car and put your hands on the hood. You're under arrest." When Arbor complied, one of the men, imitating the actions of a police officer on a television crime show, patted his body to check for weapons and then made him lie down in the bed of a pickup truck that had appeared at the scene. The men threatened to take Arbor into a wooded area to rough him up unless he gave them information about a man in a white shirt whom he had dropped off on Elm Avenue. Arbor maintained that his friend was wearing a dark shirt and they had not been on Elm Avenue. After hearing Arbor's account of the incident and calling his parents, police sent him home.

On the day following Arbor's "arrest," Mayor Randolph Martinique, City Manager Herbert Watkins, and Police Chief Bond met to discuss the situation that they decided was serious if vigilantism was arising in the city. Though not community leaders, the vigilantes were three respected business owners and a rancher. The officials did not want to let the four go unpunished for making an illegal arrest but hesitated about taking action against them that might not be supported by the community.

The officials' concern about vigilantism was heightened two days later when James J. Martin, a 24-year-old auto mechanic, shot Angelo Moreno, age 40, in an altercation over a stolen stereo. Martin suspected Moreno's son of stealing the stereo and went to his home to see if he could locate it rather than reporting the theft to police. City officials subsequently conferred with District Attorney Reginald D. Ambrose, who agreed that people taking the law into their own hands could not be tolerated. They decided that filing charges against the four vigilantes might help to deter others from forming unauthorized neighborhood watch groups bearing arms. The officials were surprised, however, when Ambrose, ardent in his support of law and order, charged the vigilantes with kidnaping, conspiracy to kidnap, feloniously pointing a weapon, using a firearm in the commission of a felony, and making an unlawful arrest.

The Metcalf *Monitor*, in its report on the outbreak of vigilantism, quoted citizens who believed the incidents were evidence of a fear of crime in the community. "I have been lucky," Diane Wager, a Main Street business owner said, "but many of my friends have been robbed of TV sets, stereos, firearms, and other things thieves can sell real quick. You can see why the town's in an uproar." Timothy Mott, whose house had been burglarized and a gun collection, television set, and stereo taken, said he would gladly join a vigilante group if someone would ask him. "Our law is broke down," he added. "The criminals are taking over the whole country." Mark Brown, a secretary in a legal office, said: "I don't know what has caused the change, but Metcalf isn't as safe as it used to be. We never used to lock our doors. Now we're making keys for the kids."

Chief Bond and District Attorney Ambrose were puzzled by the community's response, because statistics did not indicate a crime rate higher than usual. They liked a *Monitor* editorial on the vigilantism that said: "Whatever the burglary rate, police neither need nor want the undirected, armed assistance of citizen amateurs. It takes more than a gun and good intentions to assume the job of police; it takes training and professionalism symbolized by a badge. Citizens can and should lend constructive assistance to the police in any number of ways but they should not assume expertise they do not possess."

Yet the community did not completely share the *Monitor's* view. Many people felt that even though the vigilantes who terrorized young Lemuel Arbor may have been overzealous, to accuse them of so many serious crimes was not justified. They felt that the district attorney was wrong in prosecuting good citizens who merely wanted better law enforcement. If the police were doing their job, why was it that no burglars seemed ever to get arrested? You got a ticket if you overparked, but the people that stole you blind seemed never to be brought into court.

Questions and Instructions

1. How dangerous to law and order do you consider vigilante groups to be?
2. Do you think the district attorney's charges against the vigilantes were warranted?
3. Do you think that the neighborhood watch programs found in many cities would solve the crime problems in Metcalf?
4. What do you think officials should do to develop better relations between the people of the community and the police?

Selected Bibliography

Behan, Cornelius J., "Coping with Fear: Citizen Oriented Police Enforcement in Baltimore County, Maryland," *Public Management* 68 (January 1986): 2–6.

Cotter, Patrick R., "'Citizens' Satisfaction with State Government," *State and Local Government Review* 16 (Winter 1984): 17–21.

Golembiewski, Robert T., "Moving Toward Professional Certification," *The Bureaucrat* 12 (Summer 1983): 50–55.

———, "The Pace and Character of Public Sector Professionalism: Six Selected Questions," *State and Local Government Review* 16 (Spring 1984): 63–68.

———, "Professionalism, Performance, and Protectionism: A Contingency View," *Public Productivity Review* 7 (September 1983): 251–68.

Haug, Marie R., "The Deprofessionalization of Everyone?" *Sociological Focus* 8 (August 1975): 197–213.

Hummel, Ralph P., *The Bureaucratic Experience,* 3rd ed., New York: St. Martin's Press, 1987. Ch. 2, "Bureaucracy As the New Culture," pp. 61–122.

Neal, James E., "Managers and Councilmembers: Comparing Their Political Attitudes," *Public Management* 68 (January 1986): 13–14.

Sokolow, Alvin D., "Small Town Government: The Conflict of Administrative Styles," *National Civic Review* 71 (October 1982): 445–52.

19

An Authoritarian Approach to Management

Richard Patton had grown up in a small town in a largely rural Midwestern state whose economy was based on agriculture. His parents were hard-working and devout and subjected their children to severe discipline. As a boy Patton did odd jobs to pay for his own clothes and school supplies. He was a typical product of a society that valued the work ethic: disciplined, conservative, industrious, and respectful of authority.

At the university, where he studied public administration, Patton was mainly interested in those aspects of courses that he considered down-to-earth. He found theoretical and philosophical propositions boring, because he had difficulty in applying the abstract to practical matters.

Upon graduation Patton got his first job in his own state as an assistant to the director of the Social Welfare Department in Jefferson County, a rural county with about 40,000 people that was neither wealthy nor poor. Demands on social-welfare services were not great, and the problems facing the department staff of ten were readily taken care of. Patton won the respect of his director and coworkers by his conscientious work and reliability. When the director moved on after a year, Patton succeeded him in the post.

A year later Patton accepted an offer to direct a department in a large county with more industry, a more varied economy, and a more diverse population than Jefferson County. Patton became head of a department with forty staff members that was governed by the Polk County Board of Commissioners and the county Social Service Commission. Though the county had a mixed population that included Indians, Chicanos, and blacks, no members of these groups worked at the department. It was a typical public-welfare agency, administered by the county, supervised by the state, and funded by the county, state, and federal governments. Its program included Aid for Families with Dependent Children (AFDC), Work Incentive (WIN), Supplemental Security Income (SSI), and Medicaid, administered under guidelines set by the state and federal governments.

The staff members, Patton soon discovered, frequently failed to follow guidelines and even appeared unfamiliar with them, applied rules inconsistently, and were sometimes indifferent to their clients' needs. Employees often arrived late at the office, took time off without permission to take care of personal matters, left clients waiting while getting coffee or chatting with fellow employees, and in general were inefficient and lackadaisical. Patton found few of them had the education and training for their work and quickly discovered the reason: qualified people were hard to obtain because of the low pay scale, the minimum acceptable by state requirements. The county commissioners, all conservative politically and economically, held budgets to the lowest possible level. Salary levels in all county offices were not competitive with those in the private sector.

Patton's initial review of the agency revealed that three persons appeared potentially useful in establishing an organizational structure to replace the present slipshod operation. They were the assistant director and two others who had ill-defined supervisory powers.

The course of action to reform the agency appeared clear to Patton. What was needed was a highly structured and disciplined organization. He envisioned himself as keeping a finger on all the programs administered by the agency. Supervisors would be selected from within the organization. Authority would be delegated to the supervisors, and line workers would be classified according to a strict hierarchy. Jobs would be highly specialized and all employees would be trained to do their job in a prescribed manner. Weekly staff meetings would be used to review and modify work styles and to inculcate respect for authority.

In putting his plans into effect Patton rejected suggestions of the workers. He felt that their ideas on pay, job design, and office procedures had no place in a well-run operation. "If they don't like the way the office is run, they can work some other place," he said. Despite Patton's authoritarian approach to management, some improvement was beginning to be made. The office was brightened by fresh paint and the furniture was rearranged so that counselors had more privacy in discussing problems with their clients. Responsibility for certain tasks was assigned to specific people, files were kept up-to-date, and client requests were handled more quickly. Patton and his supervisors, carefully chosen from among the staff, seemed to receive proper respect from other employees.

But dissatisfaction and dissent soon boiled over. Line workers challenged Patton's edicts at staff meetings, complained about many of the imposed rules and regulations, wrangled over policies and goals, and threatened to appeal to the governing boards.

Patton's supervisors periodically approached him with suggestions for changes. Patton was upset and felt they were interfering with his prerogatives as an administrator, yet he was willing to listen to their opinions, especially because he began to fear losing his job if the extent of the objections among the staff reached the agency's governing boards.

The supervisors explained to him that many improvements had been made in the department, but they believed the administrative structure had to be made more responsive to staff personnel. They suggested that staff input in salary plans, office-procedural policies, and staff meetings be increased and that a program of upgrading jobs and pay be introduced. They thought that an administrative system could be too strict. The department under the former director had not been tightly controlled but the work got done and the public seemed satisfied as to the level of service delivery.

It was hard for Patton to believe he had been wrong in thinking the Welfare Department needed the imposition of a more rigid system, but he now recognized that his reforms had failed and that there were aspects of management to which he had been blind.

Questions and Instructions

1. Analyze Patton's conception of leadership.
2. Granted that the Welfare Department needed to be made more efficient, what course could Patton have followed to make his reforms more acceptable to his staff?
3. What needed changes in the department did Patton overlook?
4. What courses of action would you recommend for Patton to correct his mistakes?
5. Would another organizational theory and management practice have been more appropriate for the welfare department than that followed by Patton? Explain.
6. What are some of the organizational factors that can impede change? facilitate change? How can resistance to change be overcome?

Selected Bibliography

Carroll, Stephen J., and Tosi, Henry L., *Organizational Behavior,* Chicago, St. Clair Press, 1977. Ch. 13, "Managing Human Resources in the Hierarchical Organization," pp. 365–98.

Drucker, Peter F., "The Deadly Sins in Public Administration," *Public Administration Review* 40 (March/April 1980): 103–6.

Gortner, Harold F., *Administration in the Public Sector,* 2nd ed., New York: John Wiley and Sons, 1981. Ch. 11, "Control: Planning's Other Face," pp. 242–63.

Latham, Gary P., and Wexley, Kenneth N., *Increasing Productivity Through Performance Appraisal,* Reading, Mass.: Addison-Wesley Publishing

Co., 1981. Ch. 7, "Conducting Formal and Informal Performance Appraisals," pp. 149–73.

Lawler, Edward E., III, "Should the Quality of Work Life Be Legislated?" in Glueck, William F., ed., *Personnel: A Book of Readings,* Dallas: Business Publications, 1979. pp. 76–82.

Locke, Edwin A., "The Case Against Legislating the Quality of Work Life," in Glueck, William F., ed., *Personnel: A Book of Readings,* Dallas: Business Publications, 1979. pp. 83–85.

Lovrich, Nicholas P., Jr., "Participative Management Interventions Among Employees in Enriched and Nonenriched Jobs: A Research Note from a Panel Study of State Employees," *Public Administration Quarterly* 10 (Fall 1986): 257–77.

Natemeyer, Walter E., ed., *Classics of Organizational Change,* Oak Park, Ill.: Moore Publishing Co., 1978. Section VI, "Organizational Change and Development," pp. 298–362.

Present, Phillip E., *People and Public Administration,* Pacific Palisades, Calif.: Palisades Publishers, 1979. See Topic 3, "The Individual and the Organization," pp. 95–130.

Siedman, Harold, *Politics, Position, and Power,* 3rd ed., New York: Oxford University Press, 1980. See pp. 24–30 for a discussion of the strategic and tactical uses of reorganization, and pp. 191–92 for an analysis of local governmental agency response.

Terpstra, David E., "Theories of Motivation—Borrowing the Best," *Personnel Journal* 58 (June 1979): 376–83.

20

A Question of Contamination

Henry Erickson had been assistant to the director of the State Department of Environmental protection for eight years. In addition to his regular duties, he had been recently assigned by the department director, Mark Simpson, to serve as public relations representative. His new assignment was the result of a memo received from the governor's office. The governor, attempting to improve the public image of officials, directed all departments to appoint a senior employee to be responsible for improving the relationship between state government and the public. His memo emphasized the importance of providing accurate and complete information to the public with minimal delay. In addition, the public was to be informed of the responsibilities and operation of each major department. The governor hoped that his campaign of "selling government to the people" would reverse the growing trend of public criticism of state officials.

Erickson was impressed by the governor's new policy. He felt that too often government failed to be responsive to the public. However, he was aware of the difficulties of his task. To be truly effective the program required a great deal of time. On occasion it seemed to him that officials spent more time polishing their image than providing the basic services of their department. Despite these difficulties, Erickson felt the new policy was desirable and decided he would make every effort to comply.

About eight months later, the governor's new policy seemed to be succeeding. The press was becoming less critical, and Erickson noticed a slight change of attitude in people requesting information from his department. The governor had just successfully completed a primary election battle, helped, Erickson thought, by his slogan calling for "open government."

About this time, Erickson received a request for assistance from a rancher, Oscar Walton, in the western part of the state who said that in the past two weeks nearly two hundred of his cattle had mysteriously died. The rancher explained that he had analyzed the water sources on his land and the cattle's feed but could not determine the cause of death. He was afraid of losing the rest of his herd.

Erickson told the rancher that he would use all of the department's resources to help him solve the problem. During the course of his investigation, Erickson uncovered an apparent conflict of interest involving Ralph Fitzgerald, the attorney general. Fitzgerald had a large investment in a chemical company, the Fast Grow Corporation, that produced fertilizer. A year and a half before, the Department of Environmental Protection had investigated possible water pollution caused by use of the firm's fertilizer. Although there was no conclusive evidence, it was strongly suspected that certain chemicals in the fertilizer could contaminate local water-drainage areas. However, the department decided to stop its investigation. It was rumored that Fitzgerald and the Environmental Protection director, Mark Simpson, had come to an agreement.

Erickson consulted with some colleagues in his office concerning this matter. He was uncertain as to the amount of information he should provide his constituent. If the fertilizer was contaminating water-drainage areas, it would provide at least a partial explanation of the rancher's problem. If, however, he was wrong, he might face a possible damage suit from the fertilizer company. In addition, Director Simpson soon learned that new inquiries were being made into this matter and called on Erickson to ask him about the investigation. Simpson opened the meeting by saying, "I hear you have reopened the investigation on the cattle deaths at the Walton ranch." Erickson replied that he had and that it was in response to the governor's policy.

After some further talk, Simpson told Erickson, "Look, I can't go into the details, but there are too many people involved in the Fast Grow Corporation who are either prominent politicians or large financial contributors to the governor's campaign. We cannot afford to be open on this one. There could be too many heads to roll including mine and perhaps yours. We are fortunate that Fitzgerald, who wants to run against the governor next time, is involved." Erickson's dilemma had increased; he wondered if he should pursue the investigation or drop it.

Questions and Instructions

1. Where does Erickson's loyalty lie in this situation—with the public, with his department, or with his own integrity?
2. If Erickson decides to blow the whistle in this case, what would be his best course of action?
3. On the evidence he now has of the possible environmental dangers of the fertilizer, should Erickson inform the public? If so, should he leak the information to the press or identify himself as the source? What would be the likely consequences of each action?

4. In view of the governor's campaign slogan of "open government," do you think his chance for re-election would be harmed by disclosure?

Selected Bibliography

Aldrich, Howard, "Organization Boundaries and Inter-organizational Conflict," *Human Relations* 24 (August 1971): 279–93.

Aram, John D., *Dilemmas of Administrative Behavior,* Englewood Cliffs, N.J.: Prentice-Hall, 1976.

Armstrong, DeWitt C., III, and Graham, George A., "Ethical Preparation for the Public Service," *Bureaucrat* 4 (April 1975): 5–22.

Bailey, Stephen K., "Ethics and the Public Service," *Public Administration Review* 24 (December 1964): 234–43.

Blake, Eugene Carson, "Should the Code of Ethics in Public Life Be Absolute or Relative?" *Annals of the American Academy of Political and Social Science* 363 (January 1966): 4–11.

Boling, T. Edwin, "Organizational Ethics: Rules, Creativity, and Idealism," in Sutherland, John W., ed., *Management Handbook for Public Administrators,* New York: Van Nostrand Reinhold, 1978. pp. 221–53.

Caiden, Gerald E., "Ethics in the Public Service: Codification Misses the Real Target," *Public Personnel Management* 20 (1981): 146–52.

Cooper, Melvin G., "Administering Ethics Laws: The Alabama Experience," *National Civic Review* 68 (February 1979): 77–81.

Dometrius, Nelson C., "State Government Administration and the Electoral Process," *State Government* 53 (Summer 1980): 129–34.

Fletcher, Thomas W., and McGwire, John M., "Government and Private Business: New Relationships Emerging," *National Civic Review* 69 (October 1980): 491–96.

Foster, Gregory D., "Legalism, Moralism, and the Bureaucratic Mentality," *Public Personnel Management* 10 (1981): 93–97.

Frome, Michael, "Blowing the Whistle," *The Center Magazine* 11 (November/December 1978): 50–58.

Lovrich, Nicholas P., "Professional Ethics and the Public Interest: Sources of Judgment," *Public Personnel Management* 10 (1981): 87–92.

Rohr, John A., "Financial Disclosure: Power in Search of Policy," *Public Personnel Management* 10 (1981): 29–40.

"Symposium: Public Administration as a Profession," *Southern Review of Public Administration* 5 (Fall 1981): 237–391.

Walton, Richard E.; Dutton, John M.; and Cafferty, Thomas P., "Organizational Context and Interdepartmental Conflict," *Administrative Science Quarterly* 14 (December 1969): 522–42.

21

No Welcome Wagon Here

Case A. Subsidized Housing Wrangles

Park Forest, fifteen miles from the state capital, was more than just a bedroom community for its metropolitan neighbor. It was the site of Central University, which had attracted a growing technological industry, and the home of more than 60,000 people. Above average in affluence and education, Park Forest's residents usually passed bond issues for schools and civic improvements, supported increases in water, sewage, and trash-collection fees to maintain high standards of service, and fostered almost a hundred support groups ranging from Aging Services to a Youth and Family Center.

Therefore, Ronald Fleming, newly appointed executive director of the Park Forest Housing Authority Board of Commissioners, was surprised by residents' lack of concern for the public weal, demonstrated by their bitter opposition to a public housing project. He discovered it had roots in the past. Five years earlier a fifty-two unit complex had been constructed on the east side, and three years later many east-side residents objected to a second project of forty-four units that was to be located in their area. About twenty of them appeared before the Planning Commission and City Council to protest the rezoning of the proposed site from a single-family dwelling to a low-density apartment area. Let the wealthier residents on the west side, they argued, assume their share of housing the poor. They lost the battle, but city officials were careful the next time to locate an apartment complex for the elderly on the near west side.

Because east-side residents were angered by what they considered the City Council's neglect of their area, the Housing Authority thought it prudent to locate a new $2,024,980 low-income project on the west side. Suitable sites, however, were not easily found. The first choice, a five-acre tract near a shopping mall, was rejected because its construction would worsen an already congested traffic situation. The Housing Authority was forced to fall back on its second option, five acres in the far northwest section of town. This area was not entirely desirable because it was so far from downtown and was zoned as a rural agricultural district.

This choice was to provoke a controversy that made the earlier controversies look pacific. The site was a half mile from Riverside Estates, an exclusive residential area whose homeowners were outraged at the proposal. The Riverside Homeowners' Association called a protest meeting at which it was decided to fight the project by circulating a petition calling for an election on the question of declaring a moratorium on public housing.

Ronald Fleming was shocked to learn that petition circulators were telling prospective signers the project would bring undesirable people to the area, because not enough Park Forest people could be obtained for one hundred percent occupancy. The units, it was reported, would be filled by dislocated and unemployed minorities from the metropolitan area. Fleming asked the Park Forest Human Rights Commission to conduct an investigation of the discriminatory and inflammatory claims being made by the petition circulators. The commission expressed its support of the housing project but said it could not investigate. The chair, Joan Jackson, explained: "There's not much we can do. The only time we can take action is when there are people involved who cannot get housing because of discrimination. I don't know if any law has been broken by the petition circulators. I think their remarks are wrong, if they made them, but they have the right of freedom of speech."

The City Council meeting that dealt with the rezoning request was one of the longest and noisiest in recent years, packed with east and west siders, attorneys and leaders of the associations and agencies concerned, and unaffiliated members of the public.

In a response to a question posed by Mayor Thornton Vesco, city attorney A. B. Wainwright recommended delaying a vote on a motion to rezone. Pointing out that the petitions containing 4,800 signatures were sufficient to bring the moratorium issue to a vote, Wainwright said that action should be delayed until the public had a chance to speak. Wainwright's stand was endorsed by councilmember Anna Gilchrist of Ward 1 on the west side. "I consider the petition a mandate that an election should be held," she said. "The citizens of Park Forest should make the decision of whether we should continue to construct public housing projects." Two councilmembers supported Gilchrist's stand, but three others proposed that the views of proponents and opponents be heard before taking action.

Legal arguments for postponement were presented by Carlton Mason, representing several west-side neighborhood associations. His view was that though a vote favoring a moratorium might not be binding on the Department of Housing and Urban Development, the City Council should consider it a commitment to reject rezoning.

Legal Aid attorney Nathan Gold, representing low-income clients, declared that the election would be protested because of the racism expressed by petition circulators. "What we have here is an attempt to circumvent the housing authority," Gold declared. "My clients will be damaged. We will not sit idly by and see the housing money lost. My clients have little power, but their needs are there. Believe me, their rights should be protected."

Elizabeth Markham, president of the League of Women Voters, received both boos and cheers when she ended a plea in favor of the rezoning motion with the words: "It does not seem that the spirit of our community should be one that says, if you are poor, we do not want you in Park Forest."

It was Markham's view that eventually prevailed, to the relief of Ronald Fleming. The council postponed action on rezoning until an election could be held, and the vote was overwhelmingly against the moratorium. The community's decision tended to restore Fleming's faith that the people, if given the opportunity, would choose to do the right thing.

Case B. A Halfway House for Mental Patients

Occupants of the large, old-fashioned houses erected many years ago in a residential district north of Madisonville State University hardly noticed when a sign bearing the name "Friendship House" appeared on a three-story building on a street bordering the campus and their neighborhood. The building had been constructed originally as a dormitory for Roman Catholic women students and in recent years had been a rooming house under successive managements.

Before long, residents became aware that strangers were entering their neighborhood of big houses, large green lawns, and huge trees. These people, they learned, came from Friendship House, and instead of being university students they were accustomed to seeing, were former mental health patients.

When residents complained to Catherine Levinson, director of Friendship House, she wondered whether mental patients who were seeking to be self-sufficient and who were preparing themselves to return to mainstream society could be any more bothersome than college students. It was the designation "mental," she thought, that frightened the neighborhood people.

To a delegation calling at Friendship House Levinson promised to work with the concerned residents in solving problems and conducted a tour to explain the nature of the rehabilitation program. She said that the home had nine qualified staff members, seven full-time, and at least two employees were on the premises at any time. Although there were only thirty-five occupants at present, the building's facilities could accommodate as many as seventy people. Levinson explained that Friendship House was a private organization operating under contract with the State Mental Health Department and received about $25,000 a year for such services as education and therapy programs. Patients or their families paid fees that raised most of the money to meet the home's budget.

Levinson learned of further community objection to the home through an article in the Madisonville *Monitor*, which noted that residents were circulating a petition in favor of closing the program for presentation to state officials. Marie Clinefeldt, the seventy-year-old leader of the drive, was quoted as saying: "They call themselves a halfway house, but it's more of a holding tank. The building just does not lend itself to the purposes for which it is being used." Clinefeldt charged that occupants of the home wandered about the streets at all hours of the day and night, banging on doors or ringing doorbells; gathered in the shade of trees to loaf and talk for hours, leaving their soft-drink cans on residents' lawns; and annoyed children by engaging them in conversation. One outdoor party, Clinefeldt said, was interrupted by two Friendship House residents shouting obscenities. "Nobody has been hurt yet," she warned, "but people are frightened. This used to be such a nice neighborhood."

Clinefeldt presented the petition, signed by twenty-five persons, to the Mental Health Department director, Dr. Abraham Rubin. He explained to her that, though his department monitored Friendship House and forty other room-and-board homes for former mental patients, the homes were licensed by the Public Health Department. He assured her that the petition would receive serious consideration by the proper authorities.

Questions and Instructions

1. What do you think of the people in Park Forest who opposed low-income housing in their part of town? Why do you think they became so agitated over the issue of location?
2. Do you see any differences in the people who objected to low-income housing and those who objected to the home for former mental patients? What if the halfway house was for persons just released from prison?
3. What steps would you take to prepare the public for acceptance of a facility that is likely to receive public opposition?
4. What guidelines would you establish for going ahead with a project that is strongly opposed by the community?
5. Do you share Ronald Fleming's faith in the ability of the people to make the right decisions?
6. What action should Dr. Rubin of the Mental Health Department take in the case of the petition against Friendship House? Does the complaint warrant an on-the-spot investigation?

Selected Bibliography

Ahlbrandt, Roger S., and Sumka, Howard J., "Neighborhood Organizations and the Coproduction of Public Services," *Journal of Urban Affairs* 5 (Summer 1983): 211–20.

Bloom, Prescott E., "Legislative Oversight: A Response to Citizens' Demands and Needs," *State and Local Government Review* 16 (Winter 1984): 34–38.

Booth, Alan, and Higgins, Douglas, *Human Service Planning and Evaluation for Hard Times,* Springfield, Ill.: Charles C. Thomas Publishers, 1984.

Brooks, Harvey; Liebman, Lance; and Schelling, Corinne, eds., *Public-Private Partnership: New Opportunities for Meeting Social Needs,* Cambridge: Ballinger, 1984.

Cleveland, Harlan, "The Public Executive: A Sense of Responsibility for the Whole," *Public Management* 62 (December 1980): 2–7.

"Commentary: Local Government Strategies," *Public Management* 69 (May 1987): 3–18. Provides a synoptic discussion of what various U.S. cities are doing to provide shelter or housing for the homeless.

DeHoog, Ruth Hoogland, "Evaluating Human Services Contracting: Managers, Professionals, and Politics," *State and Local Government Review* 18 (Winter 1986): 37–44.

———, "Human Services Contracting: Environmental, Behavioral, and Organizational Conditions," *Administration and Society* 16 (February 1985): 427–54.

Goldzimer, Linda Silverman, "Treating Your Constituents Like Customers," *Public Management* 69 (April 1987): 2–4.

Hummel, Ralph P., *The Bureaucratic Experience,* 3rd ed., New York: St. Martin's Press, 1987. Ch. 1, "Bureaucracy As the New Society," pp. 25–60.

Immershein, Allen W.; Polivka, Larry; Gordon-Girvin, Sharon; Chackerian, Richard; and Martin, Patricia, "Service Networks in Florida: Administrative Decentralization and Its Effects on Service Delivery," *Public Administration Review* 46 (March/April 1986): 161–69.

Kahn, Alfred, "Service Delivery at the Neighborhood Level: Experience, Theory and Fads," *Social Service Review* 50 (March 1976): 23–55.

Marlin, John Tepper, *Contracting Municipal Services: A Guide for Purchase from the Private Sector,* New York: John Wiley & Sons, 1984.

Port, Ian, "Housing and the Local Council Agenda in Box Hill," *Public Management* 69 (May 1987): 20–21.

Rich, Richard C., "The Roles of Neighborhood Organizations in Urban Service Delivery," *Urban Affairs Papers* 1 (Fall 1979): 81–93.

Smith, Elton, C.; O'Toole, Laurence J., Jr.; and Burke, Beverly G., "Managing Public Housing: A Case Study of Myths and Realities," *State and Local Government Review* 16 (Spring 1984): 75–83.
Thomas, Edwin J., *Designing Interventions for the Helping Professions*, Beverly Hills, Calif.: Sage Publications, 1984.

22

A Problem of Motivation

As part of a workfare program to make mothers who were recipients of Aid to Families with Dependent Children (AFDC) self-supporting, the State Tourism and Recreation Department employed six women assigned to various divisions. Under the plan, the federal and state governments jointly paid their salaries while they underwent a six-month training program. At the end of this period, each division had the option of hiring or releasing the women based on their performances and the recommendations of their supervisors.

Julie Davis was one of the three trainees chosen for regular employment, being assigned to the Tourist Information Office. The mother of two girls, aged six and eight, Davis had received aid from AFDC since her husband was killed in an auto accident five years before. Upon her marriage she had given up her job as a receptionist and typist in a wholesale grocery firm. Not having been employed outside her home for a decade, Davis had reentered the workforce with some trepidation. Initially she displayed enthusiasm and performed her duties efficiently. After about six weeks, however, Jeff Baker, her supervisor, noticed she was developing poor working habits such as long coffee breaks, tardiness, and absenteeism.

Baker felt Davis's low performance had resulted from her association with two employees in the conventions unit of the department. Baker arranged a meeting with her and advised her of the unacceptability of her work behavior. He had received complaints from other employees that she was not carrying her share of the load. "Julie," he said, "generally your work has been very good but lately your job performance has not lived up to expectations. Although our standards are higher than other sections of this department, the chances for promotion and career advancement are a lot better for the hard-working employee. You can do a lot better than you have been doing!" After the session with Baker, Davis's work and behavior immediately improved. She volunteered to assist others whenever her own work was completed and quickly acquired the necessary skills for several other positions in the section. She often worked as a substitute in the absence of other employees.

At the end of the training period Baker recommended that the agency hire Davis at the level of Grade 5. The quality of her work remained consistently high and she continued to assist others willingly. Six months later, when she had completed a year with the agency, she was promoted to Grade 6 and assigned additional responsibilities. Indeed, a bright future seemed on the horizon.

About two months later, one of the employees Davis had been assisting resigned because of a death in her family. The announcement for the newly opened position emphasized it was limited to employees of the department. Since Davis was familiar with many aspects of the position, she discussed applying for it with Baker, who advised her that even though she was the only staff member familiar with the job her chance of being on the list of applicants supplied by the Bureau of Personnel was small because she had only fourteen months' experience instead of the required two years. He said she would make the list only if there were no applicants with the required experience. This was possible, though unlikely. Davis decided to apply and hope for the best. There were several applicants with the required experience and she did not make the list.

Davis's attitude changed immediately. She became irritable and her relationship with other staff members deteriorated. She developed intense feelings of insecurity. Each time a new employee was hired she felt as though she might be replaced. As a result of this constant fear she developed an ulcer. In another meeting with her, Baker reassured her of her abilities, explained the steps involved in employee termination, and outlined the grievance procedures available to employees should termination occur. Initially, she seemed to gain confidence and her work improved, though not to the level of her previous performance. Davis had become confused and felt angry toward Baker for what she considered to be unwarranted encouragement.

Since Baker felt he could no longer adequately motivate Davis, he recommended that she be transferred to another supervisor, Malcolm Tate. After a few weeks, her work performance and attitude improved considerably, and Tate soon considered her among the best employees he had ever supervised.

The problem in the department appeared to be resolved, but Tate might be faced with the same problem as Baker. In the next four months two employees under Tate's supervision were to retire. Both positions were at the Grade 7 level. Davis was now qualified for both, but there were others in the agency better qualified. Even if she made the list, there was a good possibility she would not be selected for the position.

Questions and Instructions

1. Was transferring Davis the best course of action Baker could have taken? What other choices did he have?
2. Do rules stating that a person must have two years' experience bear any relationship to the realities of an employee's efficiency and the needs of an organization? Should the rules be reviewed?
3. Do you feel that the manner in which Davis was hired through the workfare program affected her job performance?
4. Do you feel that Davis's home situation may have been the cause of her attitudes toward her job?
5. Should Tate encourage Davis to apply for a new position when the possibility of not being selected exists?
6. What can Tate do to prevent the recurrence of the previous situation if Davis is not selected for one of the Grade 7 positions?
7. Davis seems to be experiencing stress. What do you think could be the main cause of the stress? Is the stress-risk behavior related to the actions of others, or is it related to her own expectations? What could Baker have done to reduce the level of personal stress that Davis experienced? What could Davis do about her own situation?
8. Does Davis appear to be internally or externally motivated? What are the implications associated with both of these motivations?
9. What follow-up program should the state adopt for graduates of workfare now holding jobs?

Selected Bibliography

Brass, Daniel J., "Structural Relationships, Job Characteristics, and Worker Satisfaction and Performance," *Administrative Science Quarterly* 26 (September 1981): 331–48.

Filipowicz, Christine, "The Troubled Employee: Whose Responsibility?" *Personnel Administrator* 24 (June 1979): 17–22.

Goodman, Paul S.; Salipante, Paul; and Paransky, Harold, "Hiring, Training, Retaining the Hard Core Unemployed: A Selected Review," *Journal of Applied Psychology* 58 (August 1973): 23–33.

Herzberg, Frederick, "One More Time: How Do You Motivate Employees?" *Harvard Business Review* 46 (January/February 1968): 53–62.

House, Robert J., and Mitchell, Terence R., "Path-Goal Theory of Leadership," *Contemporary Business* 3 (Autumn 1974): 81–97.

Lehrer, Sande, "Motivating Subordinates: Making It Work," *The Bureaucrat* 15 (Summer 1986): 49–58.

Lutz, Carl F., "Efficient Maintenance of the Classification Plan," *Public Personnel Management* 2 (July/August 1973): 232–41.

Maslow, Abraham H., "A Theory of Human Motivation," *Psychological Review* 50 (July 1943): 370–96.

Mealiea, Laird W., and Duffy, John F., "An Integrated Model for Training and Development: How to Build on What You Already Have," *Public Personnel Management* 9 (No. 4, 1980): 336–43.

Paul, William J., Jr.; Robertson, Keith B.; and Herzberg, Frederick, "Job Enrichment Pays Off," *Harvard Business Review* 47 (March/April 1969): 61–78.

Radin, Beryl A., "Leadership Training for Women in State and Local Government," *Public Personnel Management* 9 (No. 2, 1980): 52–60.

Schulkind, Gilbert A., "Monitoring Position Classification—Practical Problems and Possible Solutions," *Public Personnel Management* 4 (January/February 1975): 32–37.

White, Robert N., "State Grievance and Appeals Systems: A Survey," *Public Personnel Management* 10 (No. 3, 1981): 313–23.

Yeager, Samuel J.; Rabin, Jack; and Vocino, Thomas, "Employee Perceptions of State and Local Government Evaluation and Reward Systems," *State and Local Government Review* 16 (Spring 1984): 58–62.

23

The Prank That Misfired

Phoebe Palmer, a GS-4 clerk-stenographer at Beckworth Air Force Base, was cheerful, young, and friendly. In the office in which she had worked for three years, the twenty men, all civilians, would frequently tease her in a playful, good-natured way. They delighted in playing jokes on her, for she was somewhat naive and easily fooled. She seemed to enjoy the pranks as much as the perpetrators. She was mature enough to know there was nothing malicious in their banter or jokes that reflected on her ability as a secretary. She considered herself, and was, an efficient worker.

One Friday morning shortly after Palmer reported for work, the telephone rang and a male voice asked, "What about that ad in this week's *Beckworth Bulletin?* I think we might be interested in a trade for our office."

Puzzled, Palmer replied, "Ad? I don't know anything about an ad in the *Bulletin.*"

The man on the other end of the line laughed and said, "Look it up in the want ads and you'll see." Still laughing he hung up the receiver.

Almost immediately the phone rang again. This time it was a woman. "I'm interested in that job in your office. Could you tell me about it? I think I might want to make a change."

"There's no position open in this office," Palmer replied. "I think you must have made a mistake."

"Is this 9555?" the voice asked. "This week's *Bulletin* says to call this number about a job exchange."

Replying that there must be some mistake, Palmer hung up and hurried to look in the *Bulletin,* the base newspaper published every Friday, which she had picked up from a stack on the floor when she entered the building. On page seven among the classifieds she found the following notice:

> WANTED TO TRADE
> ONE GS-4 Clerk-Steno for a GS-3 Clerk-Typist who is quiet, reserved, uses telephone to minimum extent and has no personal problems. No deposit, no return. Call 9555 for details.

Palmer, reading the notice, was slightly puzzled and also somewhat amused. It was, she thought, just another joke perpetrated by the men in the office.

But it soon ceased to be a joke. The first two calls were the opening of a floodgate. As soon as Palmer got rid of one caller, the phone rang again. Some of the callers, like the second one she had spoken to, did not see the want ad as a prank and seriously sought details about the position. Most of the callers were male employees or airmen at the base who recognized the advertisement as a prank and used it as an occasion to display their wit or to ask for a date. A few of the calls were obscene.

Almost in tears after an hour of constant telephone calls, Palmer refused to answer the phone and the men in the office began handling this chore. What had been intended as fun had become an embarrassment both for her and for the men. Everyone was uncomfortable at the end of the day, but the young woman was angry and determined to find out who had inserted the want ad. She went to the *Beckworth Bulletin* office and complained to the editor. Copy for the paper was not thrown away until a month after publication and the want ad, which was handwritten and had been mailed in, was available. Palmer recognized the handwriting immediately as being that of one of the men in her office.

On Monday, Palmer made an appointment with the director of her division, Houston Turner, and complained that the want ad in the *Bulletin* had made her the laughingstock of the entire base. It was well known that she was the only stenographer-clerk in her office. The incessant telephone calls and the wisecracks and obscenities she had had to listen to had so upset her that she could not sleep at night and she was too embarrassed to leave the house over the weekend. She did not see how she could face friends and acquaintances on the base.

Questions and Instructions

1. How should Houston Turner handle Phoebe Palmer's complaint about the prank of which she was a victim? Do you think she should be given a few days' leave to let the matter die down?
2. Since jokes played on Palmer were frequent in the office, do you think Turner was at fault for letting the situation get out of hand?
3. Do you think Palmer should demand a printed apology from the *Beckworth Bulletin?*
4. If the perpetrator or perpetrators of the prank can be identified, what reprimand should they receive?
5. Was the staff of the *Beckworth Bulletin* at fault in not recognizing the

advertisement as a joke?

6. How much kidding, joking, and banter should be allowed in an office? If, as an administrator, you think there is too much, how would you go about correcting the situation?

Selected Bibliography

Alderfer, Clayton P., *Existence, Relatedness and Growth: Human Needs in Organizational Settings,* New York: The Free Press, 1972.

Davidson, Robert E., "Professional Conflicts within Organizations," *Sociology and Social Research* 69 (January 1985): 210–20.

Dvorin, Eugene, and Simmons, Robert, *From Amoral to Humane Bureaucracy,* San Francisco, Calif.: Canfield, 1972.

Filley, Alan C.; House, Robert J.; and Kerr, Steven, *Managerial Process and Organizational Behavior,* 2nd ed., Glenview, Ill.: Scott, Foresman, 1976. Ch. 17, "Professionals in Organizations and Line-Staff Relationships," pp. 380–409, and Ch. 9, "Conflict Resolution and Problem Solving," pp. 162–82.

Galaskiewicz, Joseph, "Professional Networks and Institution Realization of a Single Mind Set," *American Sociological Review* 50 (October 1985): 639–58.

Graham, George A., "Ethical Guidelines for Public Administrators: Observations on Rules of the Game," *Public Administration Review* 34 (January/February 1974): 90–92.

Katz, Daniel, and Kahn, Robert L., *The Social Psychology of Organizations,* New York: John Wiley & Sons, 1966.

Kleeman, Rossly, "How to Stand Out," *The Bureaucrat* 16 (Spring 1987): 39–41.

Leavitt, Harold J., *Managerial Psychology,* 4th ed., Chicago: University of Chicago Press, 1978. See "The Jigsaw Puzzle of Individual Responsibility," pp. 321–23.

Likert, Rensis, and Likert, Jane G., *New Ways of Managing Conflict,* New York: McGraw-Hill, 1976.

McGowan, Robert P., "The Professional in Public Organizations: Lessons from the Private Sector?" *American Review of Public Administration* 16 (Winter 1982): 337–49.

Nanus, Burt, "Doing the Right Thing," *The Bureaucrat* 15 (Fall 1986): 9–12.

Riggs, R. Richard, "PA's Public Image," *The Bureaucrat* 12 (Winter 1983–84): 38–40.

Toren, Nina, "Deprofessionalization and Its Sources: A Preliminary Analysis," *Sociology of Work and Occupations* 2 (November 1975): 323–37.

Van Maanen, John, "People Processing: Strategies of Organizational Socialization," *Organizational Dynamics* 7 (Summer 1978): 19–36.

Weinstein, Denna, *Bureaucratic Opposition: Challenging Abuses at the Work Place,* New York: Pergamon Press, 1979.

Wilensky, Harold L., "The Professionalization of Everyone?" *American Journal of Sociology* 70 (No. 2, 1964): 137–58.

24

The Parking-Ticket Ledger

For the past five years Ronald Hughes had been employed as a radio dispatcher for the 25-member police force of Madison. Although Madison was a fairly small and quiet town, the job of radio dispatcher was demanding. Hughes was a responsible employee who had worked well under stress and equally well during occasional lulls. The duties of a dispatcher as described in Hughes's job description were:

1. monitoring and recording radio conversations with various law-enforcement agencies
2. receiving and recording police-related information on the telephone
3. typing and filing police and fire reports
4. assisting in the processing of offenders, such as fingerprinting
5. monitoring security alarms
6. maintaining security for jailed offenders

Hughes, along with four other radio dispatchers, was responsible for performing each of these duties as they arose. Hughes was also responsible for keeping the parking-ticket ledger in order. Tickets were registered and records kept of warrants and payments.

Hughes was employed Monday through Friday on the day watch (8 A.M. to 4 P.M.), which was considered the best shift by the entire department. Little police activity occurred during this shift, and most of the dispatcher's time was spent on the telephone routing incoming calls to various city offices. However, emergency situations calling for quick thinking and action did arise from time to time.

At first Hughes accepted his assignment to the day watch happily. But after five years at the same position, he had begun to feel that he was stagnating rather than developing his potential. Hughes decided to do something about his problem and conferred with Barry Grant, the city manager. "I really wish I could help you, Ron," Grant told him, "but you know what a bureaucratic mess the police force is. You go through channels, get involved in red tape, and then you end up where you started. Stick it out, Ron, your day will come." Although sympathetic, Grant's advice made Hughes feel even more discontented.

Hughes began to think he was not being fairly compensated for his work because of the extra duty of keeping the parking-ticket ledger. Each year the city set the hourly wage rates paid city employees based on their position. Only one class of dispatcher was recognized and longevity and merit were considered in the pay rate. Hughes believed his position carried more of a load than the other four dispatcher assignments and that therefore he was entitled to a higher rate of pay. If not paid more, Hughes felt he should not have to perform the extra duty of keeping the ledger.

When Hughes took this new problem to the city manager, Grant's sympathy had dwindled considerably. "I don't know exactly what to say," Grant said. "Obviously the keeping of the parking-ticket ledger is the responsibility of the department issuing the tickets. Who the department assigns to take care of it is their decision. I'm afraid, Ron, we're stuck with their decision." Hughes then took his problem to the police chief, who told him that the bookkeeping fell within the duties required of a dispatcher and that it was not an extra burden meriting additional compensation.

In general, the other dispatchers supported the city administrator and police chief's view. They insisted that the day watch involved no more work than the night watch. The late-night personnel pointed out that their shift involved activities not included in the day watch, including the booking of offenders and the surveillance of prisoners. The night people also mentioned that the work they were involved in was more stressful and required more effort and intelligence.

No agreement was reached and the conflict within the department grew as employees took sides. Finally Hughes had "had enough" and believed the only answer was to resign. He gave his two-weeks' notice and began looking for a new job.

Questions and Instructions.

1. What aspects of a career civil-service system or merit system does Madison lack?
2. Would a grievance procedure be helpful to Tom Hughes?
3. Were Grant's comment about the "bureaucratic mess in the police force" and advice to "stick it out" wise?
4. If there is a "bureaucratic mess' in the police department, does the city manager have any responsibility to straighten it out?
5. Hughes appears to be a good employee. Should the city have a career-development program for employees?

Selected Bibliography

Alber, Antone F., "How (and How Not) to Approach Job Enrichment," *Personnel Journal* 58 (December 1979): 837–41.

Britton, Donald E., "Are Job Descriptions Really Necessary?" *Personnel Administrator* 20 (January 1975): 47–50.

———, "Common Practices in Wage and Salary Competition," *Personnel Administrator* 19 (January/February 1974): 19–24.

Cohen, Stephen L., and Meyer, Herbert H., "Toward a More Comprehensive Career Planning Program," *Personnel Journal* 58 (September 1979): 611–15.

Dyer, Lee; Schwab, Donald P.; and Fossum, John A., "Impacts of Pay on Employee Behaviors and Attitudes: An Update," *Personnel Administrator* 23 (January 1978): 51–58.

Dyer, Lee, and Theriault, Roland, "The Determinants of Pay Satisfaction," *Journal of Applied Psychology* 61 (October 1976): 596–604.

Ellig, Bruce R., "Salary Surveys: Design to Application," *Personnel Administrator* 22 (October 1977): 41–48.

Fredlund, Robert R., "Criteria for Selecting a Wage System," *Public Personnel Management* 5 (September/October 1976): 323–27.

Greiner, John M., "Incentives for Municipal Employees: An Update," in *The Municipal Year Book 1980,* Washington, D.C.; International City Management Association, 1980. pp. 192–209.

Hackman, J. Richard; Oldham, Greg; Janson, Robert; and Purdy, Kenneth, "A New Strategy of Job Enrichment," *California Management Review* 27 (1975): 57–71.

Howell, Jon P., and Dorfman, Peter W., "Substitutes for Leadership: Test of a Construct," *Academy of Management Journal* 24 (December 1981): 714–28.

Lawler, Edward E., III, "New Approaches to Pay: Innovations That Work," *Personnel* 53 (September/October 1976): 11–23.

Locke, Edwin A.; Sirota, David; and Wolfson, Alan D., "An Experimental Case Study of the Successes and Failures of Job Enrichment in a Government Agency," *Journal of Applied Psychology* 61 (December 1976): 701–11.

Luthans, Fred, *Organizational Behavior,* New York: McGraw-Hill, 1973. Ch. 22, "Modern Behavioral Applications to Management," pp. 508–36.

Newstrom, John W.; Reif, William E.; and Monczka, Robert M., "Motivating the Public Employee: Fact vs. Fiction," *Public Personnel Management* 5 (January/February 1976): 67–72.

Rainey, Hal, G.; Traut, Carol; and Blunt, Barrie, "Reward Expectancies and Other Work-Related Attitudes in Public and Private Organizations: A

Review and Extension," *Review of Public Personnel Administration* 6 (Summer 1986): 50–72.

Schonberger, Richard J., and Hennessey, Henry W., Jr., "Is Equal Pay for Comparable Work Fair?" *Personnel Journal* 60 (December 1981): 964–71.

Simpson, Karl F., "Job Enrichment: Just Another Half-Truth?" *Personnel Administrator* 20 (November 1975): 42–45.

Terpstra, David E., "Theories of Motivation—Borrowing the Best," *Personnel Journal* 58 (June 1979): 376–79.

Whisemand, Paul M., and Ferguson, Fred R., *The Managing of Police Organizations,* Englewood Cliffs, N.J.: Prentice-Hall, 1978. Ch. 11, "Job Enrichment," pp. 375–406.

25

Affirmative-Action Pressures

Southwestern State University carried on its letterheads and printed in its catalogs and other publications the notice: "Southwestern State University Is an Equal Opportunity Institution." Following such a policy was important to it financially because otherwise it would not be entitled to federal funds for research, aid to students, and various special programs. Hence it engaged in vigorous affirmative-action efforts to recruit members of minorities as students and faculty members and to fill positions in administration and maintenance.

In recent years declines in enrollment and reductions in state appropriations along with increased costs in everything placed the university in a serious financial bind. A freeze was placed on new programs and increases in the administrative, maintenance, and instructional staffs, and an order was pending against filling vacancies created by retirement or resignation. The situation grew more serious in that the university had failed to meet its goals in employing members of minorities, and it faced a federal affirmative-action compliance audit. The word went out that any vacancies had to be filled by members of minorities.

In these circumstances Dwight Garfield, chief of campus security, and Captain Paul Rossi, head of campus police, were faced with the problem of finding a replacement for a black police officer who had resigned. Already understaffed, campus security would be severely handicapped if a replacement were not found before the freeze on filling vacancies was invoked. In seeking another black, Garfield had advertisements inserted in the state's newspaper published primarily for blacks, the *Afro-American,* and in commercial spots on radio stations directed toward a black audience.

Because the eligibility standards for the campus police were high—a bachelor's degree was required—and university pay scales were low, there were only a few applicants for the vacancy. After checking out the applications, Captain Rossi decided to interview Charles Blakemore, a student in a community college in the nearby town of Riverview. At his interview Blakemore impressed Garfield and Rossi favorably. He was neat in appearance; he was intelligent; and he was eager to get the job because it would enable him to continue his college education. Garfield and Rossi agreed that the requirement of a degree for the job might be waived, but that Blakemore would be required to obtain a bachelor's degree while on the job within three years of his appointment.

The director of Black Studies, the student organization the Black People's Union, and the university vice-president in charge of minority affairs also approved of Blakemore's appointment with the stipulation that he continue to work toward his degree. In the past three years Blakemore had proved himself worthy of consideration by earning his high-school diploma, attending the community college, and working part-time. With the proviso that Blakemore complete his college education within three years while on the job, Garfield and Rossi decided to hire him.

Questions and Instructions

1. Were Garfield and Rossi right in waiving the B.A. requirement and hiring Blakemore? Discuss fully.
2. Should members of minorities be hired before or instead of better-qualified nonminority people?
3. How effective is adopting a quota system in carrying out an equal-opportunity or affirmative-action policy?
4. Do you believe that "reverse discrimination" is a serious problem in government employment?

Selected Bibliography

Bellone, Carl J., and Darling, Douglas H., "Implementing Affirmative Action Programs: Problems and Strategies," *Public Personnel Management* 9 (No. 3, 1980): 184–91.

Foster, Gregory D., "Law, Morality, and the Public Servant," *Public Administration Review* 41 (January/February 1981): 29–33.

Grossman, Harry, "The Equal Employment Opportunity Act of 1972: Its Implications for the State and Local Government Manager," *Public Personnel Management* 2 (September/October 1973): 370–79.

Jreisat, J. E., and Swierczek, F. W., "Affirmative Action in Public Administration in the South: A Human Resources Approach," *Southern Review of Public Administration,* 5 (Summer 1981): 148–61.

Mintzberg, Henry, *The Nature of Managerial Work,* New York: Harper and Row, 1973.

Palmer, J. David, "Recruitment and Staffing," in Crouch, Winston W., ed.,

Local Government Personnel Administration, Washington, D.C.: International City Management Association, 1976.

Renick, James C., "The Impact of Municipal Affirmative Action Programs on Black Representation in Government Employment: Reality or Rhetoric?" *Southern Review of Public Administration* 5 (Summer 1981): 129–46.

Sherman, Mitchell, "Equal Employment Opportunity: Legal Issues and Societal Consequences," *Public Personnel Management* 7 (March/April 1978): 127–33.

26

A Cutback Emergency

Governor James Oliver appeared on the state's public television network to announce that the state's income could be $30 million short of projections by the end of the fiscal year. Not wishing to increase taxes in a declining economy and prohibited by the constitution from incurring a deficit of more than $100,000, the governor said he was ordering a 5-percent cut in the budgets of all government departments and agencies.

"I want the cuts to be uniformly made so that nobody can say I'm picking on one department or one state agency," said Governor Oliver. "Department heads will decide cuts within the agencies, and outlines of planned cuts must be in my office within three weeks."

The governor's announcement shocked Vincent Scotch, chairman of the state's Board of Regents for Higher Education. The board was responsible for the administration of the state's seven universities and colleges. Scotch called an emergency meeting of the board and outlined the problems of cutting $3.1 million from the college and university budgets. "Eighty-two percent of our funds are spent on employees," he reported, "and a labor contract with the union representing the faculty at colleges and universities forbids us from laying off tenured faculty members during the term of the contract."

The board members agreed that the best way to implement Governor Oliver's budget cuts was to order the seven college presidents to formulate a 5-percent cut at their institutions. But after the meeting, Robert Lewis, director of the faculty union, stated: "We'll go to court if necessary to prevent the regents or presidents from laying off faculty members in the current fiscal year regardless of whether they are tenured. The union contract specifically says that in all cases tenured faculty members will complete their existing appointment contracts and that nontenured faculty members may have their contracts terminated this fiscal year only if there is an emergency financial exigency. This hardly qualifies as an emergency financial exigency."

The day following the regents' meeting, Amanda T. Yarberry, president of Central State University, met with her vice-presidents for academic affairs, administration, and student services. She handed them a copy of the school's current budget and told them to formulate a plan showing a 5-percent budget reduction in each of their respective areas. (See Exhibit 1 on page 123.)

Carl Nute, vice-president of academic affairs, felt across-the-board cuts for each area were unfair. "Not every unit in this university contributes equally to the goals, purposes, and basic function of the university," he declared. "Before cuts can be made, priorities must be established and programs examined on a university-wide basis to determine the impact the cuts will have on the students, the employees, the people of the state, and the primary purposes of a university, which are teaching and research. Intercollegiate athletics and administrative-support services are secondary and they should bear the brunt of the cuts."

"I couldn't agree with you more," responded President Yarberry. "I'd like to sit down with the three of you and establish program priorities on a university-wide basis. However, I have only one week left to get these budget-reduction plans back to the regents, and participatory management doesn't work when you're dealing with budget cuts."

President Yarberry then handed each vice-president a copy of the budget cuts she had prepared for her own office. (See Exhibit 2 on page 124.)

"It's not easy cutting your own budget," she said at the end of the meeting, "but we're not being paid to make easy decisions."

The next day Vice-President Nute met with the deans of Arts and Sciences, Business, Education, Fine Arts, and Law. He informed them of President Yarberry's order and passed out a copy of their total budget classified by tenured faculty salaries, nontenured faculty salaries, and uncommitted salaries.* (See Exhibit 3 on page 125.) Nute then requested suggestions from the deans as to which programs and areas were of lowest priority and therefore should absorb the greatest share of the 5-percent cut.

Dean Walter Stark of the School of Business was quick to respond. "The first reduction has to come from uncommitted salaries," he said. "Those cuts could absorb over two-thirds of the reduction allocated to us."

"Taking $133,482 of budgeted salaries would cost Arts and Sciences four teachers of professorial rank," Dean Dale Schultz said. "We're up for accreditation this year and we need those slots filled."

"You haven't filled those positions in two years," replied Dean Stark. "Uncommitted salaries indicate waste and should always be the first target for budget cuts."

"Uncommitted salaries don't always indicate waste," retorted Dean Cax-

* Budgeted salaries for positions not filled due to late resignations or difficulty in finding qualified people.

ton Turner of Fine Arts. "In the past Dean Schultz and I were conserving our resources and now you want to penalize us for it."

The meeting soon degenerated into loud argument, but finally Nute was able to bring the group back to order. "This is getting us nowhere," he said. "I want each of you to draw up a plan to reduce your budget by 10 percent. Tomorrow we'll meet again and together prioritize your proposed budget reduction from the first to go to the last to go till we hit our target 5-percent reduction."

"That's not fair," said Dean Philip Carter of the School of Education. "Some of us will end up having our budgets reduced by 10 percent while others may have no reduction."

"Meeting adjourned," Nute said firmly.

The next day Nute met with the deans and reviewed their planned budget reductions. Not one of them had reduced his or her budget by even 5 percent. (See Exhibits 4–8 on pages 125–127.)

Questions and Instructions

1. Assume you are Vice-President Nute. What would you do next?
2. Compare President Yarberry's approach to the budget-reduction problem with Vice-President Nute's approach. Which do you prefer?
3. Do you feel the regents should have participated more in deciding specific budget cuts? Why or why not?
4. What type of contingency plan, if any, should President Yarberry prepare in the event of future budget cuts?
5. What is cutback management? What are some of the implications associated with cutting back? Explain.
6. What cutback tactics might be used in addition to mandating an across-the-board 5-percent budget reduction?
7. Are there any functions, projects, or activities that the colleges and schools might stop completely? That they can get other agencies or levels of government to carry out? Are there any areas where labor costs might be reduced by capital investment in labor-saving forms of technology? What activities might be done more efficiently at Central State University? At your own university or college? Prepare a list and discuss.
8. Social scientists have extensively researched the subjects of motivation and barriers to organizational change. Cutting back during a period of resource scarcity may bring about changes in the level of resource consumption, number of employees, level of job satisfaction and employee morale, level of employee productivity, and the attitude of employees and clients toward support of government. Is there any-

thing known about the characteristics and dynamics of change that might make it easier for Vice-President Nute to get the reduction he has asked for? Explain.

9. Are there any ethical implications associated with cutback management and politics? Does the university or any other organization or agency of government have an ethical responsibility toward its terminated employees? Toward the clients it serves? Explain.

Selected Bibliography

Behn, Robert D., "How to Terminate a Public Policy: A Dozen Hints for the Would-Be Policy Terminator," *Policy Analysis* 4 (Summer 1978): 393–413.

Blair, John P., and Nachmias, David, *Fiscal Retrenchment and Urban Policy*, Beverly Hills, Calif.: Sage Publications, 1979.

Boje, David M., and Whetten, David A., "Effects of Organizational Strategies and Contextual Constraints on Centrality and Attributions of Influence in Interorganizational Networks," *Administrative Science Quarterly* 26 (September 1981): 378–95.

Brewer, Garry D., "Termination: Hard Choices—Harder Questions," *Public Administration Review* 38 (July/August 1978): 338–44.

Cyert, Richard M., "The Management of Universities of Constant or Decreasing Size," *Public Administration Review* 38 (July/August 1978): 344–49.

Flentje, H. Edward, "Governor as Manager: A Political Assessment," *State Government* 54 (No. 3, 1981): 76–81.

Glassberg, Andrew, "Organizational Responses to Municipal Budget Decreases," *Public Administration Review* 38 (July/August 1978): 325–32.

Krebill, J. Robert, and Mosher, Ronald F., "Delaware Budgets for Productivity," *State Government* 53 (Winter 1980): 17–21.

Levine, Charles H., "Organizational Decline and Cutback Management," *Public Administration Review* 38 (July/August 1978): 316–25.

———, "More on Cutback Management: Hard Questions for Hard Times," *Public Administration Review* 39 (March/April 1979): 179–83.

Levine, Charles H.; Rubin, Irene S.; and Wolohojian, George G., *The Politics of Retrenchment: How Local Governments Manage Fiscal Stress*, Beverly Hills, Calif.: Sage Publications, 1980. Especially Chs. 2, 7, and 8.

Lindblom, Charles E., "The Science of Muddling Through," *Public Administration Review* 19 (Spring 1959): 79–88.

Pfeffer, Jeffrey, and Moore, William L., "Power in University Budgeting: A

Replication and Extension," *Administrative Science Quarterly* 25 (December 1980): 637–53.

Rubin, Irene S., "Retrenchment and Flexibility in Public Organizations," in Charles H. Levine and Irene S. Rubin, eds., *Fiscal Stress and Public Policy*, Beverly Hills, Calif.: Sage Publications, 1980. pp. 159–78.

———, "Retrenchment, Loose Structure, and Adaptability in the University," *Sociology of Education* 52 (October 1979): 211–22.

Simon, Herbert A., "Administrative Decision Making," *Public Administration Review* 25 (March 1965): 31–37.

Williams, John J., "Designing a Budgeting System with Planned Confusion," *California Management Review* 24 (Winter 1981): 75–85.

Exhibit 1. Total Budget of Central University

ACADEMIC AFFAIRS	
College of Arts and Sciences	$ 4,117,038
School of Business	1,026,997
School of Education	1,843,742
College of Fine Arts	1,023,182
School of Law	1,178,744
Vice President of Academic Affairs	77,403
Subtotal—Vice President Nute	$ 9,267,106
ADMINISTRATION	
Intercollegiate Athletics	$ 349,414
Business/Finance/Personnel	684,516
Computer Center	878,745
Educational Media Center	200,396
Central State University Research Institute	30,782
Physical Plant	2,490,589
Statewide Education Services	64,318
Vice President for Administration	45,156
Affirmative Action	18,699
Legal Counsel	7,039
Subtotal—Vice President Steel	$ 4,769,654
STUDENT SERVICES	
Student Services Administration	$ 73,257
Admissions	144,331
Alumni	12,000
Financial Aids	103,519
Registrar	153,728
University Counseling Center	117,332
University Relations	78,205
Subtotal—Vice President Ore	$ 682,372
Office of the President	$ 171,754
Convocations/Memberships	16,344
Subtotal—President Yarberry	$ 188,098
TOTAL	$14,907,230
PROPOSED REDUCTION: 5%	$ 745,361

Exhibit 2. Budget Cuts in the Office of the President

Item	*Amount*	*Consequences*
Harvard Seminar for College Presidents	$ 4,200	Breaking from policy of building professional development into the operating budget.
University Hospitality	$10,959	Reduce the level of hosting institutional donors, regents, legislators, lecturers, commencement hospitality, etc.
Retirement Seminars	$ 2,400	Discontinue a service that has been provided for individuals approaching retirement.
Campus Sign	$ 8,400	Abandon, again, a project that has been planned for four years, a project that would give attention to special campus events, etc.
Equipment Match	$ 9,600	Federal equipment funds will not be available as the result of not being able to provide matching funds.
TOTAL	$35,559	

Exhibit 3. Total Budget for Academic Affairs

	Total Budget	*Tenured Faculty Salaries*	*Nontenured Faculty Salaries*	*Uncommitted Salaries*	*Remainder*
CAS	$4,117,038	$2,400,006	$1,081,080	$133,482	$ 502,470
SB	1,026,997	720,004	236,196	1,444	69,353
SE	1,843,742	1,220,136	274,736	29,389	319,481
CFA	1,023,182	710,529	70,768	122,217	119,668
SL	1,178,744	703,645	62,548	24,562	387,989
VPAA	77,403	57,433	—	—	19,970
TOTAL	$9,267,106	$5,811,753	$1,725,328	$311,094	$1,418,931

CAS-College of Arts & Sciences, Dean Schultz
SB-School of Business, Dean Stark
SE-School of Education, Dean Carter
CFA-College of Fine Arts, Dean Turner
SL-School of Law, Dean Samuelson
VPAA-Vice President of Academic Affairs, Dr. Carl Nute

Exhibit 4. Dean Schultz's Proposed Budget Reduction for the College of Fine Arts and Sciences

Faculty Salaries	$39,313
Contractual Services	9,600
Supplies & Materials	6,000
Capital Assets	9,600
TOTAL	$64,513

A late faculty resignation in political science resulting in salary salvage of $24,913. Faculty turnover from a number of positions, either opened or filled at a lower salary level, resulted in salary salvage of $12,000. The money normally would be used to fulfill the necessary requests for added sections in English, communications, and mathematics. The sections simply will not be taught, which may mean that students cannot take the courses during the second semester. Faculty turnover in psychology resulted in salary salvage of $2,400. This money would have been used to hire additional teaching assistants in the psychology department with its two graduate degrees. Failure to provide it will mean that some potential assistants will do without or that other assistants will operate on a lower stipend. The elimination of matching funds for federal equipment grants will create a serious risk in providing these funds from remaining departmental resources if the grant applications are funded. Loss of additional operating and maintenance funds in the amount of $15,600 will greatly reduce the potential of the college to fund a great many activities, including travel and speakers.

Exhibit 5. Dean Stark's Proposed Budget Reduction for the School of Business

Faculty Salaries	$1,444

Impact:

Loss of these uncommitted salary funds would make it impossible to hire student labor.

Exhibit 6. Dean Carter's Proposed Budget Reduction for the School of Education

Faculty Salaries	$33,360
Part-Time Temporary Services	3,370
Contractual Services	2,400
TOTAL	$39,130

Impact:

A resignation in a recreational position resulted in salary salvage of $33,360. We will ease attempts to fill this vacancy created by a resignation after the start of this school year. Classes for second semester will be covered by part-time faculty and teaching assistants, as is being done in the first semester with funds budgeted for the position. Labor budget would be reduced by $3,370. Grants and external funding will be sought to accomplish the tasks expected to be covered in this funding during this year. This is a one-year reduction unless new funding sources are found, which appears very difficult for the tasks expected from these funds. The planned addition of another computer terminal for student use in the School of Education will be delayed for this academic year.

Exhibit 7. Dean Turner's Proposed Budget Reduction for the College of Fine Arts

Faculty Salaries	$45,016
Travel	1,200
Supplies & Materials	4,183
TOTAL	$50,399

Impact:

Salary salvage in the amount of $28,158 in music will be generated due to open visiting artist positions and one faculty member on leave without pay. These funds have been identified for translation into partial payment for a Steinway "B" piano. The department does not own one of these essential instruments and this was seen as an exceptional opportunity to acquire an expensive piece of equipment otherwise unattainable. This money must be returned to music-department personnel next year to return professors currently on leave to their contracted salary base. Failure to do so would necessitate terminating part-time faculty and graduate assistants. Open visiting-artist positions in art will generate salary salvage in the amount of $16,858. Loss of these funds would destroy departmental efforts to bring in artists of regional and national reputation as a supplement to the skills and experiences of the resident exposure of art students to the dynamics of the contemporary art world. This money must be available next year to cover sick-leave payment obligations. A reduction in operating and maintenance in art would impede faculty development by restricting attendance of all professional meetings and workshops. A reduction in operating and maintenance in theater would curtail faculty development, departmental outreach, and business operations. It would delay the replacement of worn and outmoded equipment and further restrict departmental ability to prepare theater majors with professional skills and knowledge.

Exhibit 8. Dean Samuelson's Proposed Budget Reduction for the School of Law

Travel	$7,200

Impact:

Travel by law-school personnel is essential for recruiting students, recruiting faculty, and keeping current in developments of the law. Loss of this money will require disapproval of some travel requests already submitted for out-ot-state attendance at law institutes, workshops or professional meetings on new legislation, court decisions, and development in the field of administrative law. Travel for recruiting and instate continuing legal education will not be reduced.

27

Retreat at Lake Clearwater

Jean Tse, director of the state land grant university's agricultural extension service, began receiving criticism of the annual three-day retreat for personnel at a resort lodge on Lake Clearwater as soon as the dates were announced. At a time when the university was on short rations because of budget cuts and the state was suffering a business slump, many people felt that the retreat was an unnecessary expense.

One of the objections was that some counties were having difficulty providing the 20 percent of financing for their extension offices. Six counties were, in fact, considering closing them. In Jackson County, commissioners could raise only $6,000 to keep their office open. The office in Madison County was saved only because citizens raised $10,000 in donations.

Tse explained to critics of the retreat that the state's financial situation itself was part of the reason why the conference was being held. "In times of stress it's especially important to keep people in high morale as best we can—our people and the people we serve, too," she said. "We had to give up the meeting last year because of the money crunch, and the effects were such that I think it was a mistake."

She regretted that some people thought of the meeting as a vacation for employees because it was held at a lake resort. "Of course we have free periods when we enjoy the recreational facilities of Lake Clearwater," Tse said, "but we also work very hard. The meeting provides important in-service training. It teaches our people to do their jobs better and to serve the public better."

Tse emphasized that the retreat was an opportunity for those employed at the university's extension center to get together in an informal setting and relaxed atmosphere with workers in the state's sixty-four counties to discuss new developments in the extension service and to exchange ideas and experiences. It was, she said, both a great morale builder and an educational opportunity for everyone involved.

Every effort was being made, Tse explained, to keep down the costs budgeted at $25,000. About $5,000 represented expected travel expenses for the field personnel in going to the retreat and about $20,000 represented the resort's off-season charges. Originally plans had been made for an attendance of 280 persons but this number had been reduced to 200.

"The various county extension directors and their staff will car-pool," Tse said. "We're strongly encouraging—mandating—cooperation in travel. We've worked out a plan whereby we won't approve employees' travel claims unless they car-pool—they've got to come together."

Questions and Instructions

1. Do you think Jean Tse presented a cogent defense of holding a retreat in the face of financial adversity?
2. What considerations should be given in selecting the persons to attend a retreat?
3. What considerations should be given in selecting the site for a retreat?
4. How important do you consider a retreat to be as a morale-builder?
5. What advantages does a retreat have over a more structured get-together such as a conference?
6. What factors in respect to purpose would you consider in choosing a name—assembly, conference, convention, convocation, workshop, and so on—for a meeting?

Selected Bibliography

Azzaretto, John F., and Smith, Howard, "Facilitating Change: An Approach That Works," *State and Local Government Review* 17 (Fall 1985): 279–83. The article discusses developing a retreat design, organizing the retreat experience, and facilitating the retreat process.

Denhardt, Robert B.; Pyle, James; and Bluedorn, Allen C., "Implementing Quality Circles in State Government," *Public Administration Review* 47 (July/August 1987): 304–09.

Kilmann, Ralph, *Beyond the Quick Fix,* San Francisco, Calif.: Jossey-Bass, Publishers, 1985.

Magnus, Margaret, "Will Someone Please Tell Me Exactly What Personnel Executives Do?"*Personnel Journal* 66 (January 1987): 40–47.

Manz, Charles C., and Sims, Henry P., Jr., "Leading Workers to Lead Themselves: The External Leadership of Self-Managing Work Teams," *Administrative Science Quarterly* 32 (March 1987): 106–29.

McConkie, Mark L., and Boss, R. Wayne, "Organizational Stories: One Means of Moving the Informal Organization During Change Efforts," *Public Administration Quarterly* 10 (Summer 1986): 189–205.

Napier, Rodney W., and Gershenfeld, Matti K., *Making Groups Work: A Guide for Group Leaders,* Boston: Houghton Mifflin Co., 1983. See Ch. 1, "The Leadership Effect: Why Some Groups Fail and Some Succeed," pp. 1–16, and Ch. 6, "Specific Interventions for Conflict Situation," pp. 175–208.

Paul, Christian F., and Gross, Albert C., "Increasing Productivity and Morale in a Municipality: Effects of Organization Development," in Bozeman, Barry and Strassman, Jeffrey, eds., *New Directions in Public Administration,* Monterey, Calif.: Brooks/Cole Publishing Co., 1984. pp. 100–11.

Sylvia, Ronald D., "An Organizational Perspective on Training and Development in the Public Sector," in Hays, Steven W., and Kearney, Richard C., eds., *Public Personnel Administration: Problems and Prospects,* Englewood Cliffs, N.J.: Prentice-Hall, Inc., 1983. pp. 137–52.

28

A Matter of Relief

For the third time in a year, Mildred Barnes, office manager of the Bryanville Department of Public Works, was faced with the task of screening applicants for the position of PBX operator-receptionist. She believed the job had a high turnover because it was tedious and offered little challenge or opportunity for advancement.

From among the applicants, Barnes hired Sue Simpson, who was young, energetic, and attractive, with a vivacious personality. Barnes congratulated herself on having filled a difficult position.

Gail Collins, Barnes's assistant, had been with the agency for fifteen years. She had initially worked as the PBX operator-receptionist for ten years before being promoted. She was respected by her fellow workers for her quiet, methodical manner. One of Collins's duties was to relieve the regular switchboard operator.

After two months on her job, Simpson began to complain to Barnes about Collins, contending that she did not relieve her as soon as she was supposed to. She hinted that Collins behaved like a martyr when she had to work the board. Barnes knew that Collins's work load was heavy and that she frequently stayed in the office through her lunch hour to complete her tasks. Nevertheless, Collins's negative attitude toward working the board was apparent.

Office practice had called for the relief operator to eat lunch at the same time as the others and then to relieve the regular operator, who took a late lunch hour. As a result, Simpson, who enjoyed office gossip and talk, had had little chance to socialize with the other workers during the lunch hour. Collins began to trade off lunch schedules with Simpson to allow her to have a regular lunch period every other day. Collins also relieved Simpson on several occasions so that she could attend office birthday, holiday, and retirement parties.

Nevertheless, Simpson still continued to complain to fellow workers about Collins, and soon others in the office began to criticize her attitude. Resentment against Collins became undisguised and one day Collins heard

Simpson say, "Even though she relieves me now, she acts put out about the work arrangement!" Mildred Barnes heard several complaints and was not quite sure what to do. Since Collins all this time had said nothing, Barnes decided to do nothing and see what happened. She noticed, though, that Collins's attitude toward her job had deteriorated even though her work remained well above average. She mentioned this to Collins. "Certainly I feel different now about taking over the board," said Collins. "Wouldn't you feel the same way if everyone had it in for you?"

Questions and Instructions

1. Is this office conflict serious enough for Barnes to take action?
2. What may have indicated to Barnes that she made a mistake when she hired Sue Simpson?
3. Why do you think that Gail Collins adopted the policy of trading off lunch schedules with Simpson? If you were Collins, would you tell Barnes what is going on?
4. What is causing the problem, Simpson's complaining and gossiping or Collins's lack of assertive behavior?
5. Since both parties, Collins and Simpson, have complaints, should a confrontation/conciliation meeting be arranged by Barnes?
6. If placed in Barnes's position, how would you go about the task of determining whether Collins is late in relieving Smith? Do you think Collins has too heavy a work load and needs to use part of her lunch period to keep up with her assignments?

Selected Bibliography

Burke, Ronald J., "Methods of Resolving Superior-Subordinate Conflict: The Constructive Use of Subordinate Differences and Disagreements," *Organizational Behavior and Human Performances* 5 (No. 4, 1970): 393–411.

Burke, Ronald J., and Wilcox, Douglas S., "Absenteeism and Turnover Among Female Telephone Operators," *Personnel Psychology* 25 (Winter 1972): 639–48.

Dunnette, Marvin D.; Arvey, Richard D.; and Banas, Paul A., "Why Do They Leave?" *Personnel* 50 (May/June 1973): 25–38.

Filley, Alan C., *Interpersonal Conflict Resolution,* Glenview, Ill.: Scott Foresman, 1975.

Kelly, Joe, "Make Conflict Work for You," *Harvard Business Review* 48 (July/August 1970): 103–13.

Klingner, Donald E., *Public Personnel Management,* Englewood Cliffs, N.J.: Prentice-Hall, 1980. Ch. 21, "Discipline and Grievances," pp. 381–402.

Likert, Rensis, "The Principle of Supportive Relationships," In Likert, Rensis, ed., *New Patterns of Management,* New York: McGraw-Hill, 1961. pp. 103–18.

Maier, Norman Raymond, *Problem Solving Discussions and Conferences: Leadership Methods and Skills,* New York: McGraw-Hill, 1963.

Maslow, Abraham H., "On Low Grumbles, High Grumbles, and Metagrumbles," in Maslow, Abraham H., ed., *The Farther Reaches of Human Nature,* New York: Viking Press, 1971. pp. 239–48.

Mathis, Robert L., and Jackson, John H., *Personnel: Contemporary Perspectives and Applications,* 3rd ed., St. Paul: West Publishing Co., 1982. See "Legal vs. Behavioral Grievance Resolution," pp. 512–14.

Morano, Richard A., "Managing Conflict for Problem Solving," *Personnel Journal* 55 (August 1976): 393–94.

Pursley, Robert D., and Snortland, Neil, *Managing Government Organizations,* North Scituate, Mass.: Duxbury Press, 1980. See "Discipline and Grievances," pp. 272–75.

U.S. Office of Personnel Management, *Employee Performance Evaluation—A Practical Guide to Development and Implementation for State, County, and Municipal Governments,* Washington, D.C.: U.S. Government Printing Office, 1979. pp. 8–22.

29

American vs. Immigrant Labor

There was nothing about the letting of a contract to provide janitorial service for a training center of the Federal Aviation Administration that indicated any problems would arise. It was all routine: the training center had been having the work done under contract to a private company for years, competitive bids were asked, and the contract was let to the low bidder.

The only new thing was that a local firm, Kleen-Sweepers, was taking over from an out-of-state firm, Magic Maintenance, which had held the contract the past three years. Kleen-Sweepers had won the contract with a first-year bid of $765,848. Acme Cleaning and Maintenance, another local firm, was second with a bid of $846,909, and Magic Maintenance was third with a bid of $876,300.

Trouble began when Darrell Sanger, manager of the procurement division at the center, learned from employees of plans by Kleen-Sweepers to replace the entire work force of Magic Maintenance by what they called "foreigners." Magic Maintenance had employed an average of sixty janitors and Kleen-Sweepers intended to reduce the number to fifty, all of them Koreans, either immigrants or persons with work permits.

Sanger did not like the idea of a 100-percent turnover of workers, especially one that replaced the present force with immigrants. The service contracting firm had the right to bring in its own workers, but in the past, as a general rule, it had interviewed and hired on a trial basis most of the old force. Sanger's chief objection, however, was that the wholesale firing of some workers and replacing them with persons of another race might stir up a storm. Five years earlier the local airport had fired a similar work force and employed Koreans, and a controversy raged for weeks. Pickets invaded the airport bearing signs and shouting slogans at the traveling public, television stations played up these activities on the news shows, unions issued denunciatory resolutions, and newspaper editorial writers condemned the loss of jobs by hard-working Americans.

In an attempt to avert a similar situation, Sanger met with Troy Ridgeway, president of Kleen-Sweepers, to persuade him to abandon the idea of mass layoffs. But Ridgeway insisted that he could not change his plans. He believed the Koreans comprised a more efficient force than one made up of Americans, in that he had found them to be more industrious, reliable, and likely to do work of high quality. Ridgeway's low bid, $81,061 under that of the closest competitor, was made possible only because his profit depended on using a small force of the most productive labor available. He already had his workers lined up, he said, and it would be unfair to tell them they would not be hired.

Discrimination and affirmative action did not enter into Ridgeway's program. The common belief that immigrants would work for lower wages than Americans also was not at issue. The wages Ridgeway would pay were the same he would have to pay any work force. Under government regulations, an agency advertising for a service contract must request from the Department of Labor a determination of a minimum wage for each of the work categories—(e.g., clerk, janitor, and so forth). The determination was usually the prevailing wage in the area and usually comparable to union scales. Persons not of United States nationality must be either naturalized citizens or hold work permits.

Sanger's fear that the employment of Asians and the firing of Magic Maintenance employees would stir up a row did not materialize. It was only a short item in television newscasts and rated only one story carried on an inside page of the local newspaper. The only outcry was raised by a radio talk-show host, who for several nights complained against policies that allowed immigrants to "swarm over the country" and "take the jobs of loyal Americans." His urging his listeners and callers to write their representatives in Congress resulted in dozens of letters to the state's delegation in Washington, who did no more than ask the training center to provide them with information about the situation and an explanation of the hiring policy.

Although there had been perhaps no great change in American attitudes since the airport incident five years before, Sanger mused, the American people were very likely becoming more cosmopolitan. Japanese management had put to shame American management, foreign investors and manufacturers, Asian and European, were pouring billions into the economy while Americans contributed to the drain of the money supply by closing plants in the United States and having work done abroad to take advantage of cheap labor. Further, Asian youngsters, especially the Vietnamese, were winning many high school and college honor awards and figuring prominently on the Merit Scholar lists. In view of these achievements, Sanger asked himself whether the firing of Magic Maintenance janitors was perhaps an instance of reverse discrimination? Perhaps, he thought, future affirmative action programs would arise for the majority to balance those for minorities.

Questions and Instructions

1. What do you think of the following stereotypes associated with the employment of foreign labor, immigrants, and displaced persons:
   That they take jobs that should go to American citizens?
   That they work for lower wages than Americans and, therefore, tend to keep down wage levels?
   That they are needed to perform the difficult or menial labor Americans avoid?
   That they are exploited because of language difficulties, lack of education or skilled training, racial prejudice, and unfamiliarity with American ways?
2. Should the affirmative-action policies established for such minorities as blacks, women, and Hispanics also apply to recent immigrants?
3. In the case of the training center, do you think the procurement manager should have protested more strongly against the replacement of the entire janitorial force by Koreans?
4. Do you agree with the opinion of the president of Kleen-Sweepers that in what many consider menial work a Korean force would be more industrious, reliable, and likely to do work of high quality than an American one?

Selected Bibliography

Berry, David P., and Appleman, Jeff T., "Policing the Hiring of Foreign Workers: Employers Get the Job," *Personnel* 64 (March 1987): 48–51.

Borcherding, Thomas E.; Pommerehne, Werner W.; and Schneider, Friedrich, "Comparing the Efficiency of Private and Public Production: The Evidence from Five Countries," *Journal of Economics* (Supplement 2, 1982): 127–56.

Collett, Merrill J., "The Federal Contracting Process," in Bozeman, Barry, and Straussman, Jeffrey, eds., *New Directions in Public Administration,* Monterey, Calif.: Brooks/Cole Publishing Co., 1984. pp. 233–40.

Ferris, James, and Graddy, Elizabeth, "Contracting Out: For What? With Whom?" *Public Administration Review* 46 (July/August 1986): 332–44.

Fisk, Donald; Kiesling, Herbert; and Muller, Thomas, *Private Provision of Public Service: An Overview,* Washington, D.C.: The Urban Institute, 1978.

Gutierrez, G. G., "The Undocumented Immigrant: The Limits of Cost Benefit Analysis," *Public Management* 62 (October 1980): 8–11.

Hayes, Edward C., "Contracting for Services: The Basic Steps," *The Privatization Review* 2 (Winter 1986): 20–27.
Hinton, Robert, "Getting Along with the Media," *Public Management* 64 (January 1982): 16–17.
Hughes, Mark, "Contracting Services in Phoenix," *Public Management* 64 (October 1982): 2–4.
Johnson, Alan, "Working with the Media: A Reporter's View," *Public Management* 69 (May 1987): 29–30.
Kolderie, Ted, "The Two Different Concepts of Privatization," *Public Administration Review* 46 (July/August 1986): 285–91.
Lourie, Norman V., and Swartz, Dale Frederick, "Managers and Migration: Pluralism, Politics, and International Affairs," *Public Management* 67 (March 1985): 3–5.
Mehay, Stephen L., and Govzalez, Rodolfo A., "Economic Incentives under Contract Supply of Local Government Services," *Public Choice* 46 (January 1985): 79–86.
Pascoe, Monte, "Libertarian Longing, Privatization and Federalism," *State Government* 55 (No. 4, 1982): 111–14.
Timmins, William M., "Impacts of Privatization upon Career Public Employees," *Public Administration Quarterly* 10 (Spring 1986): 50–59.
Valleau, Thomas F., "Good Ink," *Public Management* 64 (January 1982): 16–17.
Wingerter, Eugene J., "Refuse Collection: The Private Alternative," *The Privatization Review* 2 (Winter 1986): 28–37.
Wynne, George G., "Privatization Initiatives Around the World," *Public Management* 68 (December 1986): 19–22.

30

Supervising Job Trainees

Under a new job-training program established by the state, Layton County had received $100,000 to hire disadvantaged young people in county offices and agencies. Eligible youths were assigned to positions by the county commissioners upon the request of officials and agency heads.

Under this plan, trainees received the minimum wage for one year and then were considered qualified to hold jobs in government or private industry or business. To increase the number of people taken into the program, a time-sharing arrangement was permitted; that is, individual trainees could work half-days five days a week. Two trainees, one working in the morning and one in the afternoon, would be the equivalent of a full-time employee.

Evelyn Madison, court clerk, was assigned two trainees, Juanita Gomez and Tom Rutledge, certified to her as competent typists. Both were attending Layton County Vo-Tech School and had completed courses in typing. If they proved satisfactory, they would be of inestimable help in the court clerk's office, which was understaffed and falling behind in record keeping.

Madison was known as a demon for efficiency. She met with the trainees when they reported for work and carefully explained office procedures and regulations. The new workers were to become members of the typing pool and were expected to do the same work as regular employees: type case background summaries for reference during judicial proceedings and civil- and criminal-case action summaries, transcribe recorded dictation, and do other legal typing. Madison emphasized the need for absolute accuracy because often the documents and papers they typed would constitute permanent court records. One of the full-time secretaries of the office would supervise them during their first two weeks on the job.

After the trainees had been working three weeks, it became apparent that their performance was unsatisfactory. Unfamiliar with such legal terms as *habeas corpus, nolo contendere, affidavit,* and *writ of mandamus,* the trainees did not comprehend the matter they were copying and submitted "finished" material full of typing and transcription errors. Both trainees took up the time of other staff members asking questions and sometimes joked about the material they were copying because it seemed so outlandish. Much of Madison's time, as well as that of other staff members, was spent in checking and correcting the trainees' typing, and thus they hampered rather than helped production.

Her patience wearing thin after several weeks, Madison called the young workers separately into her office and lectured them about their performance. Their typing was careless and their work was full of errors that they themselves should have been able to spot. Moreover, their behavior was not proper for a well-run office and they disrupted the routine of other employees. Unless they improved at once they might be released from the program.

Both trainees were apologetic and expressed anxiety over the possibility of being dismissed, but each tended to blame the other for the errors and slow production rate. As a partial solution to the problem, Madison assigned separate "in" and "out" boxes to each, and they seemed pleased with this new arrangement.

In the next few weeks Rutledge increased the volume of his work but continued to make many typographical and transcription errors. Gomez's typing improved in accuracy and she took greater pains, but her output fell off and so her contribution to office productivity was minuscule.

Deciding that the trainees were taking up too much of her own and her staff's time, Madison informed them that they would be relieved of their current duties and be assigned to answering telephones and running errands. Rutledge protested, asserting that he had entered the program to develop marketable skills. In his opinion, the program was not keeping its promise and the new duties did not represent worthwhile training.

Questions and Instructions

1. Do you think Madison was justified, in the interest of office productivity, in reassigning the trainees to work involving no special ability?
2. What leadership principles might Madison have followed in dealing with the trainees to improve their work? How could she have motivated them to improve?
3. Who was at fault in assigning the two trainees to positions they were not qualified to fill? How could such misassignments be avoided?
4. What responsibilities do office managers and supervisors have toward people in training programs? Should Madison, for example, have introduced an instructional program to improve the office skills of the trainees assigned to her?

Selected Bibliography

Argyris, Chris, "Leadership, Learning and Changing the Status Quo," *Organizational Dynamics* 4 (Winter 1976): 29–43.

Committee for Economic Development, *Improving Management of the Public Work Force,* New York: Committee for Economic Development, 1978. Ch. 5, "The Role of the Manager," pp. 91–102.

Giglioni, Giovanni B.; Giglioni, Joyce B.; and Bryant, James A., "Performance Appraisal: Here Comes the Judge," *California Management Review* 24 (Winter 1981): 14–23.

Janka, Katherine; Luke, Robert; and Morrison, Charles, *People, Performance . . . Results!* Washington, D.C.: National Training and Development Service Press, 1977. Ch. 2, "Program Options and Elements," pp. 23–38.

Katzell, Raymond A.; Beinstock, Penney; and Faerstein, Paul H., *A Guide to Worker Productivity Experiments in the United States 1971–75,* Scarsdale, N.Y.: Work in America Institute, 1977. See Program 3, "Training and Instruction," pp. 13–15, for a listing of studies related to training and turnover, job success, absenteeism, attitudes, and a number of other variables.

Lee, Robert D., Jr., *Public Personnel Systems,* Baltimore: University Park Press, 1979. See "Training and Education," pp. 176–87.

Levinson, Harry, "Appraisal of What Performance?" *Harvard Business Review* 54 (July/August 1976): 125–34.

———, "Asinine Attitudes Toward Motivation," *Harvard Business Review* 51 (January/February 1973): 70–76.

Robison, David, *Alternative Work Patterns: Changing Approaches to Work Scheduling,* Scarsdale, N.Y.: Work in America Institute, 1976. pp. 17–19.

Schneier, Craig Eric, "Training and Development Programs: What Learning Theory and Research Have to Offer," in Schneier, Craig Eric, and Beatty, Richard W., eds., *Personnel Administration Today: Readings and Commentary,* Reading, Mass.: Addison-Wesley, 1978. pp. 326–47.

Schockley, Pamela S., and Staley, Constance M., "Women in Management Training Programs: What They Think About Key Issues," *Public Personnel Management* 9 (No. 3, 1980): 214–24.

31

Documentary Evidence

It was an exciting moment for Royfield Puckett as he drove his Volkswagen into the Deep Valley Children's Center parking lot with its sign: Doctors and Administrative Staff Only. Before him stood the 65-bed hospital of which today he would become the chief administrator—a modernistic structure of glass, concrete, and steel.

Only thirty-five years old, Puckett had a feeling of accomplishment as he viewed the hospital and its landscaped grounds. Only a few years before, after receiving his master's degree from Howard University, he had joined the staff of a 250-bed hospital and worked his way up to assistant director. Now he had assumed the responsibility of operating an institution serving about eight hundred disabled children across the state, providing physical, occupational, and speech therapy; social services; and dental, recreational, and dietary programs.

Yet he also felt apprehensive. Was he really qualified by experience for the top administrative post in such a center? It looked open and welcoming as he approached the entrance, but more from instinct than from knowledge he suspected it was not all it seemed to be—a happy place providing humanitarian services to young people.

His predecessor, Lester Morton, had resigned unexpectedly upon his father's death to manage a family business, Puckett had been told when interviewed by the hospital board. Puckett felt, however, that he had heard only part of the story. The guarded manner in which staff members talked with him when he was taken on a tour led him to feel that below the surface problems lurked. Or was their attitude, he asked himself, because he was black? Well, he was in charge now, he thought as he entered the building, and he would soon find out.

In his first few days Puckett devoted his efforts to familiarizing himself with hospital policies and procedures, its printed rules and regulations, and the minutiae of day-to-day operations, and to getting acquainted with staff members. All those he conferred with were friendly but hesitant in talking about the two-year administration of Lester Morton. Puckett decided that he might find out more if he read the minutes of staff meetings and of the hospital board of directors.

The minutes of the Morton staff meetings were contained in a single manila folder, and it did not take Puckett long to review them since only eight had been held, each one featuring a guest speaker or theme. Morton appeared to dominate the sessions, his remarks being reported in full. He concluded the meetings with exhortatory pep talks devoted to platitudes about the need for teamwork and good public relations. The staff was seldom consulted about policy matters and problems and there appeared to be little general discussion.

In contrast to Morton's staff meetings, those of his predecessor, Alfred Kahn, had been held weekly. Kahn would summarize any hospital news, training programs, or developments and then ask department heads to discuss their projects or problems. Puckett disliked clichés, but he decided that under Kahn the administrative staff was a team, whereas under Morton it was always being urged to become one.

Puckett also researched the rate of turnover during the Morton and Kahn administrations. He asked the personnel department to draw up a list of all positions vacated during the last three months of the Morton administration, the reasons employees gave their supervisor for leaving the center, and the reasons they gave in an anonymous questionnaire.

Meanwhile Puckett sought more information from department heads about their operations and problems. Among the first he interviewed was Martha Ritter, director of public relations. He found her friendly but somewhat cynical. After they had chatted a few minutes, Puckett asked, "Well, Martha, I'd like to know what you think we can do to improve the hospital."

Ritter looked surprised and then, stifling a giggle, replied: "Excuse me, it's just that, well, I wouldn't know where to begin."

"Don't worry," Puckett said. "Please feel free to tell me what is on your mind."

"Well, my latest nightmare is the donor list—you know, the list of four thousand people who have made contributions to the hospital," Ritter said. "It's gone."

"Gone?"

"Gone. I called up the computer center and the woman who used to run the list for me said she doesn't even work with the computer any more since they put in a new machine. 'New computer?' I said. 'No one told me about changing computers.' Needless to say the list is gone. Oh, if I'd only known we were going to change systems. But who was going to tell me? No one ever saw Mr. Morton. We rarely had staff meetings."

Ritter looked out the window and adjusted her glasses. "No, Mr. Puckett,. things started going downhill the first week Mr. Morton was here and especially after he put in the time clocks. It doesn't seem to matter any more how much you actually work so long as you're not two and a half minutes late in checking in."

Chats with other department heads confirmed what Ritter had told Puckett—Morton's administration had been a disaster. The best description of the situation came from Hester Wilson, head of nursing services: "We were a team, or better still, more like a family before Mr. Morton became the administrator. I suppose things were going too smoothly. Have you ever been in a boat, Mr. Puckett, on a calm sea? Well, you'd swear the boat is just standing still. The fact is the current below the surface is moving you right along. It must have looked to the Board of Directors like we were moving too smoothly to be making progress. They wanted a new administrator with—what's the word—pizazz, somebody who could get the center known in the state. Well, he was a good advertisement—for himself. Our duty is to handicapped children, and our services to them suffered."

Returning to his office after talking with Wilson, Puckett found a report on his desk prepared by the Department of Personnel on the employees who had left the center in the last three months. (See Exhibits 1 and 2 at the end of this case.) He studied the reasons given supervisors for leaving and the reasons given in the anonymous questionnaire. Here was documentary evidence of a situation not fully revealed in his interviews. He faced a difficult administrative problem, and it was not race-related.

Questions and Instructions

1. If you were Puckett, what are the first changes you would make as the new hospital administrator?
2. What are some of the underlying reasons for the job dissatisfaction at the hospital?
3. What generalizations can be drawn from Exhibits 1 and 2 (see pages 145–148) that might be beneficial in reducing the level of employee turnover? (The employees designated by numbers in Exhibits 1 and 2 are the same persons.) How would you classify the fourteen reasons given in Exhibit 1? In Exhibit 2? Develop a classification scheme and be prepared to discuss its strengths and weaknesses in class.
4. Item 7 on the "Employee Notice of Separation" form in Exhibit 3 (see page 149) lists items that employees might consider among the three most important "factors that contributed to your decision to leave Deep Valley Children's Center." Use this list to develop a workable classification scheme that would be useful in analyzing the reasons for employee turnover. Are there any factors that are missing? What are they and why are they important?

5. What are some of the advantages and disadvantages associated with employee separations?

Selected Bibliography

Augustine, Joseph C., "Personnel Turnover," in Famularo, Joseph J., ed., *Handbook of Modern Personnel Administration,* New York: McGraw-Hill, 1972. Ch. 62, pp. 1–12.

Dalton, Dan R.; Krackhardt, David M.; and Porter, Lyman W., "Functional Turnover: An Empirical Assessment," *Journal of Applied Psychology* 66 (December 1981): 716–21.

Dixon, Andrew L., "The Long Goodbye," *Supervisory Management* 27 (January 1982): 26–29.

Dunham, Randall B., and Smith, Frank J., *Organizational Surveys: An Internal Assessment of Organizational Health,* Glenview, Ill.: Scott, Foresman, 1979. Ch. 3, "Organizational Surveys: The Purposes," pp. 36–60.

Gellerman, Saul W., *The Management of Human Resources,* Hinsdale, Ill.: Dryden Press, 1976. pp. 121–46.

March, James G., and Simon, Herbert A., *Organizations,* New York: John Wiley and Sons, 1966. Ch. 4, "Motivational Constraints: The Decision to Participate," pp. 83–111.

Martin, Thomas N., and Hunt, J. G., "Social Influence and Intent to Leave: A Path-Analytic Process Model," *Personnel Psychology* 33 (Autumn 1980): 505–28.

Meyer, C. Kenneth, and Beville, Mitchel J., Jr., "Turnover in State Government: A Regional Assessment," *Midwest Review of Public Administration* 14 (March 1980): 51–63.

Meyer, C. Kenneth; Beville, Mitchel J., Jr.; Magedanz, Thomas C.; and Hackert, Ann M., "South Dakota State Government Employee Turnover and Work Related Attitudes: An Analysis and Recommendation," *Midwest Review of Public Administration* 13 (June 1979): 88–118.

Peters, Lawrence H.; Bhagat, Rabi S.; and O'Connor, Edward J., "An Examination of the Independent and Joint Contributions of Organizational Commitment and Job Satisfaction on Employee Intentions to Quit," *Group and Organization Studies* 6 (March 1981): 73–81.

Price, James L., *The Study of Turnover,* Ames, Iowa: The Iowa State University Press, 1977.

Stone, Eugene, *Research Methods in Organizational Behavior,* Santa Monica, Calif.: Goodyear Publishing Co., 1978. Ch. 2, "The Research Process," pp. 15–34, and Ch. 4, "Measurement Methods," pp. 61–76.

Whitsett, David A., "Where Are Your Unenriched Jobs?" *Harvard Business Review* 53 (January/February 1975): 74–80.

Exhibit 1. Item 1 of the Supervisors' Report on Employee Separation

Item 1. Information concerning the separation of this employee is necessary for the purpose of processing unemployment insurance claims. Please obtain information from the employee concerning his or her reasons for termination. Involuntary terminations must contain information supporting the reasons for termination. Voluntary terminations must include information as to why the individual has terminated and what the individual is going to do after termination. If he or she is separating to accept other employment, information is necessary indicating the type of new employment.

REASONS FOR TERMINATION

Employee 1

"Lack of job satisfaction. Frustration due to discrepancies in administrative practices. Some personal problems, but for the most part Mary was the first counseling therapist to tackle some of the demanding tasks associated with intake diagnostics. Nothing could have been done to prevent her from leaving."

Employee 2

"Henry was asked to resign for failure to obey a direct order given to him by a supervisor. He left the area telling the ward staff to call the supervisor's office telling them that he refused to work in the area. He left without reporting in with the supervisor's office."

Employee 3

"Mr. Jones left to accept a position in the private sector with greater promotion possibilities and a higher starting salary."

Employee 4

"Leaving due to better employment opportunities in the city and an opportunity to work on a special-education certification."

Employee 5

"This counselor was terminated for unnecessary roughness with the patients, agitating children by teasing them, and unacceptable work performance while on duty."

Employee 6

"Mary came into my office tearful, stating that she felt that she was not able emotionally to continue her work in caring for clients in the area to which she was assigned. She said the center was becoming a depressing place to work and she needed a little time to think about where she was going with her career."

Employee 7

"Herriott drives 56 miles to work a day and is finding that with the cost of gas it is terribly expensive. In fact, it is so expensive that she has to resign. She also is planning on the foster care facility which she has been working on for the past few months in her home, and will be providing some meals, housing, etc., for elderly persons."

Employee 8

"It was my understanding that she requested to transfer to the 8:00 A.M. to 4:30 P.M. shift. I was also informed it might be beneficial for her to work in a more closely supervised situation due to questionable job practices. Also, she needs to improve her communication skills. She also needs to set priorities that are in greater accordance to the needs of the center. She generally complied to what was requested of her, but frequently voiced discontent with numerous center policies, procedures, management, personnel, etc. She did not convey a genuinely sincere, enthusiastic, and motivated attitude. In turn, she tends to function in a rather regimented, authoritarian manner and will continue to need to strengthen her communication skills. With added experience she has the potential of becoming a more effective counselor."

Employee 9

"Voluntary termination. She stated that she only wanted to work during the week so that she would have more time to spend on extracurricular affairs."

Employee 10

"The employee is leaving because he said he cannot do this type of work."

Employee 11

"Found a better-paying job at the VA Hospital. Nothing could be done to keep her from leaving Deep Valley Center."

Employee 12

"Terminated because she found other employment. Also, she would have been terminated because she had taken leave without proper notification and because the grant she was working on is being discontinued."

Employee 13

"Conflict with supervisor over work schedule. Employee seems to be unable to compromise when the need arises. Employee can be easily replaced since he performs janitorial services."

Employee 14

"Terry Nichols seems to have serious personal family problems and it is affecting her attendance and quality of work. She is a single parent with two very young children and feels a strong responsibility to her family. Unplanned absences and chronic tardiness, however, cause serious work disruptions and have adversely impacted on the services which Deep Valley renders. Her position will be a difficult one to fill."

Exhibit 2. Item 8 of Employee Notification of Separation Form

Question 8. Please provide a brief statement of your reason(s) for termination from Deep Valley Children's Center. Your response will remain anonymous.

Employee 1
"I have been assigned to night duty for the greatest share of my employment at the Center. I have to work alone constantly and need to have regular daytime hours where I can have at least *some* contact with people."

Employee 2
"The suggestions that I made and those which other people made to improve patient care either took too long to be implemented or were never made. The day the center starts paying people and promoting them according to their abilities, then it will be able to retain employees rather than losing them."

Employee 3
"I don't feel that I'm accomplishing anything due to some conflicts of procedures and attitudes among personnel."

Employee 4
"I'm being offered my previous job and I have decided to take it. This way I'll also be able to further my education. I have no complaints toward this facility. It has progressed very much since I was here as a student four years ago. I enjoyed working with the people and the majority of them are definitely interested in their clients."

Employee 5
"Too much bureaucracy. Too many fingers in the pot. Lack of interest for advancement of fellow workers so that they can become better qualified for their positions and provide better care and counseling to the children."

Employee 6
"Poor personnel management procedures and poor training coordination. Overall, poor working conditions and low morale!"

Employee 7
"When I would tell Mr. Morton, the administrator, about the girls and boys sneaking into the lounge at night or being late for activities, he would tell me, 'What can I do about it?'"

Employee 8
"I think the separation questionnaire missed the point. I think the various units of Deep Valley Center need constant assessment of goals and objectives with restatement in clear, concise manner, and leadership responsive to ideas and suggestions of employees. Opportunities for professionals to exercise judgment in completing their job assessment are becoming fewer, thereby resulting in less motivation."

Employee 9
"I want to spend more time in a newly built home, spend more time on outdoor

activities and craft work, hobbies, etc. I do think that the salary for this particular position, and similar positions in the center, is too low for the amount of work involved. After working 10 years at this position the salary was very poor in comparison to the counselor positions with the Feds. One woman left here to work with the Feds for more than I was making after 10 years. That is embarrassing and disgusting."

Employee 10

"I feel that I couldn't handle this kind of work and of taking care of these kind of people. I guess I overestimated my own capabilities when taking the position."

Employee 11

"Direct care nurses have the most responsibility toward patients, yet they receive the lowest pay. Too many bureaucrats who are sitting on their cans, they won't understand this statement. 'Taxation without representation' law should go into effect immediately!"

Employee 12

"I was told that the grant program under which I was working was terminated and that there was no place for me in the center. In effect, I was asked to resign under threat of adverse action. Someone had better recognize the fact the center is about to go quickly down the tube!!!"

Employee 13

"The job itself was misrepresented to me by Mr. Morton. It stated that the job was 8 to 5 Monday through Friday. It did not state that nightwork or weekend duties would be required."

Employee 14

"Unfair treatment toward me for the thing that I did. A follow-up letter will be sent to the Board of Directors, State's Attorney, and the Governor."

Exhibit 3. Item 7 of the Employee Notice of Separation Form

Item 7. Reasons for Termination: Please read through the entire list before you make any mark. Then rate the factors that contributed to your decision to leave Deep Valley Children's Center by ranking the three most important factors in your decision by placing the number (1, 2, and 3) IN FRONT of the reason. Number 1 is the most important reason and number 3 is third most important reason.

1. ______ My salary was too low
2. ______ My health is poor
3. ______ I got married
4. ______ Unfriendly community
5. ______ I felt the job was too difficult
6. ______ I was asked to resign
7. ______ I am having a baby
8. ______ I got tired of working
9. ______ I was laid off
10. ______ My salary was frozen
11. ______ Training I desired was not available
12. ______ I am returning to school
13. ______ I was discriminated against
14. ______ I am retiring
15. ______ Poor working conditions
16. ______ I felt the job was too dangerous
17. ______ Poor health facilities in the area
18. ______ I didn't like the working hours
19. ______ Poor parking at work
20. ______ Poor parking in town
21. ______ My spouse found a better job
22. ______ Poor recreational facilities
23. ______ I didn't get along with my supervisor
24. ______ Job required too much travel
25. ______ Wanted to reassign me and I didn't agree
26. ______ I am starting my own business
27. ______ The job was too physically demanding
28. ______ I didn't agree with my job classification
29. ______ I can receive more money elsewhere
30. ______ I didn't like the working hours
31. ______ I failed to receive an annual raise
32. ______ Poor shopping facilities in the area
33. ______ The center was not using my abilities to best advantage
34. ______ I didn't agree with my supervisor's way of doing things
35. ______ I didn't get along with my fellow employees
36. ______ I didn't like the job
37. ______ Poor entertainment in the area
38. ______ Had to care for family member(s)
39. ______ Poor educational facilities in the area
40. ______ Poor cultural facilities in the area
41. ______ No promotional opportunities
42. ______ My career development was progressing too slowly
43. ______ Other reasons: (please specify)______________________________

32

Problems with Volunteer Workers

Because of reductions in federal aid, the State Department of Public Welfare was forced to cut drastically the budget for the agency administering educational programs for handicapped children. This created a crisis for Reginald MacArthur, director of one of the agency's facilities located in a small university town.

MacArthur considered a high staff-client ratio necessary for the proper implementation of his facility's programs. Although no staff positions actually were eliminated, no additional people could be hired and no vacancies created by resignation or retirement could be filled. The crisis was heightened when sixteen handicapped children were transferred to the facility's case load from another state agency. MacArthur applied to the director of the Department of Public Welfare for emergency assistance but did not expect any help for several months if at all.

Because of the facility's location in a university town and the nature of its services, it received many well-meaning offers of volunteer help. These offers often came from students with considerable training in special and adaptive education. In the past MacArthur tended to make only limited use of these volunteers, assigning them to duties as aides and custodians with few chances for carrying out actual instruction and training. Recently, volunteers had received special development training from the department as ombudsmen on behalf of the clients.

In view of the existing financial crisis, MacArthur decided that he would have to place greater reliance on volunteers if he was to provide adequately for the additional children. He reviewed a large number of volunteer applications and selected two persons whose backgrounds seemed the most appropriate.

One was Sharon Bowers, a graduate student in special education who expected to receive her degree within the next six months and said she hoped to work with handicapped children. She was bright and enthusiastic and established immediate rapport with both the children and the professional staff members on her introductory meeting with them. She appeared to be reliable and responsible and was recommended in glowing terms by former employers. Under the circumstances, MacArthur would be inclined to offer Bowers a full-time paid position, but at the moment she was available for only about two hours every afternoon.

The other person chosen was Alice Pearson, a socially prominent local woman with a degree in elementary education. Although she had not taught for several years and her experience had been entirely with normal children, she had excellent local recommendations and several useful political connections. She was able to devote between fifteen and twenty hours a week to the program. After being introduced to the group with which she would be working, however, she seemed overwhelmed by the magnitude of the children's handicaps.

While fitting Bowers and Pearson into the program, MacArthur received a request from Professor Paul Corkin, a faculty member of the university's Department of Education, to include the children in a study that would attempt to measure their educational development and achievement over a twelve-month period. Since the study was designed to evaluate the teaching methods used by agency professionals, MacArthur felt that participation was almost a necessity. Negative results might reveal areas where program content should be improved while positive results would be a useful budgetary negotiating tool. Either way the agency would probably benefit. The study required that some of the children and their assigned staff workers spend several afternoons each week in a controlled experimental environment and that they would be periodically tested.

MacArthur juggled his staff schedules to take best advantage of the volunteer help within the time limits imposed. This required having Bowers and Pearson work together with a group of five children during the period of the experiment. Pearson was also available to supervise during the lunch hour when the agency was particularly short-handed. Since the experiment was scheduled to start immediately, MacArthur was able to provide only a brief orientation session before the volunteers began their duties.

Several weeks passed before Professor Corkin had his first conference with MacArthur. He reported that during the experiment he had noted a great deal of antagonism between the two volunteers, Bowers and Pearson. They were barely civil to each other and competed for the children's attention. The children seemed to sense the conflict, and as a result were nervous, easily upset, and generally uncooperative. The atmosphere was adversely influencing the outcome of the experiment. The professor revealed that Bowers had announced to him her intention of quitting. He was ready to abandon the study unless some change was made.

Further investigation by MacArthur revealed that Bowers was doing an outstanding job. She had developed warm relationships with all the children with whom she worked. Pearson had largely overcome the initial feelings aroused by the contact with the severely handicapped, and was almost always able to be on hand when the agency was in critical need of additional help. She had also proved to be a valuable link with the local community and was engaged in fund-raising activities that would benefit the agency. Although she did not relate to the children as well as Bowers, she could be depended on to keep order.

MacArthur knew that his paid professional staff members were spread as thinly as possible. Altering schedules now would be nearly impossible. He also realized that community volunteers provided valuable services and financial support to the agency that he would hate to lose. He could not afford to offend members of this group yet knew he must do something to resolve this problem.

Questions and Instructions

1. In such a sensitive program dealing with handicapped children, do you think MacArthur is justified in attempting to make greater use of volunteer workers who, despite their best intentions, might harm their young charges?
2. In view of the described situation, what do you think MacArthur can do to save the experimental program?
3. If it came to making a choice between Bowers and Pearson, which do you think MacArthur should keep in the program? Why?
4. What should be MacArthur's overriding concern in resolving the problem?
5. Discuss various choices open to MacArthur as they affect the facility's long-term and short-term well-being.
6. What functions would an ombudsman for handicapped children perform?
7. Should different supervisory approaches be used for volunteer employees in contrast with paid employees? Explain.
8. How can MacArthur make better use of Pearson's and Bowers's skills and talents?

Selected Bibliography

Biddle, William W., *Encouraging Community Development: A Training Guide for Local Workers,* New York: Holt, Rinehart and Winston, 1968.

Carter, Barbara, and Dapper, Gloria, *Organizing School Volunteer Programs,* New York: Citation Press, 1974. See "Training," pp. 85–103, and "Coordination: The Key to an Effective Program," pp. 67–84.

Ferris, James M., "Coprovision: Citizen Time and Money Donation in Public Service Provision," *Public Administration Review,* 44 (July/August 1984): 324–33.

Ilsley, Paul J., and Niemi, John A., *Recruiting and Training Volunteers,* New York: McGraw-Hill, 1981. Ch. 1, "What Is Voluntarism?" pp. 1–9; Ch. 3, "Roles and Responsibilities of a Coordinator of Volunteers," pp. 17–29; Ch. 5, "Recruitment of Volunteers," pp. 44–67; Ch. 6, "Selection, Orientation, Placement, and Training of Volunteers," pp. 58–76; and Ch. 8, "Evaluation of Volunteer-Based Programs," pp. 97–116.

Janowitz, Gayle, *Helping Hands: Volunteer Work in Education,* Chicago: University of Chicago Press, 1965. Ch. 1, "Growth of Volunteer Work," pp. 1–7; Ch. 3, "Children in Need of Help," pp. 24–37; and Ch. 6, "Volunteers," pp. 76–88.

Kramer, Ralph, *Voluntary Agencies in the Welfare State,* Berkeley, Calif.: University of California Press, 1981.

Mainzer, Lewis C., *Political Bureaucracy,* Glenview, Ill.: Scott, Foresman, 1973. See "The Ombudsman," pp. 56–61.

Pollak, Otto, *Human Behavior and the Helping Professions,* New York: Spectrum Publications, 1976. Ch. 4, "The Needs of the Helper and the Client or Patient," pp. 23–31.

Scheirer, Ivan, *People Approach,* Boulder, Colo.: National Information Center on Volunteerism, 1977.

Schindler-Rainman, Eva, and Lippitt, Ronald, *The Volunteer Community: Creative Use of Human Resources,* 2nd ed., Fairfax, Va.: NTL Learning Resources, 1975.

Stanton, Esther, *Clients Come Last: Volunteers and Welfare Organizations,* Beverly Hills, Calif.: Sage Publications, 1970.

33

A Town in Trauma

Until disaster struck, the town of Canfield had enjoyed moderate prosperity and steady growth that made it the envy of other towns in the largely rural northeastern part of the state. This was because fifteen years earlier Canfield was selected as the site for a Superior Tire Company plant, creating about two thousand new jobs in the community.

Other towns of Canfield's size—about 15,000 population—and smaller towns across the state had not been so prosperous. They struggled to maintain adequate municipal services on inadequate revenue and were not able to offer many opportunities for development. These less-fortunate towns were faced with such problems as dwindling populations, declining school enrollments, abandoned buildings, and eroding business and industry.

Canfield, on the other hand, made steady but small gains. It supported just under two hundred retail business establishments that created about 1,600 jobs and had combined annual sales of more than $140 million. Its thirty wholesale business firms employed about 275 persons.

In addition to the Superior Tire Company, Canfield had about twenty other manufacturers of such products as boats, canoes, steel springs, fireplaces, concrete manholes, metal containers, coach homes, and so on. Altogether these plants employed almost a thousand persons.

Canfield was also the site of Bradford College, a junior college that was part of the state's higher-education system, with a staff of about 275 persons. A church-sponsored Northeast Health Center employed a staff of almost 350 persons, and the Municipal Hospital had a staff of ninety. The elementary, junior, and senior high schools employed 115 teachers with a student-teacher ratio of 19 to 1, 17 to 1, and 16 to 1, respectively. There was also an excellent vocational-technical school serving a tri-county area with a teaching staff of 45.

Canfield had a bonded indebtedness of only $350,000 and had no immediate need for going further into debt for capital improvements. Its water supply included seven wells, and a water plant constructed ten years ago had a capacity of 3,775,000 gallons per day. The plant could handle a maximum daily consumption as high as 3,250,000 gallons, far above the current need. The city's water storage capacity in ground and elevated tanks was 5,400,000 gallons. Also built about ten years ago was a sewage treatment plant with the capacity to handle the waste of a city of 20,000 population.

The city's transportation facilities were adequate for freight and travel. Canfield was served by two major state highways and one United States highway, and a north-south Interstate interchange was one mile from town. There was one railway with two trains a day. The transit time for rail shipments to distant trade centers was four days for Detroit, Los Angeles, New York, and Seattle. This was reduced to three days for trucks.

The disaster that struck Canfield did not come without some forewarning. At first there were rumors the Canfield plant of Superior Tire was on a list of several being considered for closure. There was not much the community could do to take preventive action, for word came shortly from headquarters that layoffs would start at once and the plant would be shut down one month later. Canfield lost the $40 million annual payroll that was the major contributor to its economy, and two thousand people began looking for work.

With many cities in the state seeking to lure industry, it did not seem likely anyone could be found immediately, or ever, to take over the Superior Tire plant. There were no other jobs available to those who had worked at the plant. Further, the closing of the plant created a decline in business in the area, and unemployment continued to increase as other firms were forced to lay off workers.

Mayor Angela Guidoboni took the first step in determining what action could be taken to counter the devastating effects of the plant's closing. She called a meeting of the City Council to confer with the city manager, Superior Tire plant officials, the head of the local of the United Rubber Workers, the president and secretary of the Chamber of Commerce, and business, financial, and civic leaders. "We've got to do something," she told the group. "We can't just sit on our hands. Maybe we can't hope to restore things to what they were, but we just can't allow affairs to go their own way."

It was decided at the meeting to establish a committee representative of the principal elements of the community to canvass all possible courses of action and decide on priorities. The committee would determine if state and federal government aid could be obtained, what official actions would be required of Canfield, what assets Canfield had for attracting new business and industry, and what facilities Canfield had—social, educational, and economic—to assist in the reconstruction program. City Manager Leonard Rascoe was directed to nominate persons for a Canfield Restoration Committee, and to outline and help implement a program that would not only tackle the city's immediate problems but plan for its future.

Questions and Instructions

1. What immediate help can Canfield expect from state and federal governments?
2. What can Canfield do itself to lessen the traumatic effect of the plant's closing?
3. As City Manager Rascoe, how would you select the members of your committee in regard to the following considerations: role as a representative of a constituency; conflict of interest; membership in various sectors of the community—business, manufacturing, labor, profession, education, and so on; minority groups; and civic, charitable, and cultural organizations?
4. What matters should Rascoe take into consideration in determining the optimum size of the committee?
5. To whom should the committee be accountable?
6. How should the expenses of the committee be borne?
7. What professional help should the committee employ?

Selected Bibliography

Averch, Harvey A., *A Strategic Analysis of Science and Technology Policy,* Baltimore, Md.: The Johns Hopkins University Press, 1985.

Ayres, Robert V., *The Next Industrial Revolution: Reviving Industry through Innovation,* Cambridge, Mass.: Ballinger, 1984.

Birch, David L., *The Job Generation Process,* Cambridge, Mass.: Massachusetts Institute of Technology Press, 1979.

Bluestone, Barry, and Harrison, Bennett, *The Deindustrialization of America: Plant Closings, Community Abandonment, and the Dismantling of Industry,* New York: Basic Books, 1982.

Bowles, Samuel; Gordon, David M.; and Weisskopf, Thomas F., *Beyond the Wasteland,* Garden City, N.Y.: Anchor Press/Doubleday, 1984.

Ferris, Nancy, "Developing a Strategic Advantage for Your Community," *Public Management* 65 (July 1983): 16–18.

Goodman, Robert, *The Last Entrepreneurs: America's Regional Wars for Jobs and Dollars,* New York: Simon & Schuster, 1979.

Jones, Bryan D., and Bachelor, Lynn W., *The Sustaining Hand: Community Leadership and Corporate Power,* Lawrence, Kan.: University Press of Kansas, 1986.

Lawson, Quentin R., and Pannullo, John N., "Using Marketing Strategies to Address Local Issues," *Public Management* 68 (June 1986): 2–4.

Leary, Thomas J., "Deindustrialization, Plant Closing Laws, and the States," *State Government* 58 (Fall 1985): 113–18.

Naisbitt, John, "Why Managers Must Be Facilitators," *Public Management* 69 (June 1987) 15–16.

Reich, Robert, *The Next American Frontier,* New York: Times Books, 1983.

Schutz, Karl, "'Changing Chemainus' Image," *Public Management* 68 (June 1986): 9–11

Scott, Bruce R., and Lodge, George C., eds., *U.S. Competitiveness in the World Economy,* Cambridge, Mass.: Harvard Business School Press, 1985.

United States Congress, Office of Technology Assessment, *Technology, Innovation, and Regional Economic Development,* Washington D.C.: U.S. Government Printing Office, 1984.

34

Discord in Rehabilitation Services

Angela Patterson was elated when, after receiving her bachelor of science degree in social work, she was employed by the State Department of Human Welfare and was assigned to the Division of Rehabilitation Services. Strongly motivated by a desire to help people, she felt that work in this area would be highly rewarding. She was assigned to Lincoln County, the State's most densely populated metropolitan area.

A few days after Patterson had been on the job familiarizing herself with the services of her new organization, the division's director, Melanie Steuben, summoned the staff to a meeting in the conference room and announced that they would hear a presentation on cancer by an insurance agent. Patterson considered this an unusual proceeding but she settled herself comfortably in her chair prepared to listen. She was mildly shocked to hear the speaker launch not into a general discussion on insurance but instead into a sales talk making use of fear tactics to persuade the state employees to take out personal cancer-insurance policies offering benefits not covered in the government's insurance program.

The following week Patterson received her permanent assignment in Rehabilitation Services—she would work in the Adults and Families Unit as one of ten counselors. Her supervisor was Amy Wagner, who appeared preoccupied when Patterson reported to her glass-enclosed cubicle in the big main office for instructions. Wagner told Patterson that she was late for a meeting on family planning and handed her a manual describing forms and procedures to study until her return.

Patterson went back to her own desk and had been reading the manual for about ten minutes when the insurance agent she had heard the week before approached, sat down, and began a sales talk and exhibited pamphlets and brochures on the danger of cancer and the need for insurance protection against the high costs of treatment. New in the unit, Patterson was unwilling to ask the man to leave, since she had seen him several times before talking to individual staff members and he appeared to have the run of the office. So she heard him out, but it was hard for her to believe that the department was allowing such a disturbance to go on.

In the days that followed, Patterson learned from fellow employees why the insurance agent was allowed to interrupt and delay their work and why they submitted to it with only subvocal grumbling: he had been given permission by the division director, Melanie Steuben. It seemed that she had been hard hit emotionally and financially by the death of her mother from cancer, and had become somewhat monomaniacal on the need for people to have adequate insurance coverage. Staff members felt that her intentions were good and put up with the agent, though they considered him a nuisance.

Patterson quickly learned the operational procedures in the unit and was satisfied with her growing ability to serve the needs of her clientele. Her client load had increased and she was handling eighty-one cases—almost more than she could manage. She had learned a great deal, she felt, from her fellow counselors, but she did not have much respect for the two supervisors in the Adult and Families Unit. The supervisor to whom she was assigned was Amy Wagner, a big, raw-boned woman who was known as a martinet. She was a stickler for paper work and records, held frequent meetings to harangue the counselors on the need for writing fuller reports, and required that forms and records be redone if they did not meet her perfectionist standards of neatness and thoroughness.

On occasion Patterson felt like revolting against Wagner's devotion to petty detail, which reduced the time the counselors could spend with their clients, but she had been able to suppress her feelings. She thought perhaps the discipline was good for her.

One morning while Patterson was on the telephone discussing the emergency medical problems of a client with Dr. Philip Casement, the head physician assigned to the Adults and Families Unit, she noticed staff members leaving their desks to gather at the end of the office where a number of chairs were grouped to form a meeting place.

Her eye was caught by Amy Wagner, who motioned for her to join the group, but when Patterson saw that the meeting was to be addressed by the insurance agent she continued her telephone conversation. When she hung up, Wagner again motioned her to come over, but she remained at her desk. The problems facing her client, she felt, were more important than listening again to an insurance agent whose message she knew almost by heart.

After the agent had completed his spiel, Wagner rushed up to Patterson's desk and shouted: "Get into my office right now!" Patterson looked up from her papers to see her supervisor red-faced in anger and in the background her fellow workers looking on in curiosity. She said nothing and followed Wagner as she marched angrily into her cubicle and slammed the door after them so hard it almost shattered the glass walls.

"I can't believe the nerve you have," Wagner shouted. "How dare you disobey orders? How do you think I feel to have you ignore me before the eyes of the whole office?" The supervisor continued her tirade for a few minutes and ended: "I assumed you wanted to go somewhere in this unit, but I guess I was wrong. You're never going to get anywhere by willfully disobeying orders."

Humiliated by the confrontation, Patterson returned to her desk and like an automaton continued to work on her client's problem. Later, when she thought the situation over at lunch, she did not know what to do, but she felt she could no longer remain in the Lincoln County office of the Division of Rehabilitation Services.

Questions and Instructions

1. Do you think Angela Patterson can be blamed in any way for the disgraceful scene involving Amy Wagner? If she sought your advice, what course of action would you recommend?
2. Perhaps there's an Amy Wagner in every large organization having some power over employees. What can or should employees do in the face of such tyranny?
3. Do you think that the employees individually or collectively should protest to Melanie Steuben, the division director, about letting the insurance agent disrupt office work?
4. To what extent do you think employees are justified in acting collectively to protest against an administrator whom they dislike or whom they regard as incompetent or unfair? What about acting collectively to oppose departmental policies or practices?
5. Suppose you are an administrator heading a department or division and you detect a feeling of antagonism among the staff toward you or certain policies and practices? What can you do to improve the situation?
6. Should solicitors, even for charitable projects, be permitted to approach employees during office hours?

Selected Bibliography

Baxter, Leslie A., "Conflict Management: An Episodic Approach," *Small Group Behavior* 13 (February 1982): 23–42.

Drory, Amos, and Gluskinos, Uri.M., "Machiavellianism and Leadership," *Journal of Applied Psychology* 65 (February 1980): 81–86.

Lipsky, Michael, *Street-Level Bureaucracy*, New York, Russell Sage Foundation, 1980. See "The Prospects and Problems of Professionalism," pp. 201–04.

Milbourn, Gener, Jr., and Francis, G. James, "All About Job Satisfaction," *Supervisory Management* 26 (August 1981): 35–43.

Neuse, Steven M., "The Public Service Ethic and the Professions in State Government," *Southern Review of Public Administration* 1 (March 1978): 510–28.

Phillips, James S., and Lord, Robert G., "Casual Attributions and Perceptions of Leadership," *Organizational Behavior and Human Performance,* 28 (October 1981): 143–63.

"Special Symposia Issue: Ethics in Government," *Public Personnel Management* 10 (No. 1, 1980): 1–199.

Stahl, O. Glenn, *Public Personnel Administration,* 7th ed., New York: Harper and Row, 1976. Ch. 18, "Discipline, Removal, and Appeals," pp. 307–17.

Stevens, John M., and Webster, Thomas C., "Human Services Integration: Toward Clarification of a Concept," *Journal of Health and Human Resources Administration* 1 (August 1978): 109–26.

Wortman, Camille B., and Linsenmeier, Joan A. W., "Interpersonal Attraction and Techniques of Ingratiation in Organizational Settings," in Straw, Barry M., and Salancik, Gerald R., eds., *New Directions in Organizational Behavior,* Chicago: St. Clair Press, 1977. pp. 133–78.

35

Coproduction for Marrsville?

Reduced grants from national and state administrations bent on cutting their expenditures, a decline in income from a 2-percent city sales tax, and other revenue losses had placed Marrsville in a financial bind. City officials took a dim view of proposals for making ends meet—reducing services, increasing the fees for services, and imposing higher taxes. The public, they believed, would accept none of these without protest.

Fresh in their minds was a rate-payers' revolt against the Electric Service Company, which recently obtained a rate hike from the State Public Utilities Commission. Marrsville residents paid an average of $36.50 for 1,000 kilowatt hours—much lower than the average of $50.75 paid elsewhere in the Midwest and of $75.66 paid in the Northeast. Nonetheless, one thousand people attended a protest rally called by LOWER (Lower Our Wild Electric Rates), hundreds turned off their lights for one hour every Wednesday night, and three hundred people carried lighted candles in a march to the local office of the Electric Service Company.

Nevertheless, in addressing the City Council on the financial situation, Mayor Wendell Hollingsworth was adamant about one principle—services rendered that were supported by fees should pay their own way. For example, he said, in no way could the monthly charge for refuse collection of $4 per residence paid a private contractor be justified when the city collected only $3.25. He appointed a task force consisting of two councilmembers, the city manager, the city engineer, and the superintendent of public works to make the refuse system more cost effective without lowering the standards of service. James Caputo, assistant to the city manager, was directed to provide staff assistance to the task force.

At one time Marrsville had its own sanitation department, which gathered and disposed of refuse, but some years ago this task was turned over to a private contractor. Citizens placed their refuse in zinc or plastic containers or polyethylene trash bags in their backyards and twice a week collectors hauled the waste away.

The operation was both costly (the contractor raised the rate each year) and unsatisfactory (residents complained of spilled trash, dogs overturning containers or tearing bags apart, missed pickups, and destructive collectors who seemed purposely to batter the zinc cans or break the lids of plastic containers so that the garbage was exposed, attracting dogs and flies and giving off an offensive smell). The city had introduced a monitoring system with fines levied on the contractor when the service fell below established standards. But this effort had not improved matters and officials concluded that the problems associated with refuse collection were insoluble.

Just out of the university with a degree in public administration and employed by Marrsville only six months, James Caputo saw his assignment on the task force as his first opportunity to demonstrate his more up-to-date approach to administrative problems than that of Winston Marbury, his superior. Marbury had been a city manager for twenty-five years and had become somewhat defeatist, in Caputo's opinion, in his attitude toward innovating civic projects.

Caputo enthusiastically began his research on refuse collection by studying articles describing various city experiences appearing in professional publications and promotional brochures from equipment companies, and by writing cities of a size comparable to Marrsville to find out how they handled the problem. Soon able to speak like an authority on the topic, Caputo could state the advantages and disadvantages of side- or rear-loader truck compactors, the best cubic-yard truck capacity, the optimum size of crews handling a truck, the arguments for and against municipal collection or contract collection of refuse, and comparative costs.

The collection of refuse, Caputo decided, offered an opportunity for implementing a concept he had heard much about in his last semester at the university: coproduction. This was defined by one scholar in typical academic gobbledygook as "an emerging conception of the service-delivery process which envisions direct citizen involvement in the design and delivery of city services with professional service agents." Broaching the subject to the city manager, Caputo said: "We need to get the public involved in city management, and refuse disposal is a good place to begin. Instead of paying men to go to the backyards of people to carry out their garbage cans or trash bags to the street for pickup, the people themselves would take their trash to the curbside."

"The people of Marrsville won't want to carry their trash to the curb," Marbury replied. "For years they've been used to putting their trash in cans or bags in their backyards and forgetting about it. Getting them to go to the trouble of taking out their trash twice a week just won't work."

"But elsewhere coproduction has worked," Caputo argued. "People want to cut down on costs. They will be willing to do things themselves that the city has been doing if they can save money."

"They might if they're forced to do it, but I don't think we've reached that stage yet in Marrsville," Marbury said. "Anyway, there's nothing new in collection systems that require people to take their trash to the curb. Many places have been doing that for years, and it's not very satisfactory. People forget what day the collection is and don't put out their trash. Or they don't have time. Besides it's unsightly having curbs lined with trash bags and cans. They're an open invitation to stray dogs to overturn the cans or tear up the bags and scatter garbage and trash about. Coproduction isn't for Marrsville."

Caputo had a more receptive audience when he talked about his plan to the mayor's refuse committee. The members were impressed by the potential savings in the cost of collection—the recent demonstration against the Electric Service Company showed that the people were opposed to paying more for public services and utilities. The problem was to persuade the people to become partners in applying coproduction to refuse removal. Caputo was asked to present his ideas in a draft program.

Questions and Instructions

1. Describe in detail a publicity and promotional program to persuade the people of Marrsville to carry their trash to the curb.
2. Do you think it advisable to conduct a pilot program before the City Council were to decide to adopt a new program of trash removal?
3. In what other areas of municipal services do you think coproduction might be adopted?
4. Do you think that coproduction would help in holding the line on, or reducing, the costs of providing adequate municipal services?
5. Comment on the following statement made by the mayor of Detroit to the City Council: "It may very well be that for the near future we will have to get used to doing things for our city that we have come to expect our city to do for us."

Selected Bibliography

Bjur, Wesley E., and Siegel, Gilbert B., "Voluntary Citizen Participation in Local Government: Quality, Cost and Commitment," *Midwest Review of Public Administration* 11 (June 1977): 135–49.

Brudney, Jeffrey L., "Coproduction Issues in Implementation," *Administration and Society* 17 (November 1985): 243–56.

Butterfield, Kevin, "The Production and Provision of Public Goods," *American Behavioral Scientist* 24 (March/April 1981): 519–44.

Clary, Bruce B., "Designing Urban Bureaucracies for Coproduction," *State and Local Government Review* 17 (Fall 1985): 265–72.

Hanrahan, John D., *Government for Sale: Contracting Out, the New Patronage,* Washington, D.C.: American Federation of State, County, and Municipal Employees, 1977.

Heretick, D. A., "Citizens Vote to Cart Their Refuse," *American City and County* 95 (July 1980): 57–58.

Jones, Bryan D., "Party and Bureaucracy: The Influence of Intermediary Groups on Urban Public Service Delivery," *American Political Science Review* 75 (September 1981): 688–700.

Levine, Charles, "Citizenship and Service Delivery: The Promise of Coproduction," *Public Administration Review* 44 (March/April 1984): 178–86.

Morgan, David R.; Meyer, Michael E.; and England, Robert E., "Alternatives to Municipal Service Delivery: A Four-State Comparison," *Southern Review of Public Administration* 5 (Summer 1981): 184–90.

O'Connor, John, "Refuse Collection Practices 1980: An Exclusive National Survey," *American City and County* 95 (April 1980): 34–38.

Olsen, John B., "Applying Business Management Skills to Local Governmental Operations," *Public Administration Review* 39 (May/June 1979): 282–89.

Rich, Richard C., "Interaction of the Voluntary and Governmental Sectors: Toward an Understanding of the Coproduction of Municipal Services," *Administration and Society* 13 (May 1981): 59–76.

Rosentraub, Mark S., and Sharp, Elaine B., "Consumers as Producers of Social Services: Coproduction and the Level of Social Services," *Southern Review of Public Administration* 4 (March 1981): 502–39.

Savas, E. S., "The Institutional Structure of Local Government Services: A Conceptual Model," *Public Administration Review* 38 (September/October 1978): 412–19.

———, *Privatizing the Public Sector: How to Shrink Government,* Chatham, N.J.: Chatham House Publishers, 1981. See Ch. 3, "The Nature of Goods and Services," pp. 29–52, and Ch. 4, "Alternative Ways to Provide Services," pp. 53–75.

Sharp, Elaine B., "Toward a New Understanding of Urban Services and Citizen Participation: The Coproduction Concept," *Midwest Review of Public Administration* 14 (June 1980): 105–18.

Whitaker, Gordon, "Coproduction: Citizen Participation in Service Delivery," *Public Administration Review* 40 (May/June 1980): 240–46.

36

Cutting Back at City Hall

The Smithville City Council meeting of June 23 had aroused more public interest than its usual weekly sessions because it was the time set for presenting the completed operating budget for the fiscal year starting July 1. The budget specified the estimated revenues and expenditures for personnel services and maintenance and operation of the city. On the table before each councilmember was a copy of the proposed budget over which department heads, the controller's staff, the city manager, and the council had been struggling for months—a neatly bound book with light blue cover containing 163 pages of tables and charts. A public hearing would be held on the proposed budget before it was presented to the council for final approval at its last regular meeting in June.

In presenting the budget, City Manager James Harmsworth said the fact that it was a balanced one was because of the hard work put into it by city employees and councilmembers. Failing revenues and higher operating costs made it seem early in the year as if there would be a shortfall ranging from a "best-case scenario" of $1,739,495 to a "worst-case scenario" of $5,139,000. State law prohibited deficit spending by municipalities, and so figuring out a budget that would meet this requirement was not an easy task. Earlier Harmsworth had presented to the council the capital budget, down about $2 million, or 39 percent, from last year. He believed the completed operations budget was equally successful.

The grim situation that Smithville, population 65,000, faced early in the year was due in part to a general business slump in the state that had affected the city's revenue. The city's income from services was down, sales tax receipts had dropped, and there was a loss in federal revenue sharing.

Early in the year Harmsworth had told the council: "This is one of the most critical times in my ten years as city manager. But the problem is a manageable one if the council will respond to it. During the year we must try to alleviate the situation. A year from now, if something isn't done, it will no longer be a manageable problem."

Recognizing that Draconian measures were needed, city negotiators had resisted demands of pay increases by the three employees' unions, the Fraternal Order of Police (FOP), the International Association of Fire Fighters (IAF), and the American Federation of State, County, and Municipal Employees (AFSCME). FOP members had asked for pay raises of 7 percent then lowered their demand to 4 percent, and finally accepted, by a 55-percent vote of the membership, no increase at all in the face of the bleak prospects presented to them. Similarly, the fire fighters had dropped their first request of an 8.5-percent increase to a 6.5-percent one and then were forced to settle for none at all, and AFSCME members had abandoned their more reasonable request of a cost-of-living increase of 3 percent.

Union leaders had objected strongly to what they considered "taking the brunt" of retrenchment, arguing that instead of lowering salaries and cutting down on personnel the city's revenue could have been raised if officials had taken proper prevention measures to offset declines in the sales tax and utilities income.

John J. Patrick, FOP president, had told a council budget study session: "It's up to City Council to determine whether they want a cut in the quality and efficiency of police services. It has known for months that sales taxes have not been up to budgeted estimates, and it could have acted to avert the present crisis by changing the city charter." He had pointed out that a charter provision required that 70 percent of the one-cent sales tax be used to fund capital improvements. "Other cities can cut on capital improvements and give their employees a little raise," Patrick had said. "Smithville has taken the wrong choice between capital improvements and employees."

Judith Weintraub, president of the employees' federation, had been critical of officials for meeting rising utility costs by taking money from the general fund. "I realize that the city charter requires residents to vote approval of increases in the water, sewage, and trash-removal rates," Weintraub had said, "but officials have allowed the present inadequate rates to go on for years."

To these criticisms officials had replied that it was difficult to persuade the public to approve increased rates for services and higher taxes in a period of business decline. Therefore, a vote on such matters at a time such as this would undoubtedly reject the needed increases, and it could be several years before the time was right for seeking a second vote.

Harmsworth briefed the council on the proposed budget and presented enlarged tables and charts on a screen. He first displayed a budget summary (see Exhibit 1, pp. 172–73) showing estimated revenues for all funds—general, capital, cable television, room tax (on hotels and motels), street and alley, revenue sharing, Smithville Municipal Authority, Smithville Utilities Authority, and the sinking fund. The budget summary revealed a total income of $35,018,179 and total expenditures of $34,710,324, well under the anticipated income.

Harmsworth presented a table comparing the projected expenditures for the new fiscal year with those for the past year that illustrated dramatically the budgetary task facing the city (see Exhibit 2, p. 174). The city had planned to spend $49,507,154 for the past year. Fortunately, it had been possible to reduce this amount by almost $12 million through using carryover funds from previous years, placing a moratorium on buying supplies, dropping training programs, eliminating travel expenses and automobile-use reimbursement, postponing the filling of vacant positions, and employing other money-saving devices.

When pressed by councilmembers to discuss the FY 1988 operations and maintenance budget of the General Fund (not itemized in Exhibit 1), Harmsworth indicated that $1,343,310 was spent for electricity, natural gas, and telephone service; $1,248,520 for landfill fees; $763,470 for gasoline, oil, tires, and vehicle and equipment repair parts; $238,800 for insurance; $376,460 for membership in the Lake Region Master Water Conservancy District; and $205,090 for water treatment chemicals. Harmsworth, as a seasoned and politically astute city manager, was quick to add that the "O & M portion of the budget would be decreased by 11.7 percent for FY '89 and that no part of the budget would remain unscathed from the sharp knife of Smithville's retrenchment plan."

Harmsworth said the worst aspect of cutting down on costs was the impact it would have on personnel—lowering the already inadequate pay of the men and women who protect the people from criminals and maintain order, who save people and buildings during fires, who collect trash and garbage, who provide a clean and adequate water supply, and who keep up the streets, parks, and public buildings. They were the human element in government budgeting, he said, and a significant proportion of the general fund went for their services (see Exhibits 3A and 3B, p. 175). Such personnel services in the new fiscal year, Harmsworth explained, were estimated to be $17,772,324 out of a total expenditure budget of $23,725,446.

The council budget committee and officials, Harmsworth continued, had worked out a plan that would save the jobs of employees—a plan calling for a reduction in force of only forty persons. Last year there had been 683 persons on the city's payrolls, the most ever employed, and the projection for the new fiscal year was 643 persons (see Exhibit 4, pp. 176–77). The reduction in force, however, would not substantially affect the essential services of the fire, police, emergency medical, and sanitation departments, whose combined work force numbered 361 persons. Instead, the forty proposed layoffs would occur in the areas of professional- and management-level employees, clerical staff, and so forth.

To minimize the salary cutback of employees, $400,000 would be transferred from the capital improvement budget and $175,000 would be saved by reducing street lighting to every other street. Additional salary funds would also be obtained from reduced health care and insurance premiums, and by deletion of a separation and retirement budget. Thus, personnel would be penalized only by a 5-percent salary reduction and a freeze on merit pay and furloughs once a month for all employees. These changes would result in net savings for the following categories: reduction, $820,000; merit raise freeze, $343,000; and furloughs, $750,000.

Questions and Instructions

1. In developing the Smithville budget, officials endeavored to make reductions easy on employees. From this standpoint, how do you evaluate their success in the following: hiring freeze, cost-of-living pay freeze, merit pay freeze, furloughs, reduction by attrition, cutting back on force, elimination of training programs, and freeze on travel?
2. Other methods of cutting back include putting ceilings on positions, load-shedding, demotions, personnel transfers, and reclassifying positions. Do you believe Smithville officials should have done more in these areas?
3. Officials could have quickly solved most of the budget-cutting problems by a 10-percent reduction in the work force. Do you think they were wiser to choose instead the complex program they did?
4. Do you consider as valid the criticism of union leaders who faulted officials for failing to attempt to alter the city charter to permit increases in utility rates or to reduce the 70 percent of the sales tax going to capital improvements when they knew long beforehand that revenue would be substantially lowered?
5. Do you agree with the president of the Fraternal Order of Police that in the Smithville budget capital improvements were allowed at the cost of "a little" raise for employees?
6. Do you think it fair not to make reductions in force for essential services such as fire and police protection and to place the burden of retrenchment almost wholly on employees providing other services?
7. Do you think it is possible that efficiency and productivity might not be better after a retrenchment program has been effected?
8. Researchers have reported what they consider negative results in retrenchment in government: (a) an increase in polarization—management vs. labor, whites vs. blacks, political appointees vs. career officials, and veterans vs. nonveterans; (b) increases in waste, fraud, and failure to maintain standards; (c) an increase in the age of the work force; (d) a higher level of organizational chaos—disruption of programs and processes; (e) a decline in morale; and (f) an increase in decision-making uncertainty. How serious are these findings?

9. Cutback practices are sometimes met with opposition from special-interest groups: trade, professional, labor, community, and business organizations; grant recipients; and clientele groups. How may interest groups help to protect programs and prevent cuts that potentially jeopardize their loss of benefits?

Selected Bibliography

Boster, Ronald S., "The Simple Politics of Gramm-Rudman," *The Bureaucrat* 15 (Summer 1986): 38–42.

Cameron, Kim S., "Strategic Responses to Conditions of Decline: Higher Education and the Private Sector," *Journal of Higher Education* 54 (July/August 1983): 359–80.

Cayer, N. Joseph, "Managerial Implications of Reduction in Force," *Public Administration Quarterly* 10 (Spring 1986): 36–49.

Colvard, James E., "Cutout: The Ultimate Cutback Management," *The Bureaucrat* 15 (Spring 1986): 6–8.

Florestano, Patricia S., "Revenue-Raising Limitations on Local Government: A Focus on Alternative Responses," *Public Administration Review* 41 (January/February 1981): 122–31.

Hamilton, Randy, "The World Turned Upside Down: The Contemporary Revolution in State and Local Government Capital Financing," *Public Administration Review* 43 (January/February 1983): 22–32.

Hirschhorn, L., *Cutting Back,* San Francisco: Jossey-Bass, Inc., 1983.

Holzer, Marc, "Workforce Reduction and Productivity," *Public Administration Quarterly* 10 (Spring 1986): 86–98.

Krantz, James, "Group Processes under Conditions of Organizational Decline," *Journal of Applied Behavioral Science* 21 (No. 1, 1985): 1–17.

Levine, Charles, ed., *Managing Fiscal Stress: The Crisis in the Public Sector,* Chatham, N.J.: Chatham House Publishers, 1980.

O'Toole, Daniel E., and Marshall, James, "Managing with Less: What Managers Can Expect," *Public Management* 66 (June 1984): 20–21.

Pfeffer, Jeffrey, and Slanacik, G. R., *The External Control of Organizations: A Resource Dependence Perspective,* New York: Harper and Row, 1978.

Reed, Sarah A., "The Impact of Budgetary Roles upon Perspectives," *Public Budgeting and Finance* 5 (Spring 1985): 72–88.

Rich, Wilbur C., "The Political Context of a Reduction-in-Force Policy: On the Misunderstanding of an Important Phenomenon," *Public Administration Quarterly* 10 (Spring 1986): 7–22.

Schneier, Craig Eric; Beatty, Richard W.; and Goktepe, Janet R., "How to Manage a Committee," *Public Management* 67 (August 1985): 20–21.

Schwab, Paul, and Wallis, Alice, "RIF Management—One Organization's Experience," *The Bureaucrat* 14 (Summer 1985): 17–21.

Shaughnessy, Cynthia, "Attitudes of Senior Personnel Officials and Employees Toward RIF Policies," *Public Administration Quarterly* 10 (Spring 1986): 23–35.

Spurrier, Robert L., Jr., "Caveat Public Employer: Selected Legal Issues in Non-Federal Agency Reductions in Force," *Public Administration Quarterly* 10 (Spring 1986): 60–85.

Weiner, Richard S., and Hendricks, J. J., "Help During Retrenchment," *The Bureaucrat* 14 (Summer 1985): 7–10.

Exhibit 1. City of Smithville Bugdet Summary: FY 1988

Estimated Revenues	*General Fund*	*Capital Fund*	*Cable T.V. Fund*	*Room Tax Fund*	*Street and Alley Fund*	*Revenue Sharing Fund*	*S.M.D. Fund*	*S.U.D. Fund*	*Sinking Fund*	*Total*
Taxes	$11,618,800	$3,417,000	$170,000	$80,000					$1,050,000	$16,335,800
Licenses and permits	486,000									486,000
Intergovernmental revenue					$460,000	$400,000				860,000
Charges for services	7,930,000						$665,050	$1,050,000		9,645,050
Fines and forteitures	752,000									752,000
Miscellaneous revenue	920,500					20,000	40,300	30,000	136,000	1,146,800
Transfer from S.M.A. fund	450,000									450,000
Transfer from cable T.V. fund	49,925	34,000								83,925
Transfer from room tax fund	21,800									21,800
Transfer from S.M.H. Sinking fund									1,051,000	1,051,000
Transfer from 1981 G.O. Bond Sinking fund									1,848,000	1,848,000
Estimated fund balance June 30, 1986	1,500,000	78,100	36,906		4,798		85,681	202,319	430,000	2,337,804
TOTALS	$23,729,025	$3,529,100	$206,906	$80,000	$464,798	$420,000	$791,031	$1,282,319	$4,515,000	$35,018,179

Proposed Expenditures										
General gov't operations	$2,490,142		$122,981	$58,200						$2,671,323
Capital		$258,976				$50,000				308,976
Planning—operations	226,340									226,340
Capital										
City controller—operations	1,057,710									1,057,710
Capital		153,566								153,566
Police—operations	5,071,195									5,071,195
Capital		46,600				206,600				253,200
Fire—operations	3,398,113									3,398,113
Capital		38,000								38,000
Park and recreation—operations	2,645,151									2,645,151
Capital		329,100				2,400				331,500
Code enforcement—operations	432,900									432,900
Capital										
Public works—operations	8,403,895			460,000						8,863,895
Capital		2,700,930				141,000		$703,900		3,545,830
Transfer to other funds			34,000						$280,500	314,500
Transfer to general fund			49,925	21,800			$450,000			521,725
Bonds, coupons, paying-agent fee							91,000	551,500	4,233,900	4,876,400
TOTALS	$23,725,446	$206,906	$80,000	$80,000	$460,000	$400,000	$541,000	$1,255,400	$4,514,400	$34,710,324

Exhibit 2. City of Smithville Expenditures Budget Comparisons: FY 1987–1989

Fund Number and Name	FY 1987 Ending Budget	Actual Expenditure Through June 30, 1988	FY 1989 Budget
10 General fund	$26,952,221.00	$24,159,870.10	$23,725,446.00
40 Capital fund	8,864,969.00	3,777,815.52	3,527,172.00
20 Cable television fund	227,751.00	171,857.33	206,906.00
21 Room tax fund	217,772.00	148,030.31	80,000.00
22 Street and alley fund	731,496.00	636,932.36	460,000.00
24 Revenue sharing fund	2,690,105.00	1,276,369.38	400,000.00
30 Sinking fund	4,061,800.00	3,092,332.67	4,514,400.00
50 Smithville municipal fund	975,931.00	909,942.60	541,000.00
Transfer to general fund*	(860,000.00)	(860,000.00)	(450,000.00)
51 Smithville utilities authority fund	5,645,109.00	3,771,213.35	1,255,400.00
TOTALS	$49,507,154.00	$37,084,363.62	$34,260,324.00

* Subtracted to eliminate duplicate expenditure.

Exhibit 3.A. City of Smithville Revenue Estimates for the General Fund Operations Budget, FY 1989

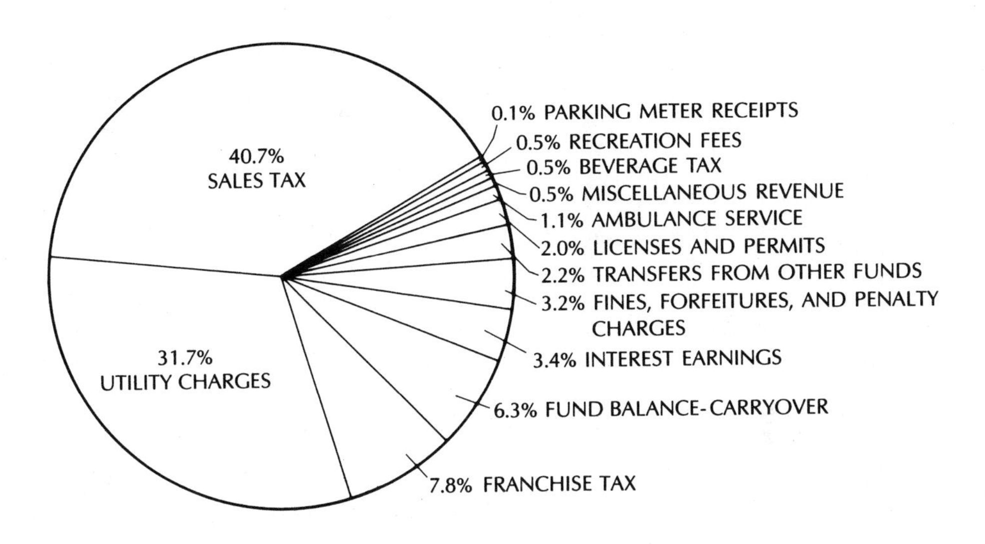

Exhibit 3.B. City of Smithville Expenditure Estimates for the General Fund Operations Budget, FY 1989

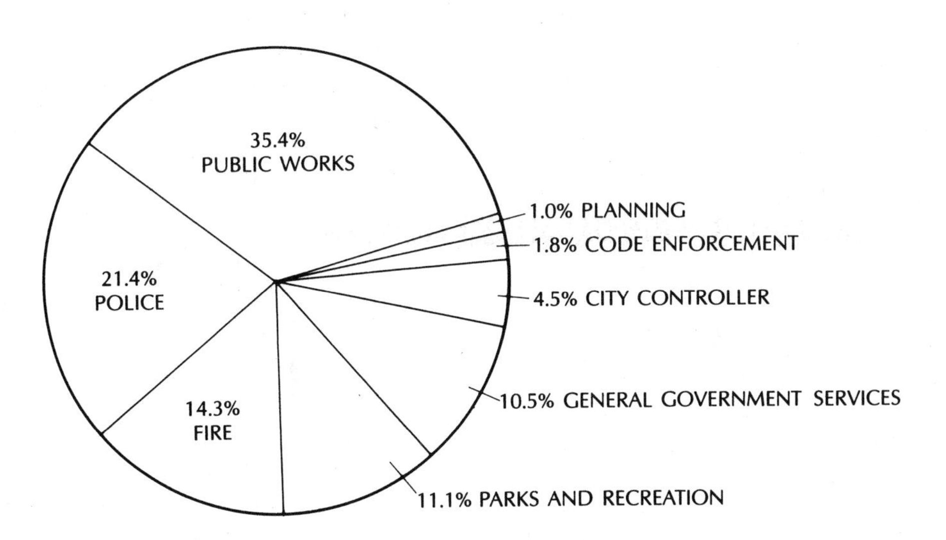

Exhibit 4. City of Smithville Department Employee Summary: FY 1986–1989

Department	FY 1986 Actual	FY 1987 Actual	FY 1988 Actual	FY 1989 Requested
City Council*	9	9	9	9
Municipal Court	9	9	9	9
General government services	31	32	33	29
City manager	3	3	3	3
Animal control	7	7	7	6
Personnel	6	7	7	4
Legal	6	6	7	8
City clerk	8	8	8	8
General government	1	1	1	0
Planning	8	8	8	6
City controller	35	34	34	31
Accounting division	5	4	4	4
Purchasing	2	2	2	1
Data processing	7	7	7	7
Utility	21	21	21	19
Police	159	159	159	156
Police	140	140	140	137
Civil defense	1	1	1	1
Emergency medical	18	18	18	18
Fire	117	120	122	119
Administration	3	3	3	3
Suppression	111	114	116	113
Prevention	3	3	3	3
Parks and recreation	80	82	82	77
Administration	6	6	6	4
Special services				3
Parks	15	15	15	14
Recreation	17	17	17	16
Forestry	3	4	4	3
Drainage maintenance	7	7	7	6
Roadside maintenance	5	6	6	5
Westwood golf and maintenance	11	11	11	10
Building maintenance	16	16	16	16
Code enforcement	18	18	18	12
Public works	210	216	218	204
Administration	7	7	6	5
Engineering	10	10	11	6
Traffic control	13	13	13	10
Maintenance administration	4	4	4	4
Street maintenance	20	20	20	17

Department	*FY 1986 Actual*	*FY 1987 Actual*	*FY 1988 Actual*	*FY 1989 Requested*
Water maintenance	17	17	17	17
Sewer maintenance	15	16	16	16
Water/wastewater administration	2	2	2	2
Water treatment	10	10	12	12
Wastewater treatment	15	15	15	15
Sanitation	78	82	82	81
Municipal garage	19	20	20	19
Employee totals	667	678	683	643

* Not included in total employee count.

37

Personnel Dilemma: Terminate or Retain

In a reorganization of the State Department of Education a planning commission was established to coordinate activities and programs of its more than fifty sections and divisions and to institute and carry out comprehensive programs for the public schools and institutions of higher learning. Commission members were the superintendent of public instruction, the secretary of the State Board of Education, and the directors of the Federal Programs, Finance, and Instruction divisions of the department. Staffing of the commission was provided by the State Board of Education, headed by Dr. Frank Jordan.

In July, Dr. Jordan received funds to hire an additional secretary to perform secretarial and clerical services for the planning commission. The board at one time had only one secretary for six professional staff persons, and she could not handle that work load and take on additional duties for the commission.

Jordan's administrative assistant, Barbara White, who served as personnel officer and supervisor of the clerical staff, began working with the Department of Personnel to classify the new position and announce the opening. She consulted with the board's office planner, Pamela Goldsmith, and the facilities coordinator, John Rodriguez, to determine the classification for the new position. No one was sure what duties would be assigned to the person hired other than that he or she act as secretary to the planning commission. The job would include making arrangements for meetings, preparing agendas, recording and transcribing minutes, and providing data and materials requested by commission members. It was thought that the person would also serve as secretary to Goldsmith and perhaps do some work for Rodriguez.

After reviewing the anticipated duties with Dr. Jordan, White submitted a job summary to the Department of Personnel requesting a Secretary Grade I classification. The qualifications for this position were graduation from high school, one year of secretarial experience, and the ability to type 45 wpm and take dictation at 80 wpm. The classification was approved and the opening was announced.

The Department of Personnel submitted to the board a list of four eligible applicants and after interviewing them Dr. Jordan and White decided to employ Edith Reichel. Her experience was not entirely what was wanted—she had held only one secretarial position and had worked the past three years as a clerk in the state auditor's office—but she was enthusiastic about getting the job and expressed a willingness to improve her skills and take on new responsibilities. In addition, she won Dr. Jordan's sympathy because she was divorced and had two small children to support.

After Reichel began working, it soon became apparent to Barbara White that employing her had been a mistake. Reichel was a heavy cigarette smoker and frequently left her desk to light up, she was restless and disrupted office work by visiting with other staff members, and she was inattentive when receiving instructions, thus often making mistakes that resulted in her work having to be redone. Moreover, the position required abilities Reichel did not have. Goldsmith was working on a comprehensive plan for reorganizing the filing system of the department and needed assistance in her studies that she could not entrust to Reichel.

Antagonism also quickly arose between the board's regular secretary, Hazel Holmberg, and Reichel. Instead of lightening Holmberg's too-heavy work load, Reichel added to the burden. Because of Reichel's inefficiency, Holmberg had to assist in collecting material for the commission meetings and, since Reichel's shorthand was poor, she had to take the minutes as well. In consequence, Holmberg complained to White and threatened to seek a transfer unless something was done.

White consulted Pamela Goldsmith about Reichel's performance and found that she too considered it unsatisfactory. They held a counseling session with Reichel, who, apologetic, blamed her deficiencies on problems with her two children and promised to improve. For some weeks her work was almost satisfactory, and it looked as though the problem was resolved. But Reichel soon slipped back into her old habits, and those most concerned with her work—White, Goldsmith, and Rodriguez—discussed getting rid of her while she was still on probation. None of the three, however, was willing to assume the responsibility for taking action.

Thus the question of whether to start proceedings to release or retain Reichel remained in limbo until near the end of the fifth month of her employment she failed to report for work one morning. The planning commission was to meet at ten o'clock, and telephone calls to Reichel at her home to find out where she had placed the data and papers required for the members went unanswered. Fortunately, these items were discovered by Holmberg just before the meeting began. Reichel called the office at eleven o'clock to say that she had taken a bus to visit friends in a neighboring town the night before and missed the bus back. She did not return to work until the next morning.

White reported to Dr. Jordan the difficulties encountered with Reichel, informing him that only a few more weeks remained in her probationary period. If no action were taken, she would become a permanent employee and it would be hard to remove her even if her work continued unsatisfactory. Although Jordan was busy trying to meet a deadline for completing the department budget, he promised to talk the situation over with Reichel. When she appeared in his office, he was so preoccupied with budgetary matters that he merely told her there had been some complaints about her work and urged her to try to improve it, which he felt sure she could.

After leaving Dr. Jordan's office, Reichel related to White what had occurred, saying that he had been "very nice" and reassuring about the quality of her work and her future in the department. Later, discussing the matter with Goldsmith, White said that apparently Jordan, rushed in getting the budget together, would not take the time to deal with such a minor matter as a Grade I secretary's deficiencies. They would have to make every effort to help her improve. To this end, White arranged for Reichel to attend a week-long secretarial training workshop to brush up on her typing and shorthand. At the end of the probationary period, Reichel became a permanent employee.

Reichel's good intentions did not last long and she lapsed again into her old ways. Other staff members, believing her poor performance placed an extra burden on them, complained of her slipshod work to employees in other offices at the capitol. Through friends, word of this got back to Reichel. She became very upset and in an emotional confrontation with White exclaimed that she wished she had never taken the job in the first place and that there had never been any fault found with her work in the state auditor's office. Dr. Jordan and White, she said, had not been honest with her.

Repeated complaints of staff members to Jordan finally persuaded him that to restore staff morale he would have to get rid of her and arrange for someone else to do the secretarial work for the planning commission. Since there was no really strong basis for firing Reichel, he decided to reclassify her position to a Secretary Grade II and reassign her to work in one of the auxiliary programs attached to the department.

Questions and Instructions

1. How would you allocate the blame in permitting Reichel to complete her probation and become a permanent staff member?
2. Would an orientation and training program and closer supervision have prevented the situation involving Reichel from developing?

3. What do you think of the manner in which the problem was finally resolved?
4. Do you think that Reichel was correct in her belief that her superiors had not dealt honestly with her?
5. Is it fair to the state for administrators to keep an employee who performs poorly out of sympathy for her or his personal problems or because they find reprimanding or firing a person too painful an experience? How tough must administrators be?

Selected Bibliography

Brim-Donohoe, Lue Rachelle, "A Case for Human Resources Development," *Public Personnel Management* 10 (No. 4, 1981): 365–70.

Brooks, Ronald A., "Don't Fire Your Executives—Trade Them," *Personnel Journal* 58 (May 1979): 308–10.

Dwoskin, Robert P., *Rights of the Public Employee,* Chicago: American Library Association, 1978. Ch. 2, "Exclusion and Dismissal from Public Service," pp. 34–79, and Ch. 6, "Procedural Due Process Rights," pp. 214–38.

Freedman, James O., *Crisis and Legitimacy,* Cambridge: Cambridge University Press, 1978. Ch. 8, "The Significance of Public Attitudes Toward Agency Goals: The EEOC," pp. 105–15.

Filley, Alan C., *Interpersonal Conflict Resolution,* Glenview, Ill.: Scott, Foresman, 1975.

Flynn, W. Randolph, and Stratton, William E., "Managing Problem Employees," *Human Resource Management* 20 (Summer 1981): 28–32.

Greiner, John M.; Hatry, Harry P.; Koss, Margo P.; Millar, Annie P.; and Woodward, Jane P., *Productivity and Motivation,* Washington, D.C.: Urban Institute Press, 1981. See "Four Important Motivational Techniques," pp. 7–9, and "Some Recommendations for Improving Employee Motivation Over the Long Run," pp. 417–23.

Huseman, Richard C.; Lahiff, James M.; and Hatfield, John D., *Interpersonal Communications in Organizations,* Boston: Holbrook Press, 1976. Ch. 6, "Communication and Conflict," pp. 89–103.

Maslow, Abraham H., "A Theory of Motivation," *Psychological Review* 50 (July 1943): 370–96.

McGregor, Douglas, *Leadership and Motivation,* Cambridge, Mass.: Massachusetts Institute of Technology Press, 1968.

Meyers, Deborah, and Abrahamson, Lee M., "Firing with Finesse: A Rationale for Outplacement," *Personnel Journal* 54 (August 1975): 432–34, 437.

Stanton, Ervin S., "The Discharged Employee and the EEO Laws," *Personnel Journal* 55 (March 1976): 128–29, 133.

Tracey, William R., "Put-Down Techniques: Are You Guilty of Them?" *Personnel Journal* 58 (May 1979): 311–13.

Truskie, Stanley D., "In-House Supervisory Training Programs: High Caliber, High Impact," *Personnel Journal* 58 (June 1979): 371–73.

38

In Whose Best Interest?

Edward Holbrook was approaching the end of his six-month probationary period as a counselor in a regional office of the Vocational Rehabilitation Service, an agency of the State Department of Human Welfare, and the time had come for his supervisor, Thomas Fuentes, to assess his work.

Holbrook held bachelor-of-arts and master-of-arts degrees with a major in history and a minor in political science. The Vocational Rehabilitation Service required a master's degree in liberal arts or science but did not specify courses in social work or sociology, though this background was considered desirable in employing people. Holbrook had impressed his job interviewers with his apparent energy and eagerness to work in vocational rehabilitation.

New counselors were employed at the Counselor I level. Their duty was to meet with the clients, assess their needs, provide information to guide them in planning their careers, and help them find suitable work. Many of the clients were just out of high school and had disabilities that would require assistance. Others needed monetary assistance while they were learning a trade or profession.

A major consideration in the evaluation of counselors at the end of their probationary period was whether they were meeting their quotas of case closures, the target being sixty case closures a year. Other considerations in the evaluation were the length of the clients' employment, their satisfaction with their jobs, and the value of the assistance given them by Vocational Rehabilitation.

Fuentes regarded Holbrook as competent enough because he had surpassed the minimum performance standards required of new counselors. He had observed that Holbrook displayed eagerness in quickly attaining case closures. The surest way to quick closure was with clients who seemed uninterested in higher education and who were willing to enter vo-tech programs that did not take long to complete and that enabled them to get jobs in a comparatively short period of time. Fuentes had noted that many of Holbrook's referrals had been for vo-tech training, but these did not seem out of line with the referrals of other counselors and he had endorsed them.

After Fuentes had drafted his assessment of Holbrook's work, a highly complimentary one, he learned from one of the service employees that Holbrook's brother owned a trade school in which Holbrook had an interest in the form of some stock given him as a wedding present. Disturbed at hearing this, Fuentes reviewed the file on Holbrook's clients and noted that a suspiciously high number were enrolled in his brother's school.

Fuentes's initial feeling was that of being trapped. He had frequently praised Holbrook for his productivity and felt that such productivity would enable him to be a competent supervisor in the years to come. Now Fuentes appeared to be faced with the problem of productivity gains at the expense of questionable activities. He decided to attend to the problem at once and wrote Holbrook a note asking him to report to his office at ten o'clock the next morning.

At the meeting, Fuentes quickly got down to the matter at issue. "Ed," he said, "I received word yesterday that you have part interest in a trade school with your brother. Is that correct?"

"Yes, sir, my brother gave me a few shares as a present."

"Well, I reviewed your case load, and I found that many of your clients are enrolled in your brother's school."

"Sir, if you think I'm being dishonest, I can assure you that I'm not. I have been concerned only about the placement of my clients and I know my brother's school is reputable and will teach a trade as well as, and often better than, some of the other training schools in town."

At this point, Fuentes remembered Holbrook's competency in all other aspects and became concerned about maintaining a compatible relationship and not making a hasty judgment. He decided the best solution would be to resolve the legal ramifications of the problem.

"Ed, I know your brother runs a quality school," he said. "However, if you remember, the rule book presented to you at the time you were employed contains a section pertaining to conflicts of interest. With you owning a part of your brother's business, it looks as if you may be guilty of a conflict of interest."

Holbrook said that this might appear to be so to an outsider and that he could see the problem. He went on to assure Fuentes that the referrals had not been made out of any monetary interest—his brother's school had a large enrollment and his referrals to it would not make or break it. "My only concern," Holbrook said, "was to help out my clients."

In a brief lecture, Fuentes stressed the need for impartiality in all counselors. Holbrook's job, he said, consisted of assessing the educational needs of a person and determining what kind of school—vo-tech or college—would be best depending on his or her interests or abilities. Holbrook should explain to clients, Fuentes said, the amount of money they could or could not receive from the state. When a client asked questions about a certain school, Fuentes said, the counselor should not be overly opinionated, since the ultimate decision was left to the client.

To remove any suspicion of a conflict of interest, Holbrook offered to return his gift shares in the school to his brother, and Fuentes accepted this as an adequate solution to the problem. He felt convinced that Holbrook had been sincere in his belief that he had always acted in the best interests of his clients and that in the future he would be particularly careful in helping them choose a school. He decided to submit his favorable report on Holbrook as a probationer.

Holbrook, for his part, was satisfied with the conclusion of the conference, but in the weeks to come he occasionally had moments of unease. He had never been called on the carpet before by supervisors, and he felt that he and Fuentes did not have the same rapport they had had before the incident. Sometimes at conferences with clients he had the feeling that Fuentes was looking over his shoulder. However, with time these feelings disappeared completely.

Questions and Instructions

1. What were some of the positive and negative aspects of Fuentes's handling of the situation?
2. How would you handle the situation as a personnel manager and what are some of the remedial actions open?
3. How does the private sector differ from the public sector regarding conflict of interest?
4. Are case closures a good indication of vocational-rehabilitation-counselor productivity? Explain.

Selected Bibliography

Committee for Economic Development, *Improving Management of the Public Work Force,* New York: Committee for Economic Development, 1978. Ch. 6, "Employee Performance and Satisfaction," pp. 103–25.

Bozeman, Barry, *Public Management and Policy Analysis,* New York: St. Martin's Press, 1979. Ch. 3, "Policy Philosophies, Public Management, and the Public Interest," pp. 60–82.

Dewey, John, *The Public and Its Problems,* New York: Holt, 1927.

Drucker, Peter F., "The Sickness of Government," *Public Interest* 14 (Winter 1969): 3–23.

Dvorin, Eugene P., and Simmons, Robert H., *From Amoral to Humane*

Bureaucracy, San Francisco, Calif.: Canfield Press, 1972. Ch. 5, "Toward a Theory of the Public Interest," pp. 36–46.

Gordon, George J., *Public Administration in America,* 2nd ed., New York: St. Martin's Press, 1982. See "Ethics, Morality, and Corruption," pp. 546–50.

Halatin, T. J., and Flannery, William T., "Keeping Your Employees Turned On—Professionally," *Supervisory Management* 26 (October 1981): 10–14.

Hersey, Paul, and Blanchard, Kenneth H., "So You Want to Know Your Leadership Style," *Training and Development Journal* 35 (June 1981): 34–54.

Jacob, Charles E., *Policy and Bureaucracy,* Princeton, N.J.: D. Van Nostrand, 1966. Ch. 8, "Public Policy and the Public Interest," pp. 192–202.

Janka, Katherine; Luke, Robert A.; and Morrison, Charles A., *People, Performance . . . Results!* Washington, D.C.: National Training and Development Service Press, 1977. Ch. 1, "What Makes Employees More Effective?" pp. 11–22.

Lipsky, Michael, *Street-Level Bureaucracy,* New York: Russell Sage Foundation, 1980. See Ch. 5, "Relations with Clients," pp. 54–70, and "Keeping New Professionals New," pp. 204–11.

Maslow, Abraham H., "The Superior Person," in Bennis, Warren G., ed., *American Bureaucracy,* Chicago: Aldine, 1970. pp. 27–37.

Morrow, Allyn A., and Thayer, Frederick C., "Materialism and Humanism: Organizational Theory's Odd Couple," *Administration and Society* 10 (May 1978): 86–106.

Murray, R. Stuart, "Managerial Perceptions of Two Appraisal Systems," *California Management Review* 23 (Spring 1981): 92–96.

Poston, Ersa, and Broadnax, Walter D., eds., "Ethics and Morality in Government: A Public Policy Forum," *Bureaucrat* 4 (April 1975): 3–65.

39

Restoring Peace at Maysville

Robert Haworth was the manager of operations for the State Department of Natural Resources, an agency that dealt with wildlife conservation, stream pollution, soil erosion, and other environmental problems. His responsibilities included supervision of more than a hundred people assigned to fifteen districts. Thirty of the employees reported directly to him. The district field offices were responsible for working with individuals, groups, municipalities, and counties in implementing programs designed to improve and preserve natural resources. The state provided funds and technical assistance for these programs.

The typical field office had a professional person as the supervisor and several para-professionals. The professional was required to have a four-year college degree and was the manager of the operation. The para-professionals were technicians receiving supervision and guidance from the professional.

Late one Friday afternoon in October, Haworth received a call from Jefferson Parsons, supervisor of the Maysville field office. Obviously upset, Parsons told him that Gary Foraker, technician at Maysville, had just stormed out of the office, declaring that he was resigning. Questioning revealed that the two men had become involved in a quarrel that had started over a minor "beef" of Foraker that he had received a citation from the state office for exceeding unit goals for which Parsons had not given him any recognition. Parsons closed the conversation by saying he thought Foraker would call Haworth that night at home and resign. "That's all right with me," Parsons said. "I don't feel I could work with him after this."

Before leaving the office that evening Haworth quickly reviewed the personnel files of Parsons and Foraker. Parsons was four years out of college and twenty-six years old. He had trained in three different locations in the state, spending only a few months in each, and had quickly risen from a trainee to his present supervisory position that he had held for fourteen months. He was manager of the Maysville office and also supervised a subunit at Hilton twenty miles away.

Haworth recalled that an experienced technician at Hilton, James Harold, had died of a heart attack in July and a new, inexperienced technician, Ernest Bart, had been hired in September. Parsons had been spending one day of each week in the Hilton office before Harold's death but was now spending three days a week there. Parsons had two other technicians besides Foraker and a woman professional trainee, Martha Sessions, twenty-three years old, who was one year out of college and had been in the Maysville office six months. Haworth had previously noted a weakness in Parsons's supervisory abilities—he seemed to have a one-track mind and disliked tackling more than one problem at a time. Haworth had discussed this with him and documented it in the file.

Foraker, Haworth noted, was forty-seven years old and had lived in the Maysville area all his life. He had worked for the agency seven years and had risen two pay grades during this time. He had only a high-school education but despite this had expressed a wish to further his education. To this end he had enrolled in two engineering courses by correspondence but had finished neither. He had two letters of commendation in his file for excellence in performance of work on special projects.

With the background of the two men in mind, Haworth went home feeling that he was prepared to deal at least temporarily with the situation should Foraker call.

[Note: Before reading the complete case history, consider the questions and instructions that follow.]

Questions and Instructions

1. What attitude do you think Haworth should take toward Foraker should he receive a call from him that night?
2. How involved should Haworth get in the situation not knowing any more details than he now has?
3. Do you think the differences between Parsons and Foraker are so deep-seated that they cannot be resolved and the two men cannot work together again?
4. With the information you have, how would you deal with Foraker when he calls?

Haworth was preparing to watch a movie on television that evening when the telephone rang and he heard Foraker's voice when he picked up the receiver. Foraker apologized for calling Haworth at home and then got down to the purpose of the call. "Mr. Haworth," he said, "Jeff Parsons and I had a row this afternoon. I don't think I want to work under him any longer and I want to resign."

"I'm sorry to hear that," Haworth replied. "I think the office at Maysville has been doing a great job. I thought we had a good team there. What seems to be the matter?"

"It's Parsons," Foraker said. "He doesn't think enough of me to keep me informed about what's happening, or the other technicians either. Also, he's not providing direction for our trainee Martha Sessions. He spends most of his time over at Hilton and doesn't give enough time to more important programs here at Maysville."

"Well, hold your horses about this," Haworth replied. "Let's not do anything hasty. Why don't I drive up to Maysville the first of the week and get together with you and Parsons and talk the situation over. I think if we let matters rest over the weekend and then sit down and talk things over we can straighten them out."

Foraker agreed to this and Haworth, to make the forthcoming conference appear less official, suggested that they meet Monday morning in Foraker's home. The next day Haworth told Parsons of the telephone call and the meeting with Foraker at his home. "I'll pick you up about ten o'clock," Haworth said, "and we'll go and see Foraker."

When Haworth and Parsons arrived at Foraker's home on Monday morning he met them at the door and invited them into the kitchen for coffee. The meeting was more like two friends visiting a third friend than a formal session to iron out an official problem. They talked about fishing, the weather, and the quail season before getting down to business.

"I think if we talk things over and get each other's viewpoint we should be able to settle matters satisfactorily," Haworth said. "I know you've been doing good work," he continued addressing Foraker, "and the Maysville office will miss you. And I'm sure Jeff won't easily find someone who knows the area as well and can step right in to do your work."

Foraker, asked by Haworth to give his view, repeated what he had said in his telephone call to Haworth. He and Martha Sessions were not receiving any guidance or direction from Parsons and they never knew what was going on at the office. The office exceeded yearly goals, he continued, and received a performance award, but Parsons had never bothered to commend the staff for the work that earned the award. "We feel we should be treated like human beings, not robots," he said.

"I'm sorry about this," Parsons said. "I just didn't know. I guess I just don't do a good job of communicating with people. I've been so busy over at Hilton trying to get things straightened out, I've just not had the time to attend to matters as I should here in Maysville."

Parsons added that he supposed he should have proposed Foraker for an award but it hadn't occurred to him. He had never been in one place long enough to learn how much such commendation meant to staff members. "This is my first supervisory position," Parsons said, "and I guess I've had too many things on my mind to take care of them all."

"Well, I can see you have a lot on your mind," Foraker said to Parsons. "I guess I went off half-cocked. I really don't want to quit the agency. I've always liked the work, helping the region I grew up in and know best."

"There's enough blame for all of us to share," Haworth interjected. "The important thing is to try to see each other's point of view and do our job."

The three shook hands and Haworth and Parsons left to return to the office followed by Foraker in his own car. Haworth had disliked spending most of the day settling a small dispute but felt the trip had been worthwhile if peace had been restored at Maysville.

Questions and Instructions

1. How do you evaluate Haworth's handling of the situation?
2. Do you think Haworth shares any blame for letting the situation develop in the first place? What can he do to prevent such situations from developing in the future?
3. What follow-up measures might it be desirable for Haworth to take in regard to Maysville?
4. Merit awards and citations are designed to reward employees for tasks well done, to build up self-esteem, to provide recognition, and to raise morale. In the situation at Maysville this purpose clearly was not fulfilled. Discuss the value of such recognition devices in management.

Selected Bibliography

Anthony, Peter David, "Work and the Loss of Meaning," *Social Science Journal* 32 (No. 3, 1980): 416–26.

Austin, Terence W., "What Can Managers Learn from Leadership Theories," *Supervisory Management* 26 (July 1981): 22–31.

Bozeman, Barry, *Public Management and Policy Analysis,* New York: St. Martin's Press, 1979. Ch. 5, "Organization Structure and Design," pp. 112–36.

Browne, Philip, and Golembiewski, Robert, "The Line-Staff Concept Revisited," *Academy of Management* Journal 17 (September 1974): 406–17.

Gibson, Frank K., and Teasley, Clyde E., "The Humanistic Model of Organizational Motivation: A Review of Research Support," *Public Administration Review* 33 (January/February 1973): 89–96.

Greiner, John M.; Hatry, Harry P.; Koss, Margo P.; Millar, Annie P.; and Woodward, Jane P., *Productivity and Motivation,* Washington, D.C.: Urban Institute Press, 1981. Ch. 6, "Special Concerns Associated with Implementing Monetary Incentive Plans," pp. 95–105.

Hall, Richard H., *Organizations: Structure and Process,* 2nd ed. Englewood Cliffs, N.J.: Prentice-Hall, Inc., 1977. Ch. 10, "Communications and Organizational Change," pp. 266–300.

Janka, Katherine; Luke, Robert; and Morrison, Charles, *People, Performance . . . Results!* Washington, D.C.: National Training and Development Press, 1977. Ch. 6, "Implementing an Effectiveness Program," pp. 73–84.

Klingner, Donald E., *Public Personnel Management,* Palo Alto, Calif.: Mayfield Publishing Company, 1981. Ch. 5, "Rewarding and Public Personnel Management," pp. 215–93.

Lee, Robert D., Jr., *Public Personnel Systems,* Baltimore: University Park Press, 1979. Ch. 11, "Motivation Theory," pp. 303–23, and Ch. 12, "Motivation in Daily Operations," pp. 325–63.

Leidecker, Joel K., and Hall, James J., "Motivation: Good Theory—Poor Application," *Training and Development Journal* 35 (June 1981): 152–55.

Nigro, Felix A., and Nigro, Lloyd G., *Modern Public Administration,* 5th ed., New York: Harper and Row, 1980. Ch. 8, "The Geography of Organization," pp. 169–89.

Palmer, Walter W., and Dean, Charles C., "Increasing Employee Productivity and Reducing Turnover," *Training and Development Journal* 27 (March 1973): 53–55.

Porter, Lyman W., and Steers, Richard M., "Organization, Work, and Personal Factors in Employee Turnover and Absenteeism," in Hammer, W. Clay, and Schmidt, Frank L., eds., *Contemporary Problems in Personnel,* Rev. ed., Chicago: St. Clair Press, 1977. pp. 362–76.

40

Equalizing Overtime Assignments

Kent Lemons had worked in the maintenance shops of the Air Force Air Logistics Center eleven years and held the rank of WG-10 journeyman mechanic when, angered at what he considered favoritism in the assignment of overtime work, he filed a grievance against his employer. A good family man and a church-goer, Lemons was usually even-tempered, but if he felt he had been treated unjustly he could be aroused to action.

Lemons's immediate supervisor, Oscar Putnam, was an easygoing fellow who was a pal to all the employees in the shop. Lax in his authority, Putnam was easily manipulated by workers who wanted soft jobs or special privileges.

Lemons was a steady worker with a good record and not prone to ask favors. Some months after being assigned to Putnam's unit, he became resentful because the supervisor did not always use the overtime roster in distributing overtime among the employees. Lemons, as well as others, had been skipped on a number of occasions.

The situation that finally aroused his ire occurred in March when four four-hour blocks of overtime were approved—two for the evening of March 17 and two for March 18—to repair four fuel-control units for jet engines on aircraft grounded as inoperable.

On the evening of March 17, two mechanics, Lane Deerfield and Adam Merryman, were working on the control units and the task was not completed when their regular shift ended—two units still were to be repaired. They were directed to continue their work and completed the repairs on the two units by the end of their four-hour overtime on March 18. According to the overtime roster, Lemons would have been next in line for overtime assignment. Five other employees also had prior rights to overtime before Deerfield and Merryman.

Two days later Lemons filed a grievance reporting what had happened and said in conclusion: "It is requested that I be paid eight hours' overtime missed because I was bypassed on the overtime roster."

Lemons received an answer to his grievance on March 30 that stated in part: "An emergency existed to get these jet engines out; thus, a violation of the union contract was not committed. Your overtime request is denied."

With the support of his union, Lemons appealed to arbitration and a hearing was conducted on May 10. The union's position was that Article XX (see Exhibit 1, p. 195) of the Labor-Management Agreement was violated when the employer failed to give Lemons an opportunity to work overtime and that no emergency situation existed that justified bypassing prescribed procedures.

The union presented several witnesses who testified that the employer failed to use the overtime roster, thereby denying Lemons his rightful turn to work overtime. In addition, the union steward argued that the employer was aware of the situation sufficiently in advance to consult and use the overtime roster and inform Lemons, who was working on the swing shift from 4 P.M. to midnight. The employees who received the overtime assignment, the steward said, were on the graveyard shift from midnight to 8 A.M.

The employer's position was that under Article XIV of the contract (see Exhibit 2, p. 195) management had clearly retained the right to take whatever action might be necessary to carry out the mission of the Air Force in emergencies. Article XX of the contract, it was contended, was not violated in assigning overtime work on the evenings of March 17 and 18 to employees who had been previously assigned critical work of an emergency nature. It was also held that even in nonemergency situations the practice in the shop was not to switch workers during the assembly of a specific unit. Finally, management contended that Lemons would not have been entitled to overtime work even if the roster had been used: on March 17 five other employees were higher on the roster.

The arbitrator reversed the decision of the grievance board and found in favor of Lemons. His findings were that the employer had the right to take whatever actions were necessary to carry out the mission of the Air Force in emergencies but had not properly raised this contention as a defense and had not adequately supported it with evidence. Therefore, he agreed with the union's contention that an emergency had not existed and this defense was not valid. Moreover, he did not subscribe to the employer's contention that Lemons was not entitled to be called for overtime and would not have been called if the overtime roster had been used, because this contention assumed a statement of facts not in evidence.

Questions and Instructions

1. What options other than filing a grievance did Lemons have? What might be the consequences to him of the actions taken?

2. What practices should management follow to avoid situations like the one that led to Lemons's filing his grievance?
3. Which verdict in the Lemons case do you think right and proper—that of the grievance board or that of the arbitrator? Justify your conclusion by analyzing all alleged facts in the case, noting any that are inconsistent or dubious, the contentions of Lemons, the union, and the employer, and Articles XIV and XX of the Labor-Management Agreement.

Selected Bibliography

Adams, J. Stacy, "Toward an Understanding of Inequity," *Journal of Abnormal Psychology* 67 (November 1963): 422–36.

Bloom, David E., "Is Arbitration *Really* Compatible with Bargaining?" *Industrial Relations* 20 (Fall 1981): 233–44.

Committee for Economic Development, *Improving Management of the Public Work Force,* New York: Committee for Economic Development, 1978. Ch. 4, "Collective Bargaining," pp. 62–90.

Garman, Phillips L., "Grievance Procedures in Health Care Establishments," *Journal of Health and Human Resources Administration* 2 (August 1979): 73–87.

Golembiewski, Robert T., "Civil Service and Managing Work," in Golembiewski, Robert T.; Gibson, Frank; and Cornog, Geoffrey Y., eds., *Public Administration: Readings in Institutions, Processes, Behavior, Policy,* 3rd ed., Chicago: Rand McNally, 1976. pp. 265–92.

Lester, Richard I., "Leadership: Some Principles and Concepts," *Personnel Journal* 60 (November 1981): 868–70.

Klingner, Donald E., "Federal Labor Relations After the Civil Service Reform Act," *Public Personnel Management* 9 (No. 3, 1980): 172–83.

Miller, George, "Management Guidelines: Being a Good Communicator," *Supervisory Management* 26 (April 1981): 20–26.

Podsakoff, Philip M., "Determinants of a Supervisor's Use of Rewards and Punishments: A Literature Review and Suggestions for Further Research," *Organizational Behavior and Human Performance* 29 (February 1982): 58–83.

United States Office of Personnel Management, *Manager's Handbook,* Washington, D.C.: United States Office of Personnel Management, 1980. Ch. 8, "Appeals and Grievances," pp. 98–105.

Zagovia, Sam, ed., *Public Works and Public Unions,* Englewood Cliffs, N.J.: Prentice-Hall, 1972.

Exhibit 1. Article XX of the Labor-Management Agreement

Overtime

Section A: The opportunity for overtime assignments will be rotated equitably among employees within the lowest organizational segment, in accordance with the particular skills determined to be necessary to accomplish the work to be performed on overtime.

Section B: In designating employees to work overtime the employer agrees to provide affected employees with advance notice when it is shown sufficiently in advance that employees may be required to work overtime on their usual days off. Employees will be notified of the overtime assignments no later than the start of their scheduled lunch periods on the day prior to the last day before their days off. The union recognizes that situations beyond the control of the employer may preclude advance notice. In these situations, the designated stewards, upon request, will be informed of the reason for the late notice of overtime assignments.

Section C: Rotational systems based on rosters established by seniority shall be utilized. Records of overtime worked and refused shall be maintained by supervisors to assure that each employee receives equitable consideration. These records may be reviewed by the designated steward upon request.

Exhibit 2. Article XIV of the Labor-Management Agreement

Management Rights

Section A: The employer retains the right in accordance with applicable laws, regulations, and the Executive Order to do the following:

1. Direct employees of the activity.

2. Hire, promote, transfer, assign, and retain employees in positions of the activity; and to suspend, demote, discharge, or take other disciplinary action against employees.

3. Relieve employees from duties because of lack of work or for other legitimate reasons.

4. Maintain the efficiency of the government operations entrusted to the employer.

5. Determine the methods, means, and personnel by which such operations are to be conducted.

6. Take whatever actions may be necessary to carry out the mission of the Air Force in situations of emergency.

41

Union Contract Negotiations in Springfield

The city of Springfield began negotiations in June with the American Federation of State, County, and Municipal Employees local for a three-year contract. The city's negotiations were conducted by City Manager Adam Arbuthnot under guidelines recommended by the labor negotiations committee of the City Council and approved by the full council. The union demanded an across-the-board wage hike of 10 percent and increased fringe benefits.

Progress in the negotiations and the positions of the local were reported regularly to the committee and council over the next several months, and the council held three special meetings each lasting more than two hours to hear from department heads and to discuss wages and benefits. The council reviewed data on wage increases for the past five years and compared these to rises in the cost-of-living index. The data revealed that nearly all employees had received pay hikes equal to, and in many instances exceeding, the rise in the cost of living during the period. Springfield's employees, according to the statistics, had fared better than workers nationally, and the council considered that its past wage actions had been reasonable.

In determining the wage increase for employees to keep up with the cost of living the council decided that increases in benefits during the year mandated by the federal government should be considered. These included the city's share in the Social Security tax increase and unemployment-compensation insurance premiums. The council also decided to take into consideration the employer's share of insurance premiums. It concluded that a wage increase for the next year should not exceed 4.59 percent for all employees.

The council was largely composed of small businessmanagers who hired only a few employees. They believed they were familiar with pay and working conditions in the community and felt that city employees were adequately compensated in comparison with employees in the private sector. They were bolstered in this belief in that there was a small turnover in nontechnical and semitechnical positions in city employment.

The city, however, was forced to modify its 4.59 percent limit on wage increases because of the union's firmness in its demands and continued rises in the monthly cost-of-living index. It increased the rate to 5.95 percent in August, to 6.3 percent in September, and finally to 6.5 percent in October. Councilmembers believed 6.5 percent was a very reasonable offer in that fringe benefits (retirement, Social Security, workers' compensation, and unemployment compensation) would raise the de facto pay and benefits increases to 7.2 percent.

Councilmembers acknowledged that the average cost-of-living index would exceed 7.5 percent but maintained that their offer was fair because last year the city had given a cost-of-living increase that exceeded the actual cost-of-living rise by 0.5 percent. In further justification, they maintained that the increases in the federally mandated Social Security tax and unemployment-compensation tax plus health-insurance cost increases raised benefits another 1 percent. The overall increase offered by the city, taking into consideration the proposed wage and benefits increase of 7.2 percent, the previous year's increase of 0.5 percent, and benefits increase of 1 percent, amounted to 8.7 percent.

By late October all issues between the city and union were tentatively resolved except for the union's insistence on a 7.5-percent, rather than the city's 6.5-percent, wage increase. An impasse having been reached, the union filed a request for conciliation and fact-finding with the state labor commissioner. Upon his recommendation, a three-year agreement calling for a 7.0 percent increase for the next year and additional increases the next two years at the rate of increase in the cost of living was accepted by both parties and signed on December 19.

Meanwhile, developments began over what seemed to be a minor matter—filling a vacancy in the Municipal Light Department—that were to upset the agreement. Two electric line workers (one the union steward and the other the secretary of the local) approached Mayor Thomas Wentwaller and asked to appear before the council to express employee concerns about employing an additional line worker. The line workers suggested that money could be made available for hiring better-qualified workers by charging for services that the city had been previously providing at no cost to electricity users. The council approved their suggestion and imposed a new service charge that permitted a pay increase for line workers.

The council believed that the increase was made with the full knowledge of the union, since the two line workers were members and officers and the president was also a line worker. Also, in the past the union had left decisions on merit increases and individual wage adjustments to the city. The council thought this situation was no different from others in which adjustments had been made and no complaints had been filed.

Although there was some grumbling about this action among the rank and file of the union, it took no formal action until April, when it filed a complaint with the state labor commissioner. It accused the city of violating collective-bargaining procedures and interfering with the union's affairs. The union contended that the city was required to hold to the 7-percent salary increase, that it had improperly given raises above that figure to a selected occupational classification (electric line workers), and that it had made special provisions for rates of pay and wages for specific individuals in the bargaining unit without inclusion of the union representative.

The union recognized the need for the city to award the pay increase to the line workers in order to compete with the private sector, especially the Southern Public Utility Corporation, but felt that competitive salary and wage problems existed in every department and that the same considerations and adjustments should be given to all employees. The union further believed that the city's unfair labor practice was creating a serious morale problem among employees that could have an adverse effect on the amount and the quality of work performed. The union asked that the city be ordered to return to the bargaining table and renegotiate rates of pay and wages for all employees covered by the bargaining unit.

The city itself saw the need for a higher percentage across-the-board increase than the 7.0 percent in the contract because of continued rises in the cost of living but decided to hold to it because of the complaint of engaging in improper practices filed with the labor commissioner. The city's defense filed with the commissioner made the following points:

1. The city's wage scales were competitive overall but a salary raise was necessary to fill the vacant line worker position.
2. The city had used benefits paid its employees as part of the percentage raise offered the union.
3. Union members had by-passed their official representatives in asking the increase for the line workers.
4. Merit raises had never before been the subject of grievances against the city.
5. The unlawful labor-practice suit was not filed until five months after the contract was signed.

Questions and Instructions

1. If you were the labor commissioner, how would you rule in the case? Why?
2. As a student learning about public personnel administration, how would you react to the following observations?

a. The line worker should not have been recognized for purposes of salary and wage negotiation by the City Council.
b. The basis for the wage increase should have been that it was a merit increase rather than an adjustment to the salary schedule.
c. The city manager was the official negotiator for the city and therefore should have been the party who conducted negotiations with the union.
d. Street Department employees are not so skilled as line workers and therefore should not expect the same salary schedule.
e. Regional competition for obtaining line workers is greater than for obtaining help in such departments as Street Repair, Sanitation, Water, and Police; the latter jobs are competitive only locally.

3. Do you think that public employees should have the right to form unions for the purpose of collective bargaining? Why?
4. Do you think public employees have the right to strike? Discuss.
5. In the area of labor-management relations, what functions should the mayor perform? the city manager? the City Council?

Selected Bibliography

Aaron, Benjamin; Grodin, Joseph R.; and Stern, James L., eds. *Public Sector Bargaining,* Washington, D.C.: Bureau of National Affairs, 1979.

Bluestone, Irving, "Emerging Trends in Collective Bargaining," in Kerr, Clark, and Rosow, Jerome M., eds., *Work in America: The Decade Ahead,* New York: Van Nostrand Reinhold, 1979. pp. 231–52.

Charles, Henry T., "Urban Manager Roles in the '70's," *Public Administration Review* 31 (January/February 1971): 20–27.

Gottlieb, Bernard, "Steadying the See-Saw of Public Sector Pay," *Personnel Management* 13 (March 1981): 32–35.

Greiner, John M.; Hatry, Harry P.; Koss, Margo P.; Millar, Annie P.; and Woodward, Jane P., *Productivity and Motivation,* Washington, D.C.: Urban Institute Press, 1981. Ch. 2, "The Nature of Monetary Incentives," pp. 17–26; Ch. 3, "Types of Monetary Incentives Used in the Public Sector," pp. 27–32; Ch. 4, "Incentives Involving Bonuses and Other One-Time Monetary Rewards," pp. 33–66; and Ch. 6, "Special Concerns Associated with Implementing Monetary Incentive Plans," pp. 95–105.

International City Management Association, *Employment Agreements Between Managers and Governing Bodies,* Washington, D.C.: International City Management Association, 1981.

Kalleberg, Arne L., "Work Values and Job Rewards: A Theory of Job Satisfaction," *American Sociological Review* 42 (February 1977): 124–43.

Lewin, David, and Horton, Raymond D., "The Impact of Collective Bargaining on the Merit System in Government," *Arbitration Journal* 30 (September 1975): 199–211.

Mosher, Lanning S., "Facing the Realities of Public Employee Bargaining," in Klingner, Donald E., ed., *Public Personnel Management,* Palo Alto, Calif.: Mayfield Publishing Co., 1981. pp. 339–44.

Schick, Richard P., and Couturier, Jean J., *The Public Interest in Government Labor Relations,* Cambridge, Mass.: Ballinger Publishing, 1977.

Stahl, O. Glenn, *Public Personnel Administration,* 7th ed., New York: Harper and Row, 1976. Ch. 20, "Collective Negotiation and Bargaining," pp. 338–56.

Stanley, David T., *Managing Local Government Under Union Pressure,* Washington, D.C.: Brookings Institution, 1972. Ch. 4, "Effect on Classification, Pay, and Benefits," pp. 60–88.

Torrence, William D., "Collective Bargaining and Labor Relations Training of State-Level Management," *Public Personnel Management* 11 (July/August 1973): 156–60.

Wellington, Harry, and Winter, Ralph K., Jr., *The Unions and the Cities,* Washington, D.C.: Brookings Institution, 1971.

42

Pariah in the Public Library

The Dale City Public Library was governed by a six-member board appointed by the mayor for two-year terms. It met standards for accreditation by the State Library Association by employing a director with a master's degree in library science, by having a minimum of fifty thousand volumes for circulation and five thousand volumes for reference, and by maintaining other requirements in staffing and facilities specified for a Class B city like Dale City. In addition to the director, the staff comprised three full-time assistant librarians, two part-time employees used chiefly at the check-out desk, and a janitor. From ten to fifteen volunteers served regularly in the library, and an association, Friends of the Library, carried on various activities for the benefit of the institution.

The previous year, the director of the library had resigned to take a similar position in a library in a larger city, and one of the assistant librarians, Suzanne Bickley, had been named acting director. Bickley was a member of a prominent family in the community and also popular with the library's clientele. While a search for a new director was under way, Bickley did outstanding work in supervising the moving of the library to a new building. Although Bickley lacked a master's degree in library science—she had a bachelor-of-arts degree with a major in English and had accumulated only six credits in library science in post-graduate work—she applied for the position of director.

Bickley's application created a dilemma for the library board in choosing a new director. It appreciated her efficiency in directing the library during the months following the director's resignation—especially her handling of the problems in the removal to a new building—and most members considered her capable of filling the position. She also had the backing of the officers and most of the members of Friends of the Library as well as her associates in the library. But if the library board were to name her director, it would mean losing state accreditation. Though a municipal library did not necessarily have to be accredited by the state, loss of accreditation would cause it to be dropped from membership in the State Association of Public

Libraries and make it ineligible for state grants-in-aid and very likely for federal grants as well.

At a meeting at which board members heard from Bickley supporters, the board voted 5 to 1 to appoint an outside candidate to the directorship mainly in order to keep the library eligible for governmental grants-in-aid. The successful candidate was Juanita Smithers, who had earned a master's degree in library science at the state university and who had two years' experience as an assistant librarian in a neighboring city. Smithers was not a complete stranger to Dale City, however, since she had attended Dale City Junior College two years before going on to the university.

Smithers's appointment caused an immediate uproar among Bickley's many supporters, who filled the letters column of the Dale City *Daily News* with protests for a week. Bickley contributed to the agitation by filing a suit in District Court against the library board alleging improprieties in the procedures followed in appointing the new director.

Smithers met with great hostility when she assumed the directorship. Bickley was openly rude, other staff members were uncooperative, the number of volunteer workers dropped, and the Friends of the Library discontinued some of its supportive activities. The situation had not improved very much after three months and Smithers was on the verge of resigning.

Questions and Instructions

1. Do you think Smithers should complain to the library board about the rudeness of Bickley and the lack of cooperation from other library employees?
2. What suggestions do you have for courses of action Smithers might institute to win acceptance in the community? To win acceptance from her staff?
3. Should the library board intervene in the situation?
4. What are some of the advantages and disadvantages of promoting from within an organization? From outside an organization?

Selected Bibliography

Alderfer, Clayton P., and Brown, L. Dave, *Learning from Changing: Organizational Diagnosis and Development,* Beverly Hills, Calif.: Sage Publications, 1975.

Caraley, Demetrios, *City Governments and Urban Problems,* Englewood Cliffs, N.J.: Prentice-Hall, 1977. Ch. 13, "City Private Elites," pp. 288–316.

Huntley, Robert J., and MacDonald, Robert J., "Urban Managers: Organizational Preferences, Managerial Styles, and Social Policy Roles," in *Municipal Yearbook 1975,* Washington, D.C.: International City Management Association, 1975. pp. 149–59.

Klingner, Donald E., *Public Personnel Management,* Englewood Cliffs, N.J.: Prentice-Hall, 1980. Ch. 7, "Job Analysis, Classification, and Evaluation," pp. 106–32, and Part 4, "Staffing," pp. 135–204.

Luthans, Fred, and Chapman, J. Brad, "The Female Leadership Dilemma," *Public Personnel Management* 4 (May/June 1975): 173–79.

Nirenberg, John, "Constraints to Effective Motivation," *Supervisory Management* 26 (November 1981): 24–29.

Provan, Keith G., "Board Power and Organizational Effectiveness Among Human Services Agencies," *Academy of Management Journal* 23 (June 1980): 221–36.

Radin, Beryl A., "Leadership Training for Women in State and Local Government," *Public Personnel Management* 9 (March/April 1980): 52–60.

Rice, Robert W., "Leader LPC and Follower Satisfaction: A Review," *Organizational Behavior and Human Performance* 28 (August 1981): 1–25.

Roos, Leslie L., Jr., and Hall, Roger I., "Influence Diagrams and Organizational Power," *Administrative Science Quarterly* 25 (March 1980): 57–71.

Schmitt, David R., "Performance Under Cooperation or Competition," *American Behavioral Scientist* 24 (May/June 1981): 649–79.

Shafritz, Jay M.; Balk, Walter L.; Hyde, Albert C.; and Rosenbloom, David H., *Personnel Management in Government: Politics and Process,* New York: Marcel Dekker, 1978. Ch. 7. "Recruitment, Selection, and Placement," pp. 117–39.

Stahl, O. Glenn, *Public Personnel Administration,* 7th ed., New York: Harper and Row, 1976. Ch. 5, "Classification of Positions," pp. 74–92.

Trounstine, Philip J., and Christensen, Terry, *Movers and Shakers: The Study of Community Power,* New York: St. Martin's, 1982. Ch. 2, "Social Science and the Study of Community Power," pp. 17–53, and Ch. 3, "A Primer in Power Structure Study," pp. 54–77.

Van Wagner, Karen, and Swanson, Cheryl, "From Machiavelli to Ms.: Differences in Male-Female Power Styles," *Public Administration Review,* 39 (January/February 1979): 66–72.

Weaver, Charles N., "What Women Want in a Job," *Personnel Administrator* 22 (June 1977): 66–71.

43

The Ordeal of Change

Alex Stone was an aggressive and determined young man with a drive to get things done quickly and efficiently. He had received a bachelor's and then a master's degree in public administration with a major in city management from a large Midwestern university. Upon receiving his second degree at the age of twenty-three and having been selected by the department as one of the most promising graduates, he turned to the network of earlier graduates known as the "True Connection" for assistance in getting a job. The alumni helped him obtain his first position as assistant city manager in Plainview, a city of about 100,000 population.

The city manager of Plainview was Frank Bartels, a member of the True Connection, who demanded much of his assistant but who took pains to teach him his job. In Plainview, Stone displayed his managerial talents best in municipal finance, job classification, and organization. He was respected rather than liked by employees, and he realized this. He never pretended to be a good politician, he would say, and preferred to leave the politicking and public relations to Bartels.

After five years as assistant city manager, Stone realized he had come to a dead end insofar as his own advancement in Plainview was concerned. He discussed his prospects with Bartels, who advised him to "strike out for his own city." Taking stock of his own assets and liabilities, Stone decided that Bartels was right. He realized that he had made some mistakes but he thought these were canceled by the recognition he had received for tasks expeditiously performed in Plainview.

Stone, as one would expect from his character, began his job search in a practical way. He prepared a comprehensive resume, passed the word among the True Connection and notified the job-placement office of his alma mater that he was looking for a new position and answered advertisements in the city-management and public-administration publications. But jobs were scarce in the central part of the state, where he hoped to locate. He did not, however, rule out going further afield. Finally, after several disappointments, he learned of an ideal opening in Sparta, a city in the state with a population of 175,000, that offered a salary of $52,000. With strong references from Bartels and Professor John McGee, the chairman of his graduate committee, and the support of the True Connection, Stone was invited to Sparta for interviews with the mayor, City Council members, and the city manager. These interviews went well, and an offer was quickly extended. Stone was elated and told Bartels on his departure from Plainview that he looked forward "to calling the shots from City Hall."

Stone found his first weeks on the job exciting. City officials, elective and appointive, were friendly and informative about municipal affairs and they welcomed a dynamic young administrator whom they thought likely to solve long-standing problems, some of which, Stone discovered, were acute. These did not worry him. He accepted the challenge of solving them, convinced that he would register his personal imprint on the city with a more efficiently operated government.

Singling out the personnel system for his first close examination, Stone asked for a summary profile of all employees and for a copy of all personnel policies, rules, and regulations. He was initially most interested in the system of job classification and pay, an area that he felt his knowledge and experience especially had prepared him to tackle.

After spending hours studying the reports, Stone discovered many disparities in job classification and many inequities in pay. The problem, he decided, was that the system, in operation for twenty-five years, had not been basically overhauled to meet the needs of a government that had assumed new services and responsibilities in recent years of rapid growth. Instead of being incorporated into the basic scheme, new classifications were added so that there was a multiplicity of them. In effect, Stone concluded, the generalizations and flexibility necessary for an adequate position classification had led to abuses within each "job family" or those jobs that were alike in the work performed and the skills needed for the required tasks. He decided, also, that misuse of seniority in making job assignments had played a part in the disparities he found in the system.

Because of the complexity of the problem, Stone felt that an outside evaluation of the personnel system by a management firm should be conducted. He submitted a request for proposal (RFP) to Public Management Consultants, a privately owned and locally based firm. It proposed that the position-classification system be examined through desk audits so that jobs could be properly grouped on the basis of job-related characteristics that pertained to satisfactory work performance.

The evaluation required two months. The report stated that "confusion is the only standard operating in the present classification system." It suggested a new hierarchical arrangement of positions based on the knowledge required, supervision given and received, complexity of the work performed, scope and effort of the tasks, physical demands of the work, and personal contacts and their purposes. Stone sent copies of the report to councilmembers and recommended its adoption. After a brief discussion of the report at a regular meeting, the council approved it by a vote of 4 to 1.

The next day Stone sent copies of the report to the director of personnel and the heads of line departments with a memo ordering them to implement the new classification system as quickly as possible. He stated that the new plan would bring about major changes in office arrangements, power and pay hierarchies, and office accountability.

City employees had been aware of the study being conducted of the classification system, but they had no idea of its extent until now. They reacted with fear and resentment. Those who held positions that would be reclassified were upset because generally they had become accustomed to doing things in certain ways and dreaded the uncertainty of new conditions. Some complained that the reclassification scheme would produce new inequities. In brief, they preferred following familiar paths to embarking on new ones.

At a meeting the department heads told Stone that implementation of the new system was encountering difficulties. Some of the more outspoken declared it would cause more problems than it would solve. Stone was shocked. He could not understand why a system worked out so carefully to introduce efficiency and economy into city operations and to correct inequities in work assignments and pay could meet with such opposition. Reform, he discovered, was easier to propose than to effect.

Questions and Instructions

1. If you were Stone, would you seek advice from Bartels? If you would not, why not? If you would, why? If you were Bartels, what advice would you offer Stone?
2. Is it fair to change job classifications for people who have tenure?
3. Would it have been desirable for Stone to have consulted with the heads of line departments before hiring Public Management Consultants? Before bringing the reclassification plan before the City Council? Before issuing the implementing order? Why?
4. What might happen to Stone's career in Sparta if he insists upon immediate implementation of the classification plan? If he backs down now, is it likely departmental heads and employees will see him as immature, inexperienced, and indecisive?
5. How is job classification related to human-resource planning?
6. What lessons should Stone have learned from this experience that might be helpful to him in making administrative and policy decisions? Discuss.
7. What appear to be Stone's basic faults as an administrator?

8. What criteria would you use in selecting an outside consultant? Should the consultant only be study oriented—that is, concerned with a personnel study—or should he or she also be process oriented—concerned with change implementation?

Selected Bibliography

Carrell, Jeptha J., "The City Manager and His Council: Sources of Conflict," *Public Administration Review* 22 (December 1962): 203–8.

Caruth, Don; Middlebrook, Bill; and Davis, Debra, "How to Communicate to Be Understood," *Supervisory Management* 27 (February 1982): 30–37.

Eddy, William B., "The Management of Change," in Powers, Stanley; Brown, F. Gerald; and Arnold, Davis S., eds., *Developing the Municipal Organization,* Washington, D.C.: International City Management Association, 1974. pp. 147–59.

Fletcher, Thomas W., "What Is the Future of Our Cities and the City Manager?" *Public Administration Review* 31 (January/February 1971): 14–20.

Frankenhuis, Jean Pierre, "How to Get a Good Consultant," *Harvard Business Review* 55 (November/December 1977): 133–39.

Ghropade, Jai, and Atchison, Thomas J., "The Concept of Job Analysis: A Review and Some Suggestions," *Public Personnel Management* 9 (No. 3, 1980): 134–44.

Jones, Pamela R.; Kaye, Beverly; and Taylor, Hugh R., "You Want Me to Do What?" *Training and Development Journal* 35 (July 1981): 56–62.

Kantor, Rosabeth Moss, "Power, Leadership, and Participatory Management," *Theory into Practice* 20 (Autumn 1981): 219–24.

Korda, Michael, *Power, How to Get It, How to Use It,* New York: Random House, 1975.

Kotter, John P., and Schlesinger, Leonard A., "Choosing Strategies for Change," *Harvard Business Review* 57 (March/April 1979): 106–14.

Lawton, Esther C., and Suskin, Harold, *Elements of Position Classification in Local Government,* Chicago: International Personnel Management Association, 1976.

Mansfield, Harvey, "Federal Executive Reorganization: Thirty Years of Experience," *Public Administration Review* 29 (July/August 1969): 332–45.

Meier, Kenneth J., "Executive Reorganization of Government: Impact on Employment and Expenditures," *American Journal of Political Science* 24 (August 1980): 396–412.

Patti, Rino J., "Organizational Resistance and Change: The View From Below," *Social Science Review* 48 (September 1974): 367–83.

Rehfuss, John, "Managing the Consultantship Process," *Public Administration Review* 39 (May/June 1979): 211–14.

Shafritz, Jay M.; Balk, Walter L.; Hyde, Albert C.; and Rosenbloom, David H., *Personnel Management in Government: Politics and Process*, New York: Marcel Dekker, 1978. Ch. 6, "Position Classification and Pay," pp. 93–116.

Solomon, Robert J., "Determining the Fairness of Salary in Public Employment," *Public Personnel Management* 9 (No. 3, 1980): 154–59.

Stromberg, Charles H., and Wilcox, Robert F., *The Urban Manager As an Agent of Planned Change*, Denver: The Graduate School of Public Affairs, University of Colorado-Denver, 1977.

Thayer, Paul W., "Personnel Challenges in the Eighties," *Public Personnel Management* 9 (No. 4, 1980): 327–35.

Thompson, John T., "Helping Line Managers to Be Change Agents," *Training and Development Journal* 35 (April 1981): 52–56.

U.S. Office of Personnel Management, *Position Classification: A Guide for City and County Managers*, Washington, D.C.: U.S. Government Printing Office, 1979.

———, *Goals and Techniques for a Merit Pay System*, Washington, D.C.: U.S. Government Printing Office, 1981.

44

Check-out for the Old Library

Stromberg, A Northwestern city of about ten thousand people, had completed the construction of a new public library, financed in part by a federal grant. The City Council was faced now with a decision on what to do with the old library building, which had been appraised at $70,000. It had been built in 1903 with a $10,000 donation from the Carnegie Library Fund. The granite-faced, two-story structure containing 4,262 square feet needed structural reinforcement and extensive repairs as well as new heating, air-conditioning, and electrical systems. The cost of rehabilitating the building had been set at a minimum of $35,000.

Discussion of what to do at a City Council meeting was so indecisive that members approved a motion that the city manager, Archibald Manders, be instructed to solicit the public's opinion by placing the following notice in the local newspaper:

> The city is considering the disposition of the old library building and land at the corner of Main Street and Elm Avenue and is seeking proposals for its use or sale.
>
> Any individual or group desiring to use or purchase it or with a good idea for its use by the community please contact Mayor Oscar Meacham at the City Hall.

At the next council meeting Mayor Meacham read three letters from among a number he had received regarding the old library building that he said represented, in his view, a significant body of public opinion.

The Stromberg chapter of the American Association of University Women (AAUW) wrote that it had gone on record in support of the preservation of the Carnegie Public Library building. "We are strongly opposed to any sale of the building," the letter said. "We feel it is a building that should be preserved as both a landmark and historic structure of Stromberg." The association suggested leasing of the building at a minimum sum to the Stromberg Area Arts Council and the Stromberg Area Teen Center.

The suggestion made by the American Association of University Women was endorsed by the Teen Center and Arts Council in a letter from Porter A. Olmstead, director of the Teen Center. "As far as we have heard, the Teen Center and Arts Council are the only service organizations that are seriously attempting to obtain the Carnegie Library, maintain it, and keep it for the community to use and enjoy," Olmstead wrote.

Mrs. Anthony A. Parrott, long a leader in social and cultural affairs, wrote strongly condemning any thought of demolition of the building. "Not only is it a landmark and eligible for registration as a historic site, but it is a major part of the cultural history of Stromberg," she pointed out. She described the structure as one of the few buildings in Stromberg of "real architectural charm and distinction." She declared that the "quartzite of the exterior and the oak of the interior could not be duplicated at any price."

Mayor Meacham also informed the council that one person had shown an interest in purchasing the old building and renovating it for office space. A representative of the library board, Mrs. Allen Bartleby, spoke in favor of selling the building and using the proceeds to purchase furniture and books for the new library. Further consideration of the building's disposition was postponed until the next council meeting.

At this meeting City Manager Manders presented a proposal at the request of a local law firm that desired to lease the library building. It offered to lease it from the city for a five-year period with rental payments of $960 a month. The firm would receive a credit of up to $380 a month for repairs and improvements it might make. The city would pay for electrical, heating, and plumbing improvements at an estimated cost of $14,400. At the expiration of the lease, the firm would retain first rights to renew the arrangement for another five-year term.

A motion approving the lease agreement between the city and the law firm was passed by a vote of 6 to 1. Those in favor held that it was the most economically sound proposal for what one councilmember called "a white elephant." The old structure, it was argued, was in such disrepair that an extra mill levy would have to be added to the property tax to pay for renovation, and upkeep of the structure would be a continuing burden. By leasing the building it would be preserved and satisfy those who valued it as an architectural asset and historic landmark. Marshall Alberts, Ward 1 councilmember, who cast the one dissenting vote, expressed his belief that public funds should not be used for private benefit and that the city should not be in "the landlord business."

The council's decision was attacked in an editorial in the next day's issue of the Stromberg *News,* and in the following week letters to the editor appeared vehemently condemning the "sell out" to the law firm and the council's failure to use the historic landmark for the benefit of the entire community. The agitation against the council's decision was climaxed by a public meeting at which councilmembers individually and collectively were denounced.

Two weeks later the city received a summons to answer in District Court a suit brought by a taxpayer, Theodore Andrews, to annul the lease on the following grounds:

1. It was beyond the defendant city's power and authority to lease its property to a private person for a private purpose.
2. The purported lease was in effect a contract for a public improvement that the city entered into contrary to the bidding procedures prescribed under municipal ordinances.
3. The lease restricted the city in the use of its property and its power to alienate the same for a period of more than one year.

Questions and Instructions

1. Should the City Council have sought the public's opinion on what to do with the old library building and then ignore what seemed to be that opinion?
2. Was it ethically proper for the city manager to present a persuasive offer for use of the building by the law firm?
3. To what extent should city officials, elective or appointive, follow public opinion in making decisions about municipal affairs? Can the public ever be sufficiently informed to pass upon certain matters? What should be the role of public opinion in governmental matters?
4. If public opinion is to be sought on a question, is an open hearing by a civic body adequate or should the question be submitted to the people in a referendum vote?
5. Besides a newspaper notice requesting ideas, a civic hearing, or a referendum, what other mechanisms for soliciting public opinion might have been useful in this situation and how would you proceed to use them? Would such mechanisms be feasible?
6. What commitment does a city owe to the past and to the future as far as historical sites and land use are concerned?
7. Should a search for outside financial or other assistance have been conducted?

Selected Bibliography

Anderson, Desmond, L., ed., *Municipal Public Relations,* Chicago: International City Management Association, 1966.

Arnold, David S., "Public Relations," in Banovetz, James M., ed., *Managing the Modern City,* Washington, D.C.: International City Management Association, 1971. pp. 377–401.

Broadnax, Walter D., "Making Public Agencies Accountable," in Vocino, Thomas, and Rabin, Jack, eds., *Contemporary Public Administration,* New York: Harcourt Brace Jovanovich, 1981. pp. 397–415.

Frederickson, H. George, ed., "Symposium of Social Equity and Public Administration," *Public Administration Review* 34 (January/February 1974): 1–51.

Huffcut, W. Harwood, ed., *Basic Techniques of Public Contracts Practice,* Berkeley, Calif.: California Continuing Education of the Bar, 1977.

Kiebola, Leo, "Government and Business: Adversaries or Partners for the Public Good," *Personnel Administrator* 20 (May 1975): 34–39.

Kline, Robert L., and Blanchard, Paul D., "Professionalism and the City Manager: An Examination of Unanswered Questions," *Midwest Review of Public Administration* 7 (July 1973): 163–74.

Lippmann, Walter, *Essays in the Public Philosophy,* Boston, Little, Brown, 1955.

———, *Public Opinion,* New York: Macmillan, 1947. See Part IV, "Interests," pp. 159–90, and Part VII, "Newspapers," pp. 317–65.

McTighe, John J., "Management Strategies to Deal with Shrinking Resources," *Public Administration Review* 39 (January/February 1979): 86–90.

Schubert, Glendon, *The Public Interest, A Critique of the Theory of a Political Concept,* Glencoe, Ill.: Free Press, 1960.

Staats, Elmer B., "An Era of Enduring Scarcity: Challenges and Opportunities," *National Civic Review* 69 (January 1980): 13–21.

Stillman, Richard J., *The Rise of the City Manager: A Public Professional in Local Government,* Albuquerque, N.M.: University of New Mexico Press, 1974.

Taebel, Delbert A., "Strategies to Make Bureaucrats Responsive," *Social Work* 17 (November 1972): 38–43.

Thomas, John Clayton, "Governmental Overload in the United States," *Administration and Society* 11 (February 1980): 371–91.

Tullock, Gordon, *Private Wants, Public Means: An Economic Analysis of the Desirable Scope of Government,* New York: Basic Books, 1970.

White, Louise G., "Improving the Goal-Setting Process in Local Government," *Public Administration Review* 42 (January/February 1982): 77–83.

Whitesett, David A., "Making Sense of Management Theories," *Personnel* 52 (May/June 1975): 44–52.

45

Meeting the Press

Readers of the *Capital Record* were shocked one morning to see under the byline of Gordon Redfield, the newspaper's chief investigative reporter, an account of the abuse of mentally retarded children in the three institutions operated by the State Department of Public Welfare. The story was announced as the first of a series.

In all three schools, the story alleged, mentally and physically handicapped residents had been subjected to repeated assaults by adult attendants who whipped, kicked, gagged, and battered them. Children unable to take care of themselves were frequently left unattended, the article continued, some to sit or lie in soiled diapers for hours.

The article quoted a former employee, a professional health-care worker, who told Redfield of one incident at the Meadowland School. After an eight-year-old girl with Down's syndrome refused to drink a glass of water, an attendant first slapped her repeatedly and then threw the water in her face.

In another incident, the former employee said, an attendant was treated for a hand injury he suffered when he struck a child at the school. "He hit the child with such force that he fractured his hand," she said.

At Hopeville School, Redfield reported, homosexuality among students was widespread and younger children were permitted to be mistreated by older residents. According to the story, residents were encouraged to assault a misbehaving child when an attendant wanted to punish a student but was worried about getting into trouble for striking him. An attendant would say, "Hey, Jimmy, go over there and show him you mean business," the story said.

The story related that at the third school, Greenbriar Center, two female attendants had submerged a retarded girl's head in a toilet bowl and flushed it while teaching her personal hygiene. Among the incidents taking place at the center were beating, "stretching," in which children were held down while their arms and legs were pulled up behind them, and controlling children by squeezing and twisting their genitals, sticking girls in the breasts with pins, and burning residents with cigarettes. "The month-long investigation of the three schools," Redfield wrote, "paints a picture of a system that condones violence while offering no support to those who attempt to report abusive, sometimes sadistic, treatment."

Television and radio news reporters, correspondents for the Associated Press and United Press International, and capitol correspondents for other newspapers eager to obtain the reaction to the allegations by officials in the Department of Welfare crowded the entranceway to the departmental offices when they opened at nine o'clock on the morning Redfield's first article appeared.

The director of the department, Jacob Christopher, arrived red-faced in anger and forced his way through the noisy crowd. "They're all lies," he shouted when asked about the Redfield charges, and he refused to answer other questions. "I've got more important things to do than concern myself with such slanders."

Later in the morning Karl Munster, Christopher's executive secretary, appeared before the reporters and fielded questions about the accuracy of the allegations and what the Department of Welfare intended to do in the way of verifying them. "The reports are replete with gross distortions and are wholly inaccurate and unjust," Munster said. "Redfield has taken bits and pieces out of context to give a completely false picture." He announced that beginning tomorrow there would be a series of press conferences at which staff members of the Welfare Department would present evidence to refute the charges in Redfield's story. "The so-called exposé," Munster said, "is doing a great injustice to staff and children in the state schools."

Because of the refusal of the Welfare Department to supply information, radio and television newscasts during the day, the afternoon newspapers, and dispatches of the wire services repeated the charges originally published in the *Capital Record.* Governor Winfield James at his noon press conference said he had "complete confidence" in the welfare director. "Only one side of the story has been given as yet," the governor said. "When the Welfare Department is able to gather information to present to the media, a different picture of conditions in the state schools will emerge."

Helen Osterman, superintendent of Meadowland School, questioned by one wire-service reporter, said that Redfield never tried to discuss conditions in the school with her. "He was here and asked a lot of questions about the school and town," Osterman said, "but he never brought up any allegations about the abuse of children. The allegations are not based on facts. We have one of the best schools for retarded children in the country." The superintendents at Greenbriar and Hopeville refused to talk to reporters, saying that they had been instructed to refer all inquiries to the Welfare Department.

At the scheduled press conference the next day reporters reacted angrily when they were told by Christopher's executive secretary, Karl Munster, that the welfare director was unable to attend. "The decision to have Mr. Christopher forgo a confrontation with the press," Munster said, "was based on the recommendation of counsel and staff." However, the director had prepared a statement about the allegations of abuse.

Christopher's statement was a blistering attack against sensationalism in the press. "It is impossible, and frankly undesirable, to answer every single slanderous and outrageous claim made by what, in my judgment, is irresponsible journalism," Christopher said. "The allegations so far made constitute a one-sided presentation of circumstances which have been thoroughly investigated by the department and remedies instituted when wrongs were found."

After Munster had read Christopher's statement, he introduced to the reporters Roswell McIntosh, Welfare Department attorney, and said that insofar as possible they would answer all questions from reporters. As the press conference continued, it soon became clear that not much information would be available. The reporters were told that many details had to be held confidential because they concerned medical matters. Munster and McIntosh sparred with reporters over whether welfare officials were going back on promises to release information, and whether they were trying to control the media through the format of an announced series of news conferences on the allegations.

"I'd give anything if we could open the complete files," Munster said. "It would make our case so much stronger. But it would be a violation of medical ethics for us to reveal information that should be held in confidence." He disclosed that he had a list of abuse reports made in the past year that had been checked by child-welfare units working with local district attorneys and not the department. Of a dozen alleged incidents, Munster said, only one was confirmed—that of the toilet-bowl incident—and the two employees involved had been fired.

The press conference ended with a promise by Munster to be prepared to give more information the next day when staff members would have had more time to obtain details. Reporters departed complaining of a cover-up by the Welfare Department. Later in the day they were further irked when they learned that the department had employed a public-relations specialist, Clyde Manfred, to help in its campaign to counter allegations surrounding the state schools for the retarded.

That the Welfare Department was more intent in protecting itself than in discovering the facts about the *Capital Record*'s charges was indicated next day when Munster opened the press conference by introducing Lester Schlegel, president of the Parent and Guardian Association at the Greenbriar Center. "We are receiving solid support from the associations of parents and guardians for the centers," he said.

Schlegel said he had visited Greenbriar unannounced several times and never saw a state employee abusing a retarded inmate. "As a parent of a child, I am appalled at the news coverage," Schlegel said. "If there was abuse going on, I would be the first person to come down on their necks." He disclosed that he was sending letters to all parents of children at Greenbriar asking them "to share my feelings of protest." "I want them to write their legislators, the newspapers, the governor—whoever it takes," he declared.

The second press conference was about as frustrating for reporters as that of the first day. Some instances of abuse cited in the *Capital Record*'s reports, it seemed, could not be clarified because of the confidentiality of medical reports, others were explained away by improbable excuses, and the stories of former employees of conditions could not be trusted. Reporters roared with laughter when Munster explained that the story of an employee who had injured a hand by striking a retarded student too hard was false. The employee apparently was so frustrated when he himself was hit by a student he was trying to control that he struck a wall and bruised his hand. However, because of the allegations made by the newspaper, the department would look further into the matter.

Munster renewed his criticism of former employees from whom reporters obtained information about abuse at the schools. Of the employee who said she saw a young girl stuck in the breasts with pins, Munster said she had been urged to provide more detailed information, including names and dates, but she had failed to do so. "If she had knowledge of a crime, she ought to be calling the police or the district attorney and not the press," Munster said. "Child abuse is a criminal offense and anyone with knowledge of such an offense should report it to the district attorney or other appropriate authorities."

Later in the day it was revealed that support of the Welfare Department was not quite so strong among parent-guardian groups as Munster had indicated at his morning press conference. Mrs. Rosa Gonzalez, president of the group at Hopeville, said she had been asked to attend the conference but had declined. "My child is receiving good treatment at the school," she said, "but I am concerned about the charges. I think the news accounts might spur more interest in the welfare of the retarded, and if it does that will be a good thing. I'm not sure that putting the retarded away in schools far from their families is a good thing. There should be a better way."

Criticism of the care of the retarded in large institutions was also expressed by Mildred Carnahan, chairman of the Council for the Mentally Retarded. "There are always going to be problems in institutional settings," she said. "That's one of the reasons why we are trying to get money to fund some sheltered workshops in the state for these people. We are trying to get two million dollars from the legislature for thirty-five such workshops."

Apparently bowing to the widespread publicity about conditions in the schools for the retarded and media charges of a cover-up, Governor James announced four days after the *Capital Record* series began that he had asked the State Bureau of Investigation to conduct a probe of the charges. The governor said that he had asked the newspaper for a complete set of its series as well as any data documenting the allegations but that his request had been denied.

James said he would not ask the welfare director or any department officials to leave their positions while the investigation was under way. It would interfere with the operations of the department, James said. "I don't think it's fair," he added, "to say you need new leadership until the investigation is completed."

Once the investigation was completed, James said, the bureau's report would be turned over to the appropriate district attorneys to determine if laws were violated and criminal charges were warranted. By law, he explained, the bureau's report could be divulged only to prosecutors and not the public, any wrongdoing to be revealed only if charges were filed.

The allegations of abuse of the retarded were also discussed in the legislature, but a resolution in the house to conduct an investigation was voted down on the ground that the Bureau of Investigation was the proper body to probe into possibly criminal matters.

Questions and Instructions

1. In general, how would you describe the Department of Welfare's relations with the press?
2. Do you think the department was attempting to conceal from the public conditions in the school or was it merely reacting naturally to adverse publicity?
3. Did the welfare director's legal counsel and staff make the right decision when they advised him not to confront reporters at the press conference?
4. Do you think the Welfare Department representatives were sincere in calling a series of press conferences to provide information or, as reporters charged, was it an attempt to manipulate the press?
5. Was it a wise move for the department to employ a public-relations specialist to advise it in dealing with the press in respect to the allegations of child abuse?
6. If you were a public-information or press-relations employee of the Welfare Department, how would you have handled the situation created by the newspaper's exposé?
7. Do you think it desirable for a government agency to employ a press-

relations or public-information specialist? If so, how would you specify his or her duties?

8. When administrators are confronted by scandals or wrongdoing in their agencies, would it be wiser for them to be frank and open with the press or to seek to conceal the facts? Discuss.
9. From the information in this case history, how would you rate the Welfare Department as to goals and practices?

Selected Bibliography

Abney, Glenn, and Lauth, Thomas P., *The Politics of State and City Administration,* Albany, N.Y.: State University of New York Press, 1986. Ch. 2, "The Tasks of State Administrators," pp. 21–39.

Anderson, Desmond L., ed., *Municipal Public Relations,* Chicago: International City Management Association, 1966.

Belk, Judy V., "What to Do When the News Is Bad," *Public Management* 62 (September 1980): 8–10.

Berkley, George E., *The Craft of Public Administration,* 3rd ed., Boston: Allyn and Bacon, 1981. See "The Questions of Secrecy," pp. 257–64, and "Public Relations," pp. 436–46.

Cutlip, Scott M., and Center, Allen H., *Effective Public Relations,* 4th ed., Englewood Cliffs, N.J.: Prentice-Hall, 1971. Ch. 17, "Working with the Media," pp. 406–28; Ch. 22, "The Practice: Welfare Agencies, Hospitals and Churches," pp. 501–27; and Ch. 23, "The Practice: Governments and Citizens," pp. 528–57.

Gilbert, William H., ed., *Public Relations in Local Government,* Washington, D.C.: International City Management Association, 1975.

Kelly, Stanley, Jr., *Professional Public Relations and Political Power,* Baltimore: Johns Hopkins Press, 1956. Ch. 7, "The Political Role of the Public Relations Man," pp. 202–35.

Linsky, Martin, "Legislatures and the Press: The Problems of Image and Attitude," *State Government* 59 (Spring 1986): 40–45.

Rabin, Jack, and Dodd, Don, eds., *State and Local Government Administration,* New York: Marcel Dekker, Inc., 1985.

Scheffer, Walter F., "The Clienteles of Executive Branch Agencies," in Vocino, Thomas, and Rabin, Jack, eds., *Contemporary Public Administration,* New York: Harcourt Brace Jovanovich, 1981. See "Public Relations," pp. 136–37.

Schmidt, Frances, and Weiner, Harold N., ed., *Public Relations in Health and Welfare,* New York: Columbia University Press, 1966.

Starling, Grover, *Managing the Public Sector,* rev. ed., Homewood, Ill.: Dorsey Press, 1982. See "Distortion," pp. 145–49.

46

Treated Like Dogs

Margaret McChesney, personnel director for the city of Oakdale, was greatly disturbed after Cranston Hume, investigative reporter for the *Daily Tribune,* left her office after telling her that the 250 employees in the Street Maintenance Division were disgruntled and talked among themselves of a violent confrontation with officials if working conditions did not improve.

She herself had heard rumors to this effect but had not realized how extensive the dissatisfaction was until Hume told her of interviews he had conducted at the maintenance yard on three evenings. It was another instance, she felt, of the poor communication between her office, the city manager, the street-maintenance director, and the business agent of the American Federation of State, County, and Municipal Employees local: it took a reporter to let one know what was going on. The situation was bad, she thought, and publicity could only make it worse.

Her fears were confirmed two days later when the *Daily Tribune* carried Hume's story under an eight-column headline on page one, "Angry Street Workers Predicting Confrontation with City," and continued for almost a full page on the inside.

"The maintenance workers are angry," Hume had written. "They're looking for respect. They want someone—either the city administration or the union to which they pay dues—to listen to their grievances and do something. More than a score of workers interviewed at quitting time at the maintenance yard complained that their supervisors treat them as if they are slaves or prison inmates."

As she read quotation after quotation from workers, McChesney's consternation grew, and nothing that other city officials and the union business agent were reported to have said indicated that they were prepared to handle the situation with understanding or effectiveness.

Some of the more telling complaints of workers appeared early in the story. "They treat us like we're in prison or something," Wayne North, an eleven-year veteran of the Street Division was quoted as saying. "A lot of people, when they get up in the morning, they just hate to go to work."

Another worker, Vincent Esposito, said: "They treat all the workers—black or white—like dogs. It's just like hell. I just hate to walk through that gate in the morning. It's the same for all of us."

Minority workers were equally vehement. Joseph Washington, a truck driver, said: "When a black gets old, they say either quit or be fired. When whites get old, they keep them on. You go in the yard and look. We've got old white workers all over this place."

A crew worker, Bobby Anderson, agreed, interjecting, "You won't see any old blacks around here."

McChesney could identify with these statements since, upon entering public service, she had suffered from discrimination against blacks in her own career.

Hester Adams, who said she was fired because she overslept one morning, was incensed over the treatment of women maintenance workers. "I do believe my job was in jeopardy from the very day I started," she said. "From the very beginning they told me I didn't want this job. They said I wouldn't be able to stand the heat. Generally, everybody fears for their job. I knew for a fact women would not advance. I was told not to even try."

But if women saw little opportunity for advancement while working in Street Maintenance, the same was true of many of the men. "If you're hired as a laborer, you stay a laborer," Ernie Devers, an employee of ten years' standing said. "You know, you want to try to better yourself. You don't want to be a laborer all your life. But you have to sneak behind your supervisor's back to get a transfer."

"You want to know how you make supervisor?" interposed Ben Costello. "Snitching. That's how."

Others complained, in respect to advancement, that the director of the Street Division, Luther Schultz, played favorites. "If you're in the clique, everything is rosy," Matthew McNeil said. "If you're not, you don't stand any more chance of getting ahead than a snowball in hell."

Some complained that promotions were based on oral examinations rather than seniority or demonstrated job skills. "They give an oral test," said Terry O'Hara. "They don't give any other test. How can you prove if you passed or flunked?"

Workers considered many of the rules governing the maintenance division as petty and criticized enforcement as inconsistent and unfair. "If you want to go to the bathroom, you have to ask your supervisor," said Martin Steinberg, a crew worker. "If your supervisor's not there, you ask the crew chief. And if the crew chief's not there, you get written up."

The news story said that written reprimands and other forms of punishment were doled out with no apparent adherence to an established policy. Martha Dolfuss, for example, was quoted as saying: "There are no rules on reprimands. One person might be late once and get a reprimand. I might be late five times and I might not get one."

A rule forbade all maintenance workers from entering stores to buy food or drink at lunchtime or during their twice-daily, fifteen-minute break periods. Nevertheless, workers complained, supervisors ignored this and other rules for themselves while they imposed them on those they supervised. "The bosses can do anything they want, can go anywhere they want any time," complained George Alfredo. "You've got to get permission to go to the bathroom. If you get a Coke while you're there, you get a reprimand."

"The rule book says 'city employees,'" said Dolfuss. "If supervisors aren't city employees, then who is?"

As she read the complaints, McChesney came to realize what most of the workers seemed to feel but seldom were able to express: they wanted to be treated like human beings. One worker, Art Matthews, put it very well: "There's a different set of rules for us than other city employees. We're treated like a bunch of machines. There's no consideration for your personal feelings whatsoever. It's like a war—it's management on one side and us on the other."

Hume's story summed up the situation: "What the Street Division is facing," the reporter wrote, "is a near-total breakdown in the established system of resolving disputes. No one in management, the workers believe, apparently wants to listen."

McChesney decided this conclusion was borne out in part by comments made by City Manager Edward Mayes, Street Division Director Luther Schultz, and even the union agent Karl Moscowitz. They did not say anything strongly adverse about the street-maintenance workers, but they were not particularly favorable either.

Mayes said that frequent complaints by citizens of lazy municipal employees and poor maintenance made it difficult to relax stringent work rules that were adopted to insure efficiency. "You may be inclined to believe the complaints you hear every day about how incompetent and dilatory the people who work for the city are," he said. "In most cases, the complaints are unfounded, but taxpayers have a right to expect people who work for them to put in a day's work for a day's pay."

Schultz belittled the notion that there was a serious labor-management problem in his division. "Any employer that has about 250 people working for him," Schultz said, "is bound to have some personnel problems. Things right now aren't any worse than in the past."

Schultz defended the use of oral examinations in deciding on promotions. He explained that these were used in order not to discriminate against employees who could not read or write well. "We do not mistreat anybody," he continued. "We treat everybody fair and equal. We expect no more than a day's work for a day's pay. If we didn't have strict work rules, there would be chaos."

The union agent, Moscowitz, shrugged off most of the complaints made by maintenance employees. "You should check the work records of some of those employees," he said. "They've got such good benefits they abuse them."

Moscowitz spoke in favor of the work rules, saying that conditions in the past had become so slack that regulations had to be adopted. "I don't necessarily agree with all the things that the city does," he said. "I try to see the employees' side—that's what they pay me for. But I also understand management's problems. I learned a long time ago that if you don't tell workers when they're wrong, you can get into deep trouble."

Reading a comment by the city manager, McChesney had to agree with him that the union had not been especially active in the workers' defense, because it informed her, as Moscowitz had not, that dissatisfaction in the Street Division had reached the stage of almost open revolt. The city manager was reported as saying: "The union is there to assure people they have some place to go with their complaints. If they can't talk to their supervisors, they should talk to their union steward. If they can't work with that person, they ought to get a new one."

McChesney had told the *Daily Tribune* reporter of her efforts to improve the labor-management communications, which received a paragraph buried deep in the news article. She had not mentioned that in her efforts she had received little cooperation from other city officials. One of the plans she had proposed was the establishment of "quality circles" in which employees would be given an opportunity to bring up their problems and suggest how they might be resolved. Her fellow managers did not think much of the idea.

She had explained to the reporter that quality circles (QCs) are small groups of people, ideally seven or eight members of an organization, who perform similar tasks in the same area and who voluntarily participate in regular meetings to identify, analyze, and solve quality, productivity, and organization problems. Although conceived in Japan, QCs have been one of the fastest-growing concepts in the United States in terms of behavioral and managerial applications. She had explained that QCs are used in government, the armed forces, hospitals, and insurance, banking, manufacturing, and public-utility firms. They are designed to reduce errors and enhance the quality of the finished goods or services, promote cooperation and teamwork, increase job involvement and employee motivation, facilitate organizational communication, and develop the leadership capabilities of managers and workers.

McChesney had urged that the city experiment in the use of QCs, but Mayes, the city manager, had objected that the plan seemed to him too time-consuming and theoretical and Schultz, the Street Division director, had said the idea would not work with street-maintenance workers—they would not want to be bothered.

That evening McChesney noted that television news reporters had followed up on the *Daily Tribune*'s article with their own interviews with workers at the street-maintenance yard. The workers seemed to be enjoying their moment in the spotlight. She went to bed with some foreboding of how the situation might develop; she did not think it would just go away.

Questions and Instructions

1. What actions might be taken by officials to ward off an immediate confrontation between the city and the street-maintenance workers?
2. What are the responsibilities of the personnel manager in maintaining labor peace? The mayor and City Council? The division directors?
3. Do you think that the newspaper and television publicity about the dissatisfactions of the maintenance workers will make a strike or confrontation more or less likely?
4. There does not seem to be rapport between the Oakdale city manager, personnel director, and division directors. Should they work together more closely to detect and prevent such situations as that arising in the Street Maintenance Division?
5. Do you think the quality-circle idea would be successful in solving the problems of worker dissatisfaction? How would you implement such a program? What city office should be in charge of such a program? Should the labor union be brought into the program?
6. What other programs—an employee publication, social affairs, sports programs, recreation clubs—might be introduced to develop better relations between the city and its employees? Discuss and evaluate.
7. What behavioral assumptions underpin participative management techniques and approaches? How do they differ from authoritarian approaches? Explain.
8. Is there any way of improving the image of unskilled-labor jobs in the eyes of the workers and the public?

Selected Bibliography

Argyris, Chris, and Cyert, Richard M., *Leadership in the 80's,* Cambridge, Mass.: Institute for Educational Management, Harvard University, 1980.

Bryant, Stephen, and Kearns, Joseph, "Workers' Brains as Well as Their

Bodies: Quality Circles in a Federal Facility," *Public Administration Review* 42 (March/April 1982): 144–150.

Contino, Ronald, and Lorusso, Robert M., "The Theory Z Turnaround of a Public Agency," *Public Administration Review* 42 (January/February 1982): 66–72.

Dewar, Donald L., *Quality Circles: Answers to 100 Frequently Asked Questions,* Red Bluff, Calif.: Quality Circle Institute, 1979.

Fisher, John E., "Dealing with Office Politics in Authoritarian-Dominated Staff Organizations," *Public Personnel Management* 8 (January/February 1979): 56–63.

Fisher, John E., "The Authoritarian As Anti-Manager," *Public Personnel Management* 7 (January/February 1978): 33–41.

Griener, John; Dahl, Roger E.; Hatry, Harry P.; and Millar, Annie P., "The Waste Collection Division and Its Incentive Plan," in Bozeman, Barry, and Straussman, Jeffrey, eds., *New Directions in Public Administration,* Monterey, Calif.: Brooks/Cole Publishing Co. 1984. pp. 269–80.

King, Albert S., "Expectation Effects in Organization Change," *Administrative Science Quarterly* 19 (June 1974): 221–30.

Klein, Gerald D., "Implementing Quality Circles: A Hard Look at Some of the Realities," *Personnel* 58 (November/December 1981): 11–20.

Lyden, Fremont J., "Power Driven Managers Make the Best Bosses," *Public Administration Review* 36 (March/April 1976): 201–2.

Monte, Rudeen, "The Productivity Environment of Trust, Autonomy, and Initiative," *Quality Circles Journal* 4 (August 1981): 13–15.

Neugarten, Dail Ann, "Themes and Issues in Public Sector Productivity," *Public Personnel Management* 9 (No. 4, 1980): 229–34.

Rosow, Jerome M., "Quality of Work Life Issues for the 1980's," *Training and Development Journal* (March 1981): 33–52.

Walker, Donald E., "When the Tough Get Going, the Going Gets Tough: The Myth of Muscle Administration," *Public Administration Review* 36 (July/August 1976): 439–45.

47

The Polygraph Controversy

Arnold Beckman, administrator of the Children's Convalescent Center, became choleric when a reporter from the *Daily News* called on him to inquire about rumors the center was not maintaining standards set for sanitation, medical care, and safety. He told the reporter the rumors were false and demanded to know who had made the accusations. The reporter replied that the information was obtained from a reliable source whose identity he could not reveal because it was given to him in confidence.

The reporter told Beckman that, according to his source, the children were given only one tub bath a week, their teeth were seldom brushed, and their bed linens went unlaundered for days. He also said faults found by fire department examiners two months before—including lack of smoke detectors, fire alarms, and emergency lighting and inoperative fire extinguishers—had not yet been corrected.

The center was one of three licensed in the state by the Department of Human Services to care for children with multiple handicaps. The deficiencies cited by the reporter were, in Beckman's view, circumstantial, which led him to believe that the information was obtained from a member of his staff. Although the center was licensed by the Department of Human Services, supervisory authority was also shared by the Department of Health and the Department of Education. The center gave long-term care to nonambulatory patients ranging from infants to children of fourteen years. At present, sixty-four children occupied beds.

Determined to discover the informant and get rid of him or her, Beckman called a meeting of his staff of forty-three persons. He told them of the reporter's visit and said he believed the informant was an employee of the center. "Such a spy and traitor in our midst cannot be tolerated," Beckman declared. "You all know that I have constantly been improving the center in the three years since I came here. We all know that things are not perfect, but perfection takes time. Nearly all of you have given me your loyal support and you care as much as I do about the helpless children in our charge. We can't have a talebearer in our midst who carries misleading stories to the outside that may give us a bad name and hinder us in our ministrations."

Beckman asked staff members to reveal to him the name of the informant, if they knew it. After his request drew no response, he interviewed all staff members but still did not discover a clue to the culprit. His anger increased by his lack of success, Beckman decided to hire a firm of polygraph experts to give lie-detector tests to all personnel.

Yuko Ineh, head nurse and second in command in the center, objected to the tests. She questioned the accuracy of such tests and believed they would have an adverse effect on morale. As a nurse she was well acquainted with the different reactions of people, particularly nervous or timid ones, to such tests which often made them unreliable. Requiring employees to undergo lie-detection tests would upset them, she argued, increase tension, and spread suspicion in the staff. Worse, the tests would be resented because people would feel they were no longer considered trustworthy. She could never approve, Ineh said, of any attempt by the center to compel, frighten, or manipulate staff members into making confessions by what she considered the unscientifically and psychologically unsound procedure of polygraph machine testing. Many might resign, she told Beckman, and seek more pleasant and better-paying jobs elsewhere. She reminded him that recruiting of new employees was already difficult and turnover was great.

Beckman was not convinced by these arguments. He pointed out to Ineh that polygraph tests were accepted as reliable evidence in the courts of about twenty states, that they were widely used in business to screen job applicants, and that they had saved business and industry millions of dollars by preventing or exposing graft and corruption. Finally, he noted, the tests were heavily relied upon by police and intelligence agencies of the government. Lie-detection tests, he maintained, were a part of life today and everybody should get used to them.

Questions and Instructions

1. Do you think Beckman was justified in seeking the identity of the informant rather than addressing himself to the deficiencies in the operation of the center?
2. What faults, if any, do you find in the way Beckman chose to discover the reporter's informant?
3. Do you think Beckman would be justified in firing the informant to stop the spread of harmful information about the center?
4. What are your views on polygraph testing of government employees?
5. Would you in Beckman's position resort to polygraph testing?

Selected Bibliography

Azzaretto, John F., "Integrating Management and Leadership," *Public Management* 68 (August 1986): 14–16.

Becker, Christine, "Improving Communication Skills," *Public Management* 69 (April 1987): 12–15.

Bellman, Geoffrey M., *The Quest for Staff Leadership,* Glenview, Ill.: Scott, Foresman, 1985.

Bettman, Ralph B., "Technical Managers Mismanaged: Turnover or Turnaround?" *Personnel Journal* 66 (April 1987): 64–70.

Herron, Daniel J., "Statutory Restrictions on Polygraph Testing in Employer-Employee Relationships," *Labor Law Journal* 37 (Spring 1986): 632–38.

Hershey, Cary, *Protest in the Public Service,* Lexington, Mass.: Lexington Books, 1973.

Honts, Charles Robert; Hodes, Robert L.; and Raskin, David C., "Effects of Physical Countermeasures on the Physiological Detection of Deception," *Journal of Applied Psychology* 70 (February 1985): 177–87.

Hummel, Ralph P., *The Bureaucratic Experience,* 3rd ed., New York: St. Martin's Press, 1987. Ch. 3, "The Psychology of Bureaucracy," pp. 123–78.

Kaufman, Herbert, "Fear of Bureaucracy: A Raging Pandemic," *Public Administration Review* 41 (January/February 1981): 1–9.

Kleinmuntz, Benjamin, "Lie Detectors Fail the Truth Test," *Harvard Business Review* 63 (July/August 1985): 36–37.

Lee, Yong S., "Civil Liability of State and Local Governments: Myth and Reality," *Public Administration Review* 47 (March/April 1987): 160–70.

Lykken, David T., "Detecting Deception in 1984," *American Behavioral Scientist* 27 (March/April 1984): 481–99.

Medina, William A., "Managing People to Perform," *The Bureaucrat* 14 (Spring 1985): 52–55.

Mischkind, Louis A., "Seven Steps to Productivity Improvement," *Personnel* 64 (July 1987): 22–30.

Peters, Thomas J., and Austin, Nancy, *A Passion for Excellence,* New York: Random House, 1985.

Peters, Thomas J., and Waterman, Robert H., Jr., *In Search of Excellence: Lessons from America's Best Run Companies,* New York: Harper and Row, 1982.

Reed, Sally, "Commitment to Employees Results in a Better-Served Public," *Public Management* 69 (April 1987): 9–11.

White, Lawrence T., "Attitudinal Consequences of the Preemployment Polygraph Examination," *Journal of Applied Social Psychology* 14 (August 1984): 364–74.

48

A Message from Al Anon

Bernard S. Baxter, director of the State Department of Health, received the following anonymous letter:

Dear Sir:

I work as a technician in the medical laboratory. We have a woman employed here who is an alcoholic. She does blood and urine chemistries and blood typing, and often makes mistakes that others find and correct. Mondays are the worst. She often comes to work with a hangover and sometimes with the odor of alcohol on her breath. Our supervisor knows of the situation and has given her many chances. The rest of us are tired of mopping up after her and keeping an eye on everything she does. I thought you should know about this situation.

Al Anon

Questions and Instructions

1. What action should Baxter take about the laboratory supervisor?
2. Should Baxter issue a memorandum to the staff to report to him privately about any alcohol or drug abuse by employees?
3. If the department has an assistance program for the treatment of alcoholism, what special provisions should be included to take care of employees in such sensitive positions as laboratory technicians?

49

Gagging City Employees

When a $5 million civil-rights lawsuit was filed challenging Reedsburg's controversial ordinance requiring some convicted drunk drivers to place stickers on their automobiles, comments by several officials were quoted in newspaper, radio, and television reports. At the request of the city attorney, the city manager issued the following memo to department heads:

> City employees should not grant interviews to newspaper, radio, or television reporters on any lawsuits brought against the city, any of its divisions, or any of its officials. Employees' comments on such lawsuits may cause embarrassment to the city and adversely influence the handling of the litigation.
>
> Employees should instead direct all reporters seeking information to the city attorney's office. Department heads are instructed to take action against violators of this policy, the nature of the action to be determined by themselves. This policy applies to all city departments, including those with public information officers.

The memo resulted in protests by some employees that it violated their constitutional right of freedom of speech, by some department heads that they should have the chance to present their side of an issue to the public, and by information officers because an important part of their job is dealing regularly with the media.

Questions and Instructions

1. Do you consider imposing a gag on employees justified?
2. Does such an order violate the right of free expression?
3. How do you react to the protests of department heads and information officers about the policy?
4. Is the public's right to information about their government violated by the order?

50

A Charge of Favoritism

Jerry Strickmore had been director of the Employment Services division of the State Employment Security Commission five years before his attention was attracted romantically to Patricia Fellows, a long-time staff member of the Special Programs section of his division. Their professional relations became personal ones and they began dating regularly.

When Fellows decided to apply for the vacant position of Special Programs director, Strickmore had no objection. To avert allegations of favoritism in the selection process, Strickmore sought to exclude himself from any involvement. He told Blanche Empson, executive director of the commission, about the situation and gained approval to appoint a five-member selection committee. Nevertheless, the committee's appointment of Fellows to the position was poorly received. Adverse comment reached even the state legislature when a frequent critic of the commission declared among other charges that the promotion "had a devastating effect on the morale of other employees."

Questions and Instructions

1. Should the head of a department date an employee?
2. Could Strickmore have done anything else to avoid criticism of the promotion given Fellows?
3. Should Strickmore respond to the criticism made by the member of the legislature.

51

An Improper Book Sale?

Two years after Jacob Wiener, controversial director of the State Department of Health, was forced to resign after a legislative investigation, a book lauding his contributions and defending his long career appeared. It was titled *Extending the Frontiers of Health: A Biography of Jacob Wiener.*

The new director, Oscar Burnside, deputy director under Wiener, photocopied an advertisement offering the book for sale at a discount to employees and sent copies to department heads with a memo asking them to take orders for the volume. Many employees felt this was an attempt to coerce them into buying the book and complained to department heads. A physician at the state's teaching hospital wrote a letter of objection to a member of the legislature in which she stated: "The attempt of the director of health to force this book on staff members is a flagrant abuse of power. I for one think he has more important things to do than trying to build up the reputation of a discredited administrator." Burnside defended his action, saying: "I was responding to requests within the department for the book about a man I admire. The cut-rate offer was made by the publisher. Employees have not been asked to buy the book. They have only been made aware of its availability at a discounted price."

Questions and Instructions

1. Do you think Burnside acted improperly in announcing the discount offer?
2. Should he have used department facilities in copying the advertisement?
3. Do you think an administrator should ever promote among employees his or her personal interests unrelated to their work?

52

A Thief among Us

Alicia Clodfelter, director of the Trauma Care Unit of Westport Veterans Medical Center, was troubled by an increasing number of staff complaints of lost or stolen personal articles and money while on duty. Inclined to respond quickly to problems, Clodfelter prepared the following memorandum to members of the TCU staff:

> Attention! There's a thief at large in the Trauma Care Unit! During the past month money and valuables totaling more than $200 have been stolen from staff members while at work.
>
> Please take the precaution of securing all valuables brought to work and leave large sums of cash at home, because their security cannot be assured by the unit. I know such precautions may be troublesome, but they are necessary so long as a socially maladjusted, morally catatonic throw-back is abroad in the land!"

Questions and Instructions

1. What other methods could Clodfelter have employed to apprise employees of theft in the workplace?
2. Does her memorandum provide sufficient information on the nature and magnitude of the thefts so that preventive measures can be taken?
3. What, if anything, was wrong with the Clodfelter memorandum?

53

A Prophylactic Measure

As director of personnel services for the Elmwood Department of Public Works, Margaret Ladd had periodically issued informational leaflets for a series called "Life-styles and Employment" on such varied topics as stress management, sexual harassment, self-relaxation techniques, burnout, alcohol and drug abuse, retirement, and affirmative action. They had been well received, she thought, but she was worried about the response to her latest publication dealing with sexually transmitted diseases (STDs). It was entitled "Use of the Condom." Following the policy urged by the U.S. surgeon general, Ladd dealt realistically with the topic and avoided the euphemisms and vague expressions employed by some in presenting the dangers of STDs to the public. She believed the television warnings on STDs were so "tastefully" done in their effort not to offend moral sensitivities that they often did not reveal the real dangers.

Ladd's article outlined the magnitude and gravity of acquired immune deficiency syndrome (AIDS) and other STDs and instructed employees on the use of condoms and spermicides to prevent contracting and spreading the diseases. Employees were urged to limit sex partners and to use condoms for all genital contact until both partners were committed to a long-term monogamous relationship. Recognizing the contemporary freedom in sexual practices, the article also explained how to select a contraceptive on the basis of convenience, effectiveness, safety, cost, life-style, and patterns of sexual activity.

Questions and Instructions

1. Is Ladd's concern about employees' life-style misdirected?
2. Is "Use of the Condom" a topic that the personnel department should address? Why or why not?
3. Should Ladd have sought the opinion of others before issuing the leaflet?

54

Racial Insults

Robert Martinez, executive director of Amcare, the city's ambulance service, was appalled when an angry black employee brought to his office a poster highly insulting to members of his race that he had taken from a bulletin board. He told Martinez it was one of several similar items that had been recently posted. Martinez immediately sent a memo to employees stating his regret that such "horseplay" was taking place and that an investigation was under way to discover the culprit or culprits.

The guilty person turned out to be Jerry Younger, a white male driver with a good working record. Unsure of what action to take against him, Martinez met with Younger and a group of black employees, who were asked to recommend an appropriate punishment. Martinez was surprised the blacks did not demand that Younger be fired but suggested instead that he be suspended to think over the problem of racism and to develop an employee training course in interracial relations. Two days before Younger was to present his plan, he resigned.

Questions and Instructions

1. Do you think "horseplay" is the right word to describe this incident?
2. What do you think of Martinez's decision to submit the question of punishment to black employees?
3. What might be included in a training course in improving race relations?
4. If you were in Martinez's position, what action would you have taken about the incident?

55

Diagnosis: Burnout

Ralph de Rivera, a foreign-policy analyst with the United States Department of State, had always been viewed as a superior and innovative staff member during his fifteen years of employment and had received several awards for excellent performance and distinguished service. As a specialist, he was frequently sought out for his advice on data-analysis techniques and sociopsychological factors associated with terrorism, but he was also highly respected for his broad knowledge of international affairs and world history and his fluency in four languages—Spanish, German, Russian, and Japanese.

Hans Bogart, de Rivera's supervisor, had recently noticed, however, a change in his willingness to undertake responsibility for projects or assignments. In the past prompt, reliable, and conscientious, he now was becoming a problem because of absenteeism, tardiness, complaints about physical aches and pains, and his irritability in dealing with coworkers. His productivity had slipped and his reports, formerly carefully prepared, were now poorly organized and lacking in necessary details. Recently, during a coffee break, de Riviera had complained to Bogart of being fed up with State Department protocol and of being mentally and physically exhausted. Bogart diagnosed de Rivera's problem as burnout and began thinking about what might be done to rejuvenate a once highly valued employee.

Questions and Instructions

1. Should Bogart talk confidentially with de Rivera about his problems and urge him to reform?
2. Should Bogart recommend that de Rivera seek psychological help?
3. Would reassignment of de Rivera to different work restore his incentive to accomplishment?
4. Develop a plan that would help identify employees suffering from burnout and that would suggest means of dealing with them.

56

The Slot Machine To-do

When Glenville police raided a private club, the Bison Lodge, and confiscated fifteen slot machines, the incident did not provoke much comment until it was disclosed that City Manager Oscar J. Lottinville was the club's vice president. Although it had been rumored for years that gambling went on in the club, the police had done nothing about it. The only reason they had acted now was that they had gone to the club in response to a burglary report and happened to see the slot machines in a back room while investigating how illegal entry was obtained.

It seemed inappropriate to some townspeople that the city manager, charged in the city charter with "the faithful execution of all laws and ordinances of the city and state," should be an officer in an organization that was breaking the law. But Mayor John Dilling told the press: "For some reason it just doesn't seem to bother me greatly. I think I need to talk to the city attorney to find out his thoughts on the matter before I comment further." And several members of the City Council said they felt no deep concern about the propriety of Lottinville's holding office in the club. Lottinville himself declined to comment to reporters.

Town talk about the matter subsided after police charged only Clarence MacArthur, club manager, with the misdemeanor of possessing the illegal devices. "MacArthur was the only one I could charge under the statutes," District Attorney Jeffrey Wrightsman said. "Police had no actual proof that club officers knew of the slot machines. MacArthur was charged because he was on the premises when the slot machines were discovered."

Questions and Instructions

1. Does the city manager owe the public an apology for his association with the club?
2. Should he resign from the office or from the club?
3. Does such an incident as this cause disrespect for law and order?
4. What do you think of the light-hearted attitude taken by city officials about the matter?

57

Tokens of Friendship

Charles Grayson, director of procurement for Richmont, a city of 500,000 population, was pleased with reports he received about the work of his new assistant, Peter Atkinson, who had been employed upon his graduation from college with a B.A. degree in public management. In his first few months on the job Atkinson had familiarized himself with the internal procedures involved in procurement and was given greater responsibility in dealing with contractors and others seeking to do business with the city. Atkinson, according to reports reaching Grayson, was clear and concise in informing dealers of the city's requirements and specifications, and was praised for his promptness and efficiency in processing the paperwork in seeking bids and awarding contracts.

After awhile, however, adverse reports began to reach Grayson. Atkinson and his wife often were guests at parties and dinners given by persons dealing with the city, enjoyed the facilities of a country club at their invitation, and Atkinson received small gifts—a wristwatch, a magnum of champagne at Christmas, a leather wallet on his birthday—from them. Called on the carpet about the favors, Atkinson denied that they influenced his handling of the city's business. He thought he should maintain pleasant relations with dealers, and such gifts as he had received were tokens of friendship or appreciation that it would be rude not to accept.

Questions and Instructions

1. Should all gifts—a dinner, a cocktail, tickets to a football game—be refused as bribes?
2. Is it wise for public employees to carry on social relations with persons they are able to help because of their position?
3. Can a line be drawn between a friendly gift and a bribe?
4. As director of procurement, what policies would you adopt governing gifts and favors?

58

Security in the Workplace

A decision of the State Human Welfare Department to disarm security guards and to make the wearing of uniforms optional was protested by employees in the city's northeast welfare office situated in a high-crime area.

"I think someone could be killed," a claims processor said. "The majority of clients are fine people, but we do have some under the influence of alcohol or drugs." A security officer expressed fear of what might happen if the policy were not revoked. "I can't take care of myself," he said. "I was attacked recently by a man under the influence of drugs who had become upset with his social worker. My gun was the only reason why clients in the lobby didn't back up the man attacking me."

A petition asking that the new policy be revoked was signed by 153 of the 340 employees at the office. The director of field operations for the Welfare Department explained that the policy had been adopted because of incidents involving careless handling of firearms. "There were some close calls," she said. "Employees and welfare clients would be endangered if guards drew their guns and started shooting to subdue an angry or disturbed client. Guards don't need guns to handle dangerous situations, and they are allowed to carry nightsticks."

Questions and Instructions

1. What is your opinion about the need for armed security guards in welfare offices?
2. What would be the advantage of requiring guards to wear uniforms?
3. If you were an administrator, would you want to accept the responsibility for supervising armed guards?

59

Questions about Layoffs

Because of a cut in funding for the Department of Public Works, Ravi Singh discovered he must invoke a reduction in force of twenty unskilled or semi-skilled employees in the several departments under his direction: sanitation, street maintenance, sewer maintenance, engineering division, sewage treatment plant, and water treatment plant. The easiest plan was to operate on a "last-in, first-out" basis. But Singh did not like the idea because layoffs based on longevity could result in the worst employees being retained and the best being let go. He preferred an alternative method basing layoff decisions on an employee's performance. The drawback to this, however, was that the Public Works Department had not developed an appraisal system that would be objective and unbiased for these workers and to establish such a system would take time. Furthermore, Singh feared layoffs based on this principle might result in lawsuits from those believing they were unfairly fired. He considered a third possibility: furloughs; that is, giving workers short, forced vacations without pay. Furloughs, he thought, might bring about short-term relief but would not be adequate if the fund shortage continued as he believed it would.

Questions and Instructions

1. If you were in Singh's position, what would you do?
2. Which of the three layoff principles mentioned do you consider fairest to workers?
3. Which would be in the best interest of the city?
4. How would you go about establishing an appraisal system for laying off employees of the caliber being considered by Singh?

60

Equal Opportunity at Sea

Owners and crews of tuna fishing boats operating from California ports were upset when the U.S. Department of Commerce ruled that they must accept both male and female observers aboard their craft. Under the Marine Mammal Act, federal observers are required aboard vessels for complete trips, sometimes lasting two or three months, to make sure that excessive numbers of porpoises are not killed.

In response to complaints of being forced to accept women aboard the fishing boats, officials insisted it was necessary in order not to violate the 1964 Civil Rights Act making it unlawful "to limit, segregate, or classify employees according to race, color, religion, sex, or national origin."

The mariners opposed the ruling because their all-male crews shared four- to six-person bunk rooms, toilets, and bathing facilities. Special quarters would have to be provided if a woman came aboard. To provide such quarters would be an added expense and take up valuable space in the small boats. They maintained further that the attempt to bring a woman observer aboard would violate their right of privacy. In the course of their work, the mariners became soaking wet with sea water, and it was their practice to strip on deck and to change into dry clothing. They felt that a female observer would inhibit them from doing so. Also, a woman sharing their mess and the cramped living space on a boat, they argued, would interfere with the crew's freedom to engage in the sometimes profane and boisterous camaraderie typical of men separated from women and families.

Questions and Instructions

1. Do you think officials should waive the rules for equal opportunity employment under the conditions of tuna fishing?
2. Should they urge upon the tuna boatowners the need for hiring female crew members?

3. Are there other situations in which it might not be desirable to mix male and female workers?
4. Which should be the governing factor in the tuna-fishing dispute—the right of women to equal employment or the rights of privacy and freedom of the tuna fishers?

61

The Baby-Sitting Dispute

When does a baby-sitting service become a day-care center? This question was faced by Annabel Ballinger, programs supervisor for the Department of Human Services, when a group of Martinsville mothers protested what they called unwarranted interference by the state in the right of working mothers to choose whomever they wanted to baby-sit their children.

The question arose when Ballinger, acting on violations reported to her, ordered that Mrs. Orville Anderson, who had been taking care of children in her trailer home "off and on for fifteen years," must become licensed or discontinue her baby-sitting service. "I do not claim to be a day-care center," Anderson had objected. "I'm strictly a baby-sitter. I don't advertise my services and the children I care for are mostly those of friends."

Anderson's stand was defended by the mothers of the eleven children who on occasion were taken care of by Anderson. "This is a woman in her own home," one of them said. "We pay our own money. We feel our rights are being violated. We all know Mrs. Anderson. I just don't think it's any of the state's business."

But Ballinger maintained that she was merely following the law, which required licensing of all persons who, in exchange for compensation, kept five or more children in their homes on a regular basis. In the interest of the health and safety of children, Ballinger felt she must require Anderson to meet the standards established by law.

Questions and Instructions

1. Do you think Ballinger is right in insisting that Mrs. Anderson be licensed? Why or why not?
2. Is this dispute over licensing an instance of what many consider the government's intrusion into private affairs?

3. How much leeway do you think officials should have in enforcing regulations? Give examples.
4. Apparently, the mothers employing Mrs. Anderson are satisfied their children are receiving proper care, but would it not be better if her home was subject to the health and safety inspections required of licensed services?

APPENDIX

Case Histories Keyed to Topics

The text gives major emphasis to topics marked by asterisks.

1. It's Not Easy at the Top
   *Delegation, *Managerial Style, Motivation, Power and Authority, Responsibility
2. If It's Legal, It's O.K.
   Dishonesty and Corruption, *Ethical Questions, *Legal Requirements, Political Relations, Rules and Regulations
3. Special Privileges for Officials?
   Ethical Questions, Fairness, Flexitime, Morale, Professionalism, *Rules and Regulations, Whistle Blowing
4. An Illegal Order
   *Conduct Codes, Conflict of Interest, *Ethical Questions, Fairness, Legal Requirements, Managerial Style, Political Relations, Professionalism
5. Managerial Conflicts
   Communication Problems, Compensation and Fringe Benefits, Grievances, *Interpersonal Relations, *Job Classification and Placement, Job Satisfaction, Managerial Style, Morale, Motivation, *Power and Authority, Stress Management
6. Going Bare
   Fiscal-Budgetary Matters, Intergovernmental Relations, *Liability, *Risk Management
7. An Equitable Sick-Leave Plan
   *Compensation and Fringe Benefits, Fiscal-Budgetary Matters, Motivation, Program Evaluation, Retrenchment, Rules and Regulations, *Union-Management Relations
8. The Far Side of Fifty
   Equal Employment, Job Satisfaction, Performance Evaluation, *Promotion Policies, *Recruitment
9. A Campaigner for Equal Rights
   Employee Rights, *Equal Employment, Grievances, Interpersonal Relations, Managerial Style, Union-Management Relations

10. Parking Meters—A Perennial Problem
Communication Problems, Complaints of the Public, *Legislative Relations, News-Media Relations, *Planning and Goal Setting, *Public and Community Relations, Publicity and Promotion
11. A $5,000 Anonymous Phone Call?
Centralization-Decentralization, *Complaints of the Public, Conduct Codes, Discipline, Employee Rights, *Field-Central Office Relations, Professionalism, Public and Community Relations, Resignations
12. To Quit or Not to Quit
Clientele Relations, Employee Rights, Interpersonal Relations, Job Satisfaction, Morale, *Resignations, Retrenchment, *Termination Policies, Union-Management Relations
13. Pressing a Harassment Suit
Employee Rights, *Equal Employment, Professionalism, *Sexual Conduct and Harassment
14. A Leave of Absence
*Ethical Questions, Incompetence and Inefficiency, Interpersonal Relations, *Managerial Style, Morale, Productivity
15. The Good/Bad Administrator
Communication Problems, *Discipline, Employee Rights, Fairness, *Interpersonal Relations, Job Satisfaction, *Managerial Style, Morale, Performance Evaluation, Protests Organized by Employees, *Teamwork and Cooperation
16. An Indecisive Decision
*Clientele Relations, Ethical Questions, Fairness, Public and Community Relations, *Recruitment
17. No Clean Sweep in Winchester
Complaints of the Public, Contracting for Service, *Fiscal-Budgetary Matters, Planning and Goal Setting, *Program Evaluation
18. A Vigilante Arrest
Complaints of the Public, Professionalism, *Vigilantism
19. An Authoritarian Approach to Management
Change, Clientele Relations, Interpersonal Relations, *Job Satisfaction, *Managerial Style, Morale, Motivation, *Organization and Structure, Participatory Management, Power and Authority, Productivity, Quality of Work Life
20. A Question of Contamination
Clientele Relations, *Conflict of Interest, *Dishonesty and Corruption, Ethical Questions, Legal Requirements, Political Relations, Public and Community Relations, Secrecy and Confidentiality, *Whistle Blowing
21. No Welcome Wagon Here
*Administrative Advocacy, Clientele Relations, Complaints of the

Public, Fairness, Intergovernmental Relations, Interest and Pressure Groups, Planning and Goal Setting, Policy Making and Implementation, Publicity and Promotion

22. A Problem of Motivation
    Communication Problems, Job Satisfaction, *Motivation, *Performance Evaluation, Productivity, *Stress Management, *Workfare
23. The Prank That Misfired
    Employee Rights, *Professionalism
24. The Parking-Ticket Ledger
    *Compensation and Fringe Benefits, Grievances, *Job Classification and Placement, *Job Enrichment, *Job Satisfaction, Morale, Motivation, Resignations
25. Affirmative-Action Pressures
    *Equal Employment, Ethical Questions, Fairness, *Interest and Pressure Groups, Recruitment
26. A Cutback Emergency
    Delegation, *Fiscal-Budgetary Matters, *Interagency and Intra-agency Relations, Interpersonal Relations, Planning and Goal Setting, *Retrenchment
27. Retreat at Lake Clearwater
    *Morale, Public and Community Relations, Training, *Organization Development
28. A Matter of Relief
    Communication Problems, *Interpersonal Relations, Job Satisfaction, *Morale, Motivation, *Teamwork and Cooperation
29. American vs. Immigrant Labor
    Complaints of the Public, *Contracting for Service, Employee Rights, *Immigrant Employees, Interpersonal Relations, News-Media Relations, Policy Making and Implementation, Public and Community Relations, Recruitment
30. Supervising Job Trainees
    Discipline, *Incompetence and Inefficiency, Managerial Style, Motivation, *Training
31. Documentary Evidence
    Communication Problems, *Exit Interview, Job Satisfaction, Managerial Style, Morale, Motivation, Program Evaluation, Secrecy and Confidentiality, Teamwork and Cooperation, *Turnover
32. Problems with Volunteer Workers
    Clientele Relations, Interpersonal Relations, Ombudsmen, Recruitment, Teamwork and Cooperation, Training, *Volunteer Workers
33. A Town in Trauma
    *Committee Management, *Economic Development, *Intergovern-

mental Relations, Public and Community Relations, Public Marketing, Teamwork and Cooperation

34. Discord in Rehabilitation Services
Clientele Relations, *Discipline, *Interpersonal Relations, Managerial Style, *Power and Authority, *Professionalism, Rules and Regulations
35. Coproduction for Marrsville?
Clientele Relations, Contracting for Service, *Coproduction, Managerial Style, Policy Making and Implementation, *Public and Community Relations, *Publicity and Promotion
36. Cutting Back at City Hall
Fiscal-Budgetary Matters, *Interagency and Intra-agency Relations, Planning and Goal Setting, Public and Community Relations, *Retrenchment, Union-Management Relations, *Reduction in Force
37. Personnel Dilemma: Terminate or Retain
Communication Problems, Discipline, *Incompetence and Inefficiency, Interpersonal Relations, *Job Classification and Placement, Motivation, *Power and Authority, Productivity, *Termination Policies
38. In Whose Best Interest?
*Clientele Relations, *Conduct Codes, *Conflict of Interest, Discipline, Ethical Questions, Legal Requirements, Performance Evaluation, Professionalism, Supervisor-Staff Relations
39. Restoring Peace at Maysville
Centralization-Decentralization, Change, *Communication Problems, Field-Central Office Relations, Interpersonal Relations, Morale, *Motivation, Productivity, Resignations
40. Equalizing Overtime Assignments
*Fairness, *Grievances, Legal Requirements, Power and Authority, Rules and Regulations, *Union-Management Relations
41. Union Contract Negotiations in Springfield
*Compensation and Fringe Benefits, Fairness, Fiscal-Budgetary Matters, *Grievances, Interagency and Intra-agency Relations, Job Satisfaction, Legal Requirements, Morale, *Union-Management Relations
42. Pariah in the Public Library
*Interest and Pressure Groups, *Interpersonal Relations, Legal Requirements, News-Media Relations, Power and Authority, Professionalism, Public and Community Relations, *Recruitment, Volunteer Workers
43. The Ordeal of Change
*Change, Communication Problems, Compensation and Fringe Benefits, *Consultants, Fairness, Interpersonal Relations, *Job Classification and Placement, Managerial Style, Organization and Structure, Political Relations, Power and Authority, *Reorganization

44. Check-out for the Old Library
Fiscal and Budgetary Matters, Interest and Pressure Groups, *Legal Requirements, News-Media Relations, Political Relations, *Public and Community Relations
45. Meeting the Press
*Clientele Relations, Complaints of the Public, Ethical Questions, Managerial Style, *News-Media Relations, *Political Relations, Public and Community Relations, Secrecy and Confidentiality, Whistle Blowing
46. Treated Like Dogs
Communication Problems, Employee Rights, Interagency and Intra-agency Relations, *Job Enrichment, Job Satisfaction, Managerial Style, Morale, Motivation, News-Media Relations, *Quality of Work Life, *Quality Circles, Union-Management Relations
47. The Polygraph Controversy
Employee Rights, Grievances, *Managerial Style, *Polygraph Test, Quality of Work Life, *Secrecy and Confidentiality, Turnover, Whistle Blowing
48. A Message from Al Anon
*Alcohol and Drug Abuse
49. Gagging City Employees
*Employee Rights, News-Media Relations
50. A Charge of Favoritism
Fairness, *Promotion Policies, Sexual Conduct and Harassment, *Supervisor-Staff Relations
51. An Improper Book Sale?
*Conflict of Interest, Power and Authority
52. A Thief among Us
Communication Problems, Dishonesty and Corruption, *Theft
53. A Prophylactic Measure
Communication Problems, *Life-style Issues, Sexually Transmitted Diseases (STDs)
54. Racial Insults
*Participatory Management, Quality of Work Life, *Racism
55. Diagnosis: Burnout
*Burnout, Job Satisfaction, Morale, Motivation
56. The Slot Machine To-do
*Dishonesty and Corruption, Legal Requirements, Political Relations, Public and Community Relations
57. Tokens of Friendship
*Conflict of Interest, Dishonesty and Corruption, *Ethical Questions
58. Security in the Workplace

Public and Community Relations, Quality of Work Life, *Workplace Security

59. Questions about Layoffs
    Employee Rights, *Furlough, Reduction in Force
60. Equal Opportunity at Sea
    Employee Rights, *Equal Employment, Job Classification and Placement
61. The Baby-Sitting Dispute
    *Administrative Discretion, *Policy Making and Implementation, Public and Community Relations